Y0-BQT-395

The Heart of History

SUNY Series in Transpersonal and Humanistic Psychology
Richard D. Mann and Jean B. Mann, Editors

THE
HEART
OF
HISTORY

Individuality in Evolution

JOHN WEIR PERRY

State University of New York Press

Photo credits: Figures 1–3 originally appeared in John Perry, *The Self in Psychotic Process*, Berkeley, University of California Press, 1953; Figures 4–8 appeared in John Perry, "Reconstitutive Process in the Psychopathology of the Self," in the *Annals of The N.Y. Academy of Sciences*, vol. 96, January 1962, pp. 853–76; Figure 9, courtesy of the British Museum, London; Figure 10, courtesy of the Institute of Comparative Research in Human Culture, Oslo; Figure 11, courtesy of the Asian Art museum of San Francisco; and Figure 12, courtesy of the Museo Nacional de Arqueologia, Mexico City.

Scattered excerpts in the text are from James B. Pritchard, ed., *Ancient Near Eastern Texts: Relating to the Old Testament*, 3rd ed., © 1969, Princeton University Press. Reprinted by permission of Princeton University Press.

Published by
State University of New York Press, Albany

© 1987 State University of New York

For information, address State University of New York Press,
State University Plaza, Albany, N.Y., 12246

Library of Congress Cataloging-in-Publication Data

Perry, John Weir.
  The heart of history.

  (SUNY series in transpersonal and humanistic psychology)

  Includes index.
  1. Culture. 2. Individuality. 3. Myth. I. Title.
II. Series.
HM101.P456 1987   306   86–14428
ISBN 0-88706-399-3
ISBN 0-88706-400-0 (pbk.)

10 9 8 7 6 5 4 3 2 1

Contents

Preface

In these times, our culture's familiar myth has lost its vitality. The immense crises we face raise questions which find no answer from that spiritual level. This book is an examination of how great myths have been born in the course of history, and what the trend of human development has been as seen through them. For myth is at the heart of historical development.

The way we lost our myth is familiar. We now live in a cosmos quite different from that of our forefathers. No longer can we have the comfort of knowing ourselves as God's special creation, descended from Adam, and inhabiting a world that was his unique masterpiece. No longer is it taking the middle position in a three-storied universe, between a heaven to be won and a hell to receive us if we fail the test of our sojourn here in this proving ground. Instead we look out upon the staggering vastness of a seemingly endless crowd of galaxies composed of countless suns and planetary systems, and recognize our earth as a minuscule speck among them. We have appeared to shrink incredibly in our estimation of our value in this new scale of creation. Yet there awaits us a far grander mythic rendering of our place in all this, one that can stir the heart even more deeply than the one we have outgrown.

In this leap of our knowledge, what, after all, can be the place for mythic thinking? Myths are nonrational, it may be objected, and the triumphs of our culture have come by the use of reason. Our new world view, we used to say, has been the work of "science" which then has displaced "religion" as our mode of understanding the creation and the meaning of our life here. Yet these are not, in fact, the elements really concerned in our question of what we are here for. Science is a method of investigation, not a creed, and religion is the practice of a faith. Myth is another matter, having a different function.

History shows that great myths are formed in times of dire urgency and in minds of gifted visionaries. In their altered states of consciousness they perceive the play of images arising from the deepest levels of the psyche whose natural language is mythic. It expresses meaning in the form of archetypal processes so charged with emotion as to render them a compelling impressiveness.

Whenever persons are faced with new conditions for which the habitual outlook and responses are no longer adequate to provide meaningfulness and motivation, this deep level of the psyche is roused into activity and manifests itself in vivid dreams, fantasies, visions, or disturbances of varying degrees of severity. Hence, when an entire aggregate of persons, a culture, finds itself in such straits, this activation of the psyche produces leads for new orientation and purpose. The consequent myth forms provide guidelines for the energies and motivations to handle the new challenges.

Individuality has lost its guidelines and become problematic. We live in an age in which, since the exciting awakening of the Renaissance, individuality is so prized that the aims and goals of a person's life are pursued in large part at the expense of the welfare of the society to which he or she belongs. Indeed, the very experience of belonging seems to be dwindling. The part thus tends to act without regard to the needs of the whole. Since cultures are losing their myths, today's values are founded largely upon material well-being. Similarly, whole societies are tending to seek their welfare at the expense of the natural setting to which they belong. We have been tending to forget, until recently, that mankind is only a part in the whole of the eco-system in which he participates. In many ways we are beginning to recognize that we are on the verge of crisis in this respect — the spawning ground of new myth-making.

This volume examines the myth and ritual forms that reveal the evolution of individuality in various societies. Born out of the urgency of change, the myths have tended to generate fresh crises through an unbridled assertion of this individuality. In antiquity, at the time of the first city cultures, a species of individual consciousness appeared amid the new conditions of the Bronze Age. It was projected upon the sacral kings for them to personify as "Unique Men" as part of their regal station and function. Before long, this royal prerogative filtered out to the aristocracy and then to the common man. It threatened to prove disastrous when these privileges were asserted by the lesser rulers without the sense of the protective responsibility that had been part of the sacrality of the original kings. Some societies were almost destroyed in consequence of their predatory warfare.

There followed then, in times of troubles, prophets and philosophers in various cultures who recognized that the essential qualities and functions of the kingship in actuality belonged to the inner psychic life of gifted individuals, to be cultivated in their spiritual development in practices that were derived from the royal ceremonial. This gave rise to the Age of Democratization of the kingly forms.

In this frame of thought, by what was a society to be held in order? These visionaries perceived quite clearly that by this practice of spiritual cultivation a different principle than that of power and dominance by strong rules would be brought into effect. The mid-first millenium B.C. saw the birth of the concept of human-hearted caring and compassion as the desirable bonding force in social cohesion, evoked among the people spontaneously. The intent in gathering these historical materials is to explore the source and psychological dynamic of the principle of compassionate brotherhood as it plays its part in the ongoing evolution of mankind. Through these mythic visions, history was finding its heart.

Myth, Ritual, and Visions   I

The Psyche and the Evolution of Cultures

1

W̲e find ourselves today in a critical predicament of modern culture, faced with an urgent need to reassess our relation to the planet and to those who inhabit it. It is not only the inclination but the obligation of all of us who ponder the alternatives ahead to speak from our various fields of experience and expertise, offering whatever may be of relevance in groping our way into a future full of forebodings. Since I have busied myself during the past three decades in dealing with individuals in turmoil and crisis, observing the psyche in its developmental process trying out solutions to problems, and investigating in the history of cultures various parallels to these inner processes, I have found certain patterns which I feel to be relevant to our efforts to handle our dilemma.

Our Cultural Predicament and the Psyche's Response

In the technological age that has been developing and refining its methods so dramatically over the past five centuries, our principal mode of investigating nature has been governed by the drive to mastery and power over it, to learn its laws in order to be able to control it and wrest from it what we need for our use. It is easy for us to feel a sense of triumph and pride in the success of the endeavors, in the miracles that have been accomplished, and thus to assume that the human condition has never been so well off. Yet when we stand back and allow the complete picture to come to consciousness, we discover to our dismay its other, darker aspect. We recognize that we are not only exhausting the earth's resources by the efficiency with which we extract and spend them, but even depleting the life forms that inhabit this world with us. On top of all of this, we find ourselves endangering the various matrices in which these life forms exist, poisoning the atmosphere, the waters, and the soil itself. While all this progress is intended to benefit human life, we are so effective in preserving that life from disease and death, supporting it in numbers heretofore un-dreamed of, that we may well exceed the possibility of sustaining so many billions of human beings on so small a world. As populations rise, so does competitiveness with each other to attain the rich benefits that present themselves so attractively. We are learning to our bewilderment that as the crowding mounts, the order in our society crumbles. We are becoming frightened of each other within our cities and among our nations.

The facts are familiar to all of us, spelling a crisis in our world-wide, technologicaly oriented culture. The flowering of our achievements is so wondrous and the triumph so brilliant that we find it easy to lull ourselves into complacent confidence that there is nothing we cannot remedy, and to relegate the sense of uneasiness to a shadowy unconsciousness. Yet even if we may fail to acknowledge our predicament in a conscious way, the psyche does register its recognition of it on deeper levels, and makes moves to generate new possibilities of outlook and ways of living that might allow our survival.

A New Look at Visionary States

I have made it my special task during the past three decades and more to watch these deepest operations of the psyche when they are intensely activated, that is, in the visionary states that so often find a psychotic form. In these disruptive turmoils one finds frequently a myth-forming activity that gives rise to vivid imagery with regularly recurring features.[1] In light of my training, I had expected that in a person's deep regression to early experience the personal problems of parent and sibling relationships would predominate and fill the field with the turbulent emotions surrounding early hurts. But surprisingly, the play of themes in the chaotic images and emotions most often concerned itself instead with the pressing questions of cultural ideologies. The most urgent collective issues of society in any decade were felt fully as deeply as those that sprang from an individual's life story: in the 1950s, the clash of democracies and communism; and in the 1970s, the conflicts between those who are polluting the planet and those who work for ecological concerns. The fear of destruction of the planet at the hands of wrongly motivated agencies prevailed, usually with the terror of the nuclear blast woven throughout these misgivings. These individuals impressed me as being souls so sensitive to the climate of the times that they were overwhelmed by the magnitude of the collective plight. As a result, colorful messianic ideation would arise. Such imagery is easy for a therapist to dismiss because of its grandiosity and its transparent compensation for feelings of inadequacy; yet if taken seriously, it can be found to be highly significant in revealing an awareness of the cultural predicament and in envisioning programs of reform.

Listening to the visionary experiences in which these persons were engrossed at the expense of their relation to the everyday, mundane reality, raised for me a host of puzzling questions. They were obviously undergoing a process of reorganization in which an old form of the self was being outgrown and supplanted by a renewed form. But the means of accomplishing this were surprising. Themes of death and rebirth ran parallel with those of world destruction and world regeneration; time was set back to the beginnings of one's own life in parallel with those of the creation; the place was identified as the world's center; clashes of political and moral forces were portrayed on a cosmic scale, and opposites of all sorts were brought into collision, reversal into each other, and finally into union; expressions of worldwide mission of leadership and reform reached exalted dimensions.

Learning from Myth and Ritual Parallels

What, I wondered, do all these eruptions of cosmic ideation have to do with reorganization of one's psyche and its effort to bring it to maturity? If all this sequence is a myth-making process, what are the mythic parallels from history that might be found to give some orientation to the meaning? Some years went by before I encountered what I was seeking. On reading Mircea Eliade's brilliant book, *The Myth of the Eternal Return*,[2] I was electrified to see it all laid out in full, all the elements of the process in ancient ritual practices of the Ncar East. From this start, I was led into extensive readings in the myth and ritual forms of the first city cultures of that part of the world in its Urban Revolution of five thousand to three thousand years ago.[3] Exploring these ceremonial forms has led me to recognize the function of myth and ritual in the efforts of cultures to weather the turmoils and crises of the profound changes in their transitions from one kind of structural organization and economy to a new one — for example, from an agrarian and clan form to a city one of the Bronze Age.[4] Specifically, the function of the sacral kingship is found to be the principal key to an understanding of the great religions of antiquity all over the newly urbanized world.

I was reminded of an encounter while I was a medical student with Professor Mercer, a leading Egyptologist; to my grasping at this opportunity to learn something of mythology, he responded with the statement, "You won't understand Egyptian mythology without a knowledge of the practices of kingship there." From my newly acquired exposure to Jung's writings I thought, "Oh, too bad, he doesn't appreciate the psychology of mythic imagery of the unconscious!" It took me fifteen years to realize how dead wrong I was, for by then I was finding that, indeed, all the great religions of that ancient world were concerned primarily with the sacral kingship and government.

The myth and ritual sequence was uncannily similar to what I was seeing in my patients. In Mesopotamia, for example, the annual New Year Festival was a reenthronement rite for renewal of the king and the kingdom. Symbolically, the place was the center of the world, the time, that of the creation. The king underwent a ceremonial humiliation and death for three days in a ceremonial mountain while the entire populace mourned in lamentations to the sound of flutes. A ritual combat between the forces of order and chaos, or life and death, ended in a victory that released the king from his sojourn in the underworld, which was then celebrated in triumphal processions and rejoicings. The reading of the creation myth marked the world's regeneration. The king was then reenthroned as ruler of the universe, and a festive banquet was followed by the rite of the Sacred Marriage in a booth of greenery atop the stage tower (representing the union of Heaven and Earth and other opposites) to reinvigorate the land, its people, and the livestock and crops. Finally, the will of the gods for the society's near future was divined in a reading of the Tablets of Destiny.

How can it be, I reflected, that these ritual programs of antiquity can reappear in the psyche of people today with such faithfulness to the pattern? The patriarchal ceremonial governance and its theology were new at the time of the Urban Revolution. Has this mythic imagery been "coded into" our inherited psychic repertory ever since, as the basic pattern of reorganizational and renewal processes in times of stress?

Even more intriguing to me was a further question arising out of these. I had been observing that there was a trend in the content of my patients' visionary experiences during the several weeks of their process. They typically started with grossly grandiose claims to unusual power and prestige as heroes and heroines, saviors of the people, even rulers or divinities with cosmic powers. Gradually the emphasis shifted from such power concerns to a new awareness of their capacities for loving relatedness, and their messianic program for reform was colored by a preoccupation with compassion, lovingness, and brotherhood.

This seemed to me to imply that such persons were starting in their visionary turmoil with an orientation to their world that was consonant with the bias of our culture toward prestige, power, or control — a way of life that was reflected in their parental conditioning. This prevailing psychic dynamic was then being led from an active-directive-dominative mode toward one which concerned itself with sensitive relating, empathy, and receptiveness. The goal of reorganizing the self in this process therefore seemed to be that of engendering not only their own capacities for intimate relationship but also of envisioning a culture in which these values would predominate.

This suggested the picture of the psyche in myriad individuals occasionally undergoing, by their unconscious process in dream and fantasy, this transformation of values and motivations, one that is the very urgent task of the collective culture. After all, the culture as a whole cannot accomplish this change unless the persons composing it do so. Is not this cultural change an aggregate of individual changes? I was aware that a similar shift in values occurred in some ancient cultures on the heels of the initial enthusiasm for power and dominance in the early Urban Revolution, and so I wondered whether the sacral kingship ideology could also have been the vehicle for this transformation of values toward those of brotherhood and compassion.

Cultural Functions of Myth and Ritual

These questions were leading me toward an inescapable conclusion that myth and ritual not only give expression to what is occurring in the deep levels of the psyche at any time, but they also function to guide the emotional energies of societies into new channels required by changing conditions, such as those of an urban culture as it emerges out of the village life that preceded it, in the transition from an agrarian economy to a Bronze Age. Myth in this case gives form and expression to the meaning of the powerful realities of human experience in times of reorientation and culture change. The accompanying ritual provides the means to transform and channel emotional and motivational energies into new directions. It was becoming clear that wherever cultural forms are due for an overhauling, the inevitable distress of bewilderment tends to be resolved by the revelation of new meaning through the medium of myth.

The ideology of the sacral kingship is going to provide a main thread in the gradual unfolding of the evolution of the psyche as I trace it out to answer the questions being raised in this review of the initial observations that motivated my investigation of cultural histories. Making so much of the sacral kingship might seem curious since several widely read scholars have presented it in the light of grandiosity and tyranny on the part of arrogant bullies who used their power to oppress the people, or worse, who were the proponents of a fatal step in the direction of the patriarchy from which we are at last struggling to free ourselves. Such vilification misses the essential point, however. What is most significant about the sacral kings in the evolutionary perspective is that they embodied the psychic image representing the full potential of unique individuality in its nascence, awaiting its realization eventually among the many. In early China, as we shall observe, he was called the Unique Man; in early Egypt, the only man whose immortal soul could be transfigured in death; and in early Mesopotamia, his title of "Lugal" connoted the supreme man.

With the kingship, too, a new member of the male pantheon came into being in the Near East: the storm or warrior god. As king-god, he personified the mythic image of a new species of consciousness, one that was motivated toward ambition for ever-increasing power, dominance, and mastery: in the case of rulers, creating ever new worlds of aggrandized kingdoms and empires theretofore undreamed of; in the case of the common citizen, singling himself out from the common social matrix and building his own personal empire of property and prestige.

All too soon, however, this new individuality showed itself to be seriously problematic. The prerogative of kings was coveted and then mimicked by the acristocracy, and thus diffused out from the strong central monarchy into the hands of petty princes and barons. In Egypt and in China, most notably, the firm order of the reign from the center gave way to a multiplicity of competing local governments in a feudal scattering of power. The sacrality of the governing office dropped away, and with secularization came also a loss of the sense of protective responsibility toward the people who, no longer finding their lord a benign father, found themselves instead being oppressed and plundered amid the shifting fortunes of war-makers.

Out of these anguishing "Times of Troubles," to use Toynbee's term,[5] there appeared manifestations of reform that have impressed me as remarkable demonstrations of the capacity of the human psyche to respond to crises with creative visions of its healing potentials. For the ceremonial forms of the sacral kingship, I found, subsequently underwent a sequence of metamorphoses from era to era representing not only the maturation of cultures but at the same time the differentiation of the human psyche.

The changes in this developmental sequence were the outcome of the work of visionary insights on the part of reformers, prophets and seers, giving direct voice to the myth-making work of the deep levels of the psyche. It was astounding to me to discover how clearly, in their new teaching, it was indicated that while the actual rulership was becoming secularized, the sacred royal figure was being internalized; that is, what he had represented in ceremony was increasingly being perceived as happening within the individual member of the society. The familiar ritual forms now were becoming the symbolic language of inner psychic and spiritual processes. It thus was evident to me that this functioning of the mythic image of the kingship is what we still see today in the dreams and visionary experiences of individuals.

The Thrust of Evolution

The thrust of evolution through this history that I was exploring could therefore be construed as starting with the outwardly concretized myth and ritual forms of collective expression, and moving then toward inwardly realized images coming into play in individual spiritual cultivation. This internalization was at the same time recognizable as a "democratization of the kingly forms," as I have called it. This produced a remarkable transformation of values. The royal ideology had begun with such a high esteem for the new scale of power, dominance, and empire building that these motivations were sacralized. With the democratization, on the other hand, the supremacy of these values yielded place to newly conceived spiritual ideals of compassion, brotherhood, and personal piety. That is, the bonding and cohesion of society, at first imposed upon the people in the modes of power and dominance, became now recognized as springing from the capacities of individuals for compassion and mutual caring. In many cultures, the earlier image of the kingdom as a corporate entity embodied in the person of the sacral king gave way to the concept of the inner kingdom of the spirit, in which social cohesion would take place instead through the development of the sense of oneness with one's fellow beings. Along with this, the awareness of moral responsibility that had at first been carried solely by the king then became a task for the individual to realize.

I was struck by the observation that the advances of this evolution were in each culture born out of turmoil and crisis, out of the stress and strain of change, and the peril, bewilderment, and demoralization in the face of uncertain futures. This presented a powerful picture of the role of the visionary mind as one of mankind's most potent adaptive functions, activated typically in situations of puzzlement in times of transition.

The social order and organization at first projected out in the myth and ritual practices of the governing figure had a symbolic shape. The King was located symbolically at the cosmic axis or world center, and characteristically surrounded by a city-state that was constructed in the form of a quadrated circle (a mandala) as the pattern replicating the shape of the world or cosmos. With the democratization of the kingly forms, this center was now to be found within, the mandala now the shape of the soul when it accomplishes its wholeness, and above all, rule now appearing as self-government, that is, psychic integration.

The mythic processes of death and rebirth, world destruction and world creation, the clashes of opposing forces and their resolution, the establishing of renewed order in society, and the generating of life-giving powers, all the work of the earlier annual ceremonial process of renewal, now became recognized as the various aspects of the spiritual task of self-cultivation. Each of these elements that had been perceived as applying to the societal world now could be seen as representing one's relation to one's cultural world and also to one's psychic world.

This history then suggests that the ordering of a society starts with a reorganizational process expressed in the psyche's symbolic imagery, whether in myth and ritual or in the corresponding intuitive mode of thinking. As a culture outgrows its past state and enters a new one, the restructuring thrust represents a healing in terms of self-organizing process, just as it happens also in the individual organism.

In this framework we can recognize the pattern of the evolutionary process in the development of the psyche and of the cultures it creates. This evolutionary process can be clearly traced through the differentiation of psychic potentials expressed in mythic imagery, and specifically through the development of mankind's relation to the image of the center. This "archetypal" center, to use Jung's language,[6] is the source of each of the steps in psychological growth as the mainspring and governing function of the psychic organism's experience.

The cultural studies in Part II are explorations of the major turning points in four ancient cultures from which I draw the conclusions I am speaking of, ones in which there appeared the earliest dawning realization of the possibilities in the mode of human-hearted compassion for the ordering of whole societies as they democratized the kingship. Added to these are investigations of the romantic reiterations of these motifs in the twelfth and nineteenth centuries.

What Led to these Investigations

My motivation in undertaking this exploration began a long time ago. Exactly fifty years ago, even in the same season of the year in which I am writing this, I spent the months of summer vacation reexamining my beliefs and my understanding of the part we play in creation. I was aware that classical philosophies have consistently had their footing in a cosmology and cosmogony; so I began there, reviewing the current sciences of various sorts to help answer the question of where we have come from and where are we going in the creative process. At the end of a few months, what I was looking for came through to me in a highly exhilarating moment, out under the dome of a starry sky where I was reviewing these reflections. I was filled with the sense of wonderment at the grand panorama of the creative process, building upon itself layer by layer, atoms combining into molecules, these clustering to form living unicellular creatures, and cells joining cooperatively to construct the tissues of ever more complex organisms. The question pressing itself all the while was where is it going next? This time, in one of those transports that Maslow has described as "peak experiences,"[7] I perceived that the thrust of evolution toward higher levels of order and complexity was now pointing toward its next phase, the creation of a new superorganism. I saw that if the highest achievement of this creative process so far has been the extraordinary configuration of energies that form mankind's consciousness, then surely the next step is that of bringing together these individual psyches into an organic whole, which I saw as the "social organism." Of course, today this is not news, since the publication in the 1950s of Teilhard de Chardin's beautiful rendition of the cosmic process and formulation of the noosphere;[8] but in 1934 there was nothing in any literature that I knew of that spoke this way.

The gift of this vision of creation I not only treasured; I found in it my vocation. This was to explore the dynamics of social and psychic evolution, and, I hoped, to reach some comprehension of how it could be that society might become increasingly such an organism whose members lived cooperatively for the well-being of the whole. My question was that if this is indeed our evolution's next level of order and complexity, where in the human psyche would the dynamics originate that might motivate individuals toward furthering such a future? I had already the glimmering recognition of some sort of cohesive principle running through and governing the whole process of creation. It came to me that we human beings have the distinction of being endowed with a highly developed consciousness by which we are able to experience this cohesive principle at work and apperceive it as lovingness. It is an example of the observation that through mankind's awareness the universe becomes conscious of itself. At the lower levels of organization and complexity this cohesiveness is only dimly yet justifiably perceivable, suggesting to me a beautiful vision of the driving force in the evolutionary process. It then made sense to me that in the Christian teaching "God" is not only the "Creator" but also is "Love"; that is, that love is this deity.

The goal of my newly found vocation was clear. It was to explore this question: From what source in the psyche does the energy derive that motivates individuals toward this kind of lovingness that might make of human society an organism? Clearly, on this level, such a body has transcended the laws governing biological nature (though including them), and instead is psychic in its makeup. Therefore, for me it was clear that an understanding of the psyche must provide the vehicle for exploring the nature of this superorganism. At first I wondered whether the Freudian psychology would give the right lead; that is, whether the sexual libido goes through various sublimations and differentiations to serve at last the purposes of human-hearted caring and fellowship in society. I could see that, searching into the function of myth and ritual and their present-day counterparts in psychic depth, psychology would be the avenue to pursue.

When I set out with these aims in the 1930s, the habits of thought concerning myth were different than those of today. The exciting revelations were reductive in character. Frazer's *Golden Bough*,[9] in exploring the archaic manifestations of king-killing and of the death and rebirth process, as expressions of the vegetational and seasonal round of the life-giving cycle, promised to account for similar themes in the higher cultures and religions. One might then be tempted to "explain" the Christian crucifixion in terms of the motif of the dying gods such as Tammuz of the earlier Mesopotamian myths and rituals. Solomon Reinach, in his *Orpheus*,[10] accounted for the nature of the gods of the pantheon of antiquity by their animal forms in which he found them to have their origins. Lord Raglan, head of the British Royal Anthropological Society, in *The Hero*,[11] made a painstaking comparative study of that motif as a demonstration of the diffusionist frame of thought that finds the occurrence of myth forms to be due to their spread from culture to culture, following the lead given by Elliot Smith and W.J. Perry earlier.[12] Raglan, in *Jocasta's Crime*,[13] was bold enough to go the limit and set up a hypothetical scenario of a supposed first original ritual form that was then the source in remotest prehistory of all the later variations and permutations of myths of the hero that followed! After all, in the causal-reductive framework there has to be a starting point! This was the climate of thought in which Freud in his *Moses and Monotheism*[14] conceived the notion of a first guilty act that could then survive in human experience as an archaic heritage, reappearing in each succeeding generation as the proclivity toward suffering guilt in the Oedipus constellation of parent-child triangles. The first supposed act was the murder of the father by the sons in the primal horde of the remotest past.

These efforts to establish first causes would be far more justifiable if presented as myths to account for mythology rather than as scientific propositions! If a problem is fraught with mystery because of its obscurity, then the mythic image is always ready at hand to provide an orientation and approach toward more clarity.

In those years, I found Jung's escape from such causal-reductive pitfalls truly exhilarating. His early essay, *On Psychological Understanding*,[15] was a clear-headed and titanic declaration of an alternative to causal thinking. In it he pointed out that such investigations into past occurrences render only half the picture of what a dream or myth contains; the other part is provided by what he called a synthetic-constructive standpoint that looks for that with which the imagery is trying to experiment in probing into future possibilities and potentials. Herein is brought to light the creative work of the primordial images and their culture-making proclivities. In this view the deep psyche is the well-spring of creativity.

Looked at in this spirit, for example, the Arthurian mythology is explained in part perhaps by the exploration of the origins of its heroes in ancient Celtic gods of Ireland and Wales. Yet the true significance of the tales, and the source of the fervor with which they proliferated when they did, are to be found rather in their relevance to the new culture of the twelfth century in Angevin France (as we shall see in chapter 8).

In respect to evolutionary theory, I was struck with a similar contrast between reductionist thinking and the new trends. Darwin's *Descent of Man*[16] had dealt a blow to the concept of humanity, so ennobled in the phrasing of the Psalms as "a little lower than the angels," now picturing the human as a little higher than the apes from which he was descended (to borrow Whitehead's phrasing). The theory of the survival of the fittest was having a similar impact on social and economic motives in justifying man's crudest strivings toward competition and dominance. It was therefore exhilarating once more to encounter Henry Drummond's *Ascent of Man*,[17] in which he compensated this trend toward degrading the role of the spiritual in mankind's strivings. In this (and in his *Natural Law in the Spiritual World*)[18] he rendered the first glimmerings of the principle governing the direction of evolutionary development, in the increasingly ascending levels of order and complexity. He perceived, too, that the laws operating at any higher level were not reducible to those of the lower. I found this to be close to Jung's synthetic-constructive standpoint.

I enjoyed the privilege of attending classes given by A. N. Whitehead [19] and L. J. Henderson, [20] both of which were like launching pads into new dimensions of cosmological perspectives. Henderson explicated the model of the ascending orders of complexity and organization, illustrating it with his "box-spring" metaphor for the interrelations of factors in blood chemistry: A change in any part of the whole system affects all the others, a vivid introduction to the principles of systems as against the linear account of separate entities. To listen to Whitehead was to have one's mind stretched and opened to the new outlook of today, recognizing process as the fashioner of form, in a framework of sequences in time and envelopes in space, in a cosmos in which every monad is inter-related with and reflects the nature of the whole.

A particular delight was an encounter with Joseph Needham on a rain-soaked monsoon day by the Burma Road in China in the mid-1940s. He put in my hands the galley proofs of his *Time, the Refreshing River*,[21] a work on evolution, and we compared notes on our quests after an understanding of the social organism as the crown-ing phase of evolution, and the role of love as the bonding principle running through this process. He had recently outgrown his allegiance with La Mettrie's mechanistic view of biological and human nature and was gathering materials for his monumental *Science and Civiliza-tion in China*,[22] a veritable "Summa Scientifica" of Far Eastern thought in which he found a world view that gave an ideal framework for evolutionary thinking.

Through these several fortunate encounters I was reassured that I was on the right path in my pursuit of an understanding of evolution by investigating it at close range in psychological work. Since then cir-cumstances have followed one upon another in a way to keep me remarkably on track in the pursuit of this quest, even though I would not have been able to foresee the plan ahead of time. Upon my return from training in analytical psychology in Zurich, I was assigned a case that by good fortune opened up the entirely new recognition of the self-healing process in acute psychosis. This was surprising enough to send me into an investigation of such acute disturbances for a decade, finding in them an open window into the spontaneous myth-making process of reorganizing the self. Discovering the myth and ritual parallels in the sacral kingships soon provided the recognition of the image sequence I have termed the "renewal process."

All this opened two avenues to explore which have occupied me for the past twenty-five years. One came out of an appalling recogni-tion of the damage done to persons in acute episodes by our "treatment" of them in suppressing the natural self-healing work of the psyche. Seeing this so clearly led me into several efforts to provide methods to handle cases of this kind in such a way as to give the psyche full freedom to attain its own ends in its own modes. They were beautiful and rewarding experiences which were possible in the 1970s and unfortunately now have become unrealizable in the conditions of cautious conservatism of the 1980s. The other avenue arose out of a realization that the myth and ritual I was writing about were expressions of self-reorganizing processes by which whole cultures were embarking upon new futures. Reform of revolutionary proportions was again and again turning out to be the work of visionaries. It began to come through to me that in our time we are at a point of transition of critical proportions, needing our own new myth to express the still unfamiliar future as we stand upon its threshold.

With these considerations, a host of questions presented themselves about our psychological and psychiatric outlook, with its preoccupation with the rational and the normal. Do we have ways of recognizing our new myth if and when it appears? What are we doing with our visionaries? How many of them are we labelling psychotic and putting away in confinement under medication, or relegating to poverty as eccentric artists, or curing of their "symptoms" by therapy?

Composing this Exploration

By this very circuitous route, through many years and many issues to investigate, I have found myself encountering once more the original objective of my calling: to gain an understanding of human evolution. The several psychiatric and scholarly concerns and endeavors that have led me along this path have each time been expressions of the main aim, consistently remaining focused on the pursuit of the evolutionary process, and in it, the role of the dynamic of lovingness.

When the time finally arrived for the task of laying out in writing all that had been coming to light in these explorations, I found myself in no small quandary. There seemed to be several histories to recount. One was the metamorphosis of the sacral kingship expressing the differentiation of the image of the center; another, the role of visionary states in culture-making; again another, the phenomenology of rapid culture change and its psychological consequences; then there were the ways lovingness has been seen as a means of social bonding; there was the problem of our present cultural transition and its demands to avoid disaster; and all the while, there was the task of relating psychic evolution to its biological counterpart. Each of these issues seemed to deserve a full treatment in its own separate book. I sketched out one on kingship, one on visionary states, and one on acute culture change. Yet, with each, its thesis clearly necessitated some introduction of the other motifs, since all were so interdependent as to be unclear without one another. The present volume therefore is about all of these issues. As it began to emerge into its present shape, my image was one of holding half a dozen strands requiring an intricate interweaving. My hope is that in the form of this single, compact book the themes may be clear and not taxing to read, and their interrelating already accomplished.

The Design of this Exploration

The design of this exploration begins, then, with some observations from the psychological anthropologists concerning the crises of rapid culture change out of which myth and ritual are born through visionary experience. There follows a discussion focusing upon a predominant element of such visions, that of the motif of world images and world regeneration as a core feature of the renewal process occurring either on the societal or the individual level.

Concentrating further again on what is placed at the center of such world images, in Part II the myth and ritual role of the sacral kingship is reviewed in a number of cultural forms. These are selected to bring into relief the striking transformation of this myth form when it was found to belong to mankind's inner psychic life as well as to his outer societal structure. Each example demonstrates how it was that out of this internalization was born the democracy expressing the new awareness of individuality and personal sense of responsibility for the welfare of one's society. The kernel of this achievement of spiritual awareness emerged clearly as the realization, new to mankind at that time, that the emotions of lovingness could operate as the inner dynamic of social cohesion. The last of these examples shows that in the poetry of Shelley all these developmental trends were brought into play in his myth forms, ones that could have their ritual accompaniment in political action in the nonviolent mode, eventually to be carried out in actual practice a century later by Gandhi.

The selection of the historical materials to be investigated might be questioned when it is found that I have omitted certain cultures and their ways of thought about democracy and the emotions involved in societal cohesion. For example, the mythology of Greece and the dialogues of Plato are not brought into this discussion because the metamorphosis of the kingship there became lost in historical obscurity and did not lead over clearly into its internalization. For the same reason, anosticism also has not been included in this study of visionary material, even though it is replete with it. My intention has been to cleave only to the framework provided by the evolution of the imagery of kingship, of the center it personifies, and of its subsequent democratization.

The final chapters in Part III offer some psychological comments. They hold always to the spirit of the myth and ritual imagery itself in order not to do violence to its nature, which is sufficiently eloquent to render its own meaning in terms of human experience.

I am intentionally avoiding "interpreting" the myth forms into psychological language until these final chapters. A myth speaks for itself, and conveys its own meaning most clearly the nearer one is to the style of mentality of the culture that gave rise to it. If I am reading a primitive south sea island people's tale about the witchetty grub, I find myself unmoved; it takes a little time to love the Native American trickster, Coyote; but the Mesopotamian Gilgamesh suffers passions about friendship, death, and the wiles of the goddess with which we can all empathize without hesitation. Myth requires a mental process that Jung calls "amplification"[23] for its understanding, meaning simply that the more one is familiar with the language of symbolization, the more clearly the significance comes through. Amplification is essentially a means of enriching our conscious associations to these motifs in order to be able to resonate to them with the sense of comprehension. If we pick up a volume of Blake's rather wild and passionately colorful mythic poetry, we may draw a blank at first until we familiarize ourselves with the entire context of this thought and of the cultural setting in which it evolved and to which it was addressed; but with this, we find in it a wondrous critique of his age.

I therefore am holding entirely to the phenomenological data of observation when I speak of the "center" or "cosmic axis" as the locus in which renewal processes take place in dramatic form, whether in the individual or the collective dimension, or when I say that it thereby becomes the motif through which the evolution of mankind's differentiation of consciousness becomes traceable. Psychological theory only alerts me to the possibility of the meaningfulness of this motif; it is what prepares me even to think it valid to expect to grant it such a role in the evolutionary process.

In Part III, then, the first chapter describes the psychology of individuality and its evolution, emphasizing the role of the archetypal center in this process. The tension between individuality and social sensitivity is brought into focus, conceived in terms of a complementarity. The lesson of history emerges, that individuality can become so destructive that it requires compensation in the form of a full awareness of the feeling for one's fellow beings. In this the feminine principle is shown to balance the bias of the patriarchy, and the receptive to balance the overly assertive-aggressive motivations. This history is then put in the context of some current concepts of evolution and self-organizing systems.

There follows a discussion relating these cultural and mythological findings to the perils of our own day, in which nuclear nemesis threatens us so mortally. Mythic images underlying this emotional crisis are found in several motifs, in the thunderbolt representing the explosive weapon, in the end of the known world as a mark of profound culture change, and in the enemy as the projection of our own dark aspect. The rise of the feminine and the receptive mode of experience are seen as our contemporary myth form in the psyche's attempt to compensate our dangerous bias toward dominance and mastery over nations and over nature.

The last chapter is an attempt to evaluate these lessons of history in respect to the prospect ahead, considering the question of the separateness, created by individuality, in balance with the sense of oneness with out fellow beings, gained through the very fulfillment of that individuality.

I invite the reader now into the same journey of exploration and discovery that I have been enjoying for the past twenty-five years.

Lo! They Beheld

2

When embarking upon a discussion of visionary experience, I find myself mindful of the rather lowly place to which our culture has relegated it. The very words that once were used to convey awe and respect for it now have been degraded to the level of trivialities. For instance, a recent article on the newsstands was entitled "Ten Great Myths About Physical Fitness," by which was meant ten horrendous misconceptions due to erroneous information. According to current usage, "myth" signifies a falsehood, belonging to a context of common-sense thinking that regards myth as composed of "unreal" persons and events. The mention of "visions" nowadays suggests phenomena that rouse dark misgivings that something like hallucination is involved, and mistrust results. The term "visionary" has fared a little better in a way, referring now to anyone daring enough to have new ideas, especially in politics. As for the expression "Lo and behold," however, that has become a common joke referring to something like pulling a rabbit out of a hat.

It is revealing, contrary to present-day biases for reality-based, rational, common-sense thinking, to contemplate the expression "Lo!" and open our minds to its flood of suggestive meanings. When the word is uttered, it induces a particular state of mind, inviting wonderment for the strange things one is about to "behold," visions of the extraordinary, images of otherworldly import. At such a moment, there occurs an inflow of mythic happenings. To perceive them one must relax one's usual consciousness geared for the acuity of thought, feeling, and perception needed for dealing with the mundane world, and instead, give reign to the play of images arising out of the deep psyche. It is somewhat like the ceremonial entrance into the world of fairy tales, "Once upon a time," where one leaves the world of the ordinary and enters the realm of other beings. Such an induction invites a feeling that is full of expectation, one that is prepared for the magical, the mythic, or the devine. At the end of the story, an equally functional expression, "And they lived happily ever after," exhorts us to "snap out of it," to bring that state to a close and reenter the mundane world. For we are speaking here of "altered states of consciousness," the most intense of which are the "visionary states."

While the fairy tale excites this special state of wonderment in a playful spirit, the forebears of such tales were myth and ritual forms that had a far more serious import. In ancient cultures, in their early years at least, these were regarded as necessary to both the spiritual and the material well-being of a people, and the narration of these oral literatures, together with their representation in dramatic form on regularly repeated occasions, were considered absolutely vital for maintaining in their due order the forces at work in nature and in society.

Origins of Myth and Ritual

To show how alive with urgency those practices were, this chapter is given to probing into the moments of origin of some myths and into the conditions in which they were born into the world. I have found, to my surprise, that myth-making characteristically has not occurred in the placidity of contemplative states amid stable and quiet circumstances, but rather in the turmoil of crisis and cataclysm.

We do not know for certain about the origins of myth and ritual in prehistoric times but can surmise that in the era of the Neolithic Revolution, to use Gordon Childe's term, the advent of new agriculture transformed societies and gave rise to drastic changes, comparable to the kinds of effects produced by the Urban Revolution some six thousand years later (ca. 3000 B.C.), in the way of life of peoples. Within historical times, at least, we can say with some assurance that new myths are the product of stress amid changing conditions.

Profound change is sensed as hazardous to the continuity of the familiar, and hence to life itself, whether individual or collective. Cultures, as well as the individual, have alarm reactions designed to preserve the life of the organism. Altered conditions threaten the integrity of the *ethos* and *eidos* of a society, its system of values and of meanings. Whether by invasion or diffusion of new elements from outside, or by the creation of new ones from within, drastic change challenges the viability of a culture. In rousing its response to such a stimulus, a certain course of events tends to occur, registering the distress and the effort toward establishing some new equilibrium.

This process of "acculturation" in rapid culture change has received the attention of anthropologists in recent decades and presents to psychology the task of formulating the laws that govern the psyche's modes of handling crises. Their research throws into a new perspective the phenomenon of the activation of psychic depths, whether in "visionary states" or in their "psychotic" equivalents. I put it this way because I have found in observing several hundred episodes of this nature that the acute "psychotic" process is a myth-making one in which the imagery symbolizes the leaving of old ways and the embarking on new ones as the psyche strives to reorganize.

The Groundplan of Visionary Experiences

For an example, I will cite a case of "psychotic" visionary experience that I have already published[1] to indicate how closely it approximates the making of prophets.

A young lady at the moment of her "psychotic decompensation" found herself dying and entering the afterlife, and she believed the people around her were the dead returned to life. She was immediately thrown back, in her imagery, to the world's beginning and felt herself to be Eve in the Garden of Eden and also to be a new Virgin Mother of a divine child. A little later, she sensed herself caught up in plots and counterplots at the world's center between two opposing world factions engaged in a power struggle for power and supremacy. One day, she looked out the window upon a storm and saw in the play of thunder and lightning the vision of a series of three holy men: Moses, Paul, and Luther. It was revealed to her that she was chosen to be the fourth in this lineage and thus was to become the leader of a new religious era, as the reincarnation of the same great divine spirit that had entered history three times before. Then, a further wonder appeared to her. She saw the Bay Area in a cataclysmic upheaval, opening up and dropping under to become a new Hell. A new world order descended in spaceships from the sky to establish a new version of the heavenly city, a "New Bethlehem" at the center of the world. There was to be no one savior, but each oldest son was to be a Son of Man, all perfect and, as children, knowing everything of importance so as to have the wisdom to live sensibly together in peace.

The parallels between the visionary experiences of such "psychotic" individuals and those of prophets are so numerous and so close that they will become readily apparent as I narrate various instances of the formation of new cults. Themes of seeing visions in thunderstorms, of death and resurrection, of the return of the dead, of the dropping away of the old world and creation of the new, of conflict between cultures, of the election of a prophet as a new version of an old and venerated one, and of the formation of a new society of an elect, all may be found in the initiatory visions of famous reformers, just as they were in the young lady's experience.

As an example, in South Africa at the time when certain Zionist cults were forming, one of their prophets, Shembe, was a savior among the Zulus.[2] In his early years and through his adolescence, he had visions, always in thunderstorms, which made known to him his religious calling: He was to leave his family and follow the Lord, from whom he would receive the gift of healing. In one of these states, Shembe beheld his own body lying dead and decomposed; after this he became a miracle-worker. He proclaimed himself a new Moses, a leader of his people and a King of the Nazarenes in the manner that Christ had been King of the Jews. He was called the Black Christ and established a center of worship on a sacred mountain, as a New Zion and Holy City. When he died, he was buried as a saint.

Another such black prophet founded the Church of the New Salem and advocated a New Jerusalem.[3] During thunderstorms he had visions, perceiving a Lightning Bird as the Voice of Jehovah. He beheld his own dead body, understanding it to signify his old native culture which was destined to die and rise again in a different form, one that would reject both paganism and white Christianity.

We find further similarities between prophets' and "psychotics'" experiences in the Western Hemisphere in the latter part of the last century. The Ghost Dance, a phenomenon that took place among the Native Americans promising them a new hope of survival, swept through the tribes from coast to coast. Its earliest prophet was one Wodziwob, who lived in the tribes of western Nevada.[4] In a revelation he had on a mountain top, the Great Spirit announced to him a major cataclysm to come which would shake the entire world. The earth would open up and swallow the white men, who would drop through and vanish forever from the Amerindian land; their goods, however, would remain for use by the Amerindians. In further visions,[5] he saw that the earth rolled up like a carpet, and also that a rift appeared which would engulf the people in a chasm, but the followers of the new cult would come back to life in a few days. They would find themselves living and mingling in the presence of the Great Spirit and the ancestors risen from the dead. With all these events, a new heavenly era would be established. The Ghost Dance gave cultic expression to this new myth and a new spirit of hope to the people.

It should be evident, then, in these various instances, that the experiences of persons in visionary states bear remarkably close resemblances to one another in their contents and motifs, whether these men or women be regarded by their cultures as "psychotic" or as "prophetic." In the crisis of reorganization, the psyche draws each time upon the same repertory of images that expresses its own processes.

The Work of Prophets

I am assuming that most readers are as unfamiliar with the myth-forming process in tribal, preurban cultures as I was when I set out upon these investigations. Because of recent events such as the disaster at Jonestown, where the community's fanatical devotion to a cult leader with obviously destructive motivations led to mass-suicide, it is difficult for our generation to consider such phenomena with sympathetic understanding; indeed, we are skeptical toward cults. The history of prophetism is replete with stories of unfortunate appearances of cults that one can only lament as mistaken. These occurrences, however, do not detract from the equally noteworthy fact that history has more ample instances of myth and cult that have marked the turning point of their cultures from spiritual impoverishment to enrichment and fresh vigor. Without the visionary work of prophets to reanimate their people in such conditions of demoralization, cultures have been prone to disintegrate and even disappear.

I suppose, too, that most readers share in a modern frame of mind that expects really practical reforms to come only by the work of clear reason. Myths, after all, though poetic and colorful in their suggestive meanings, are not rational, at least in the orthodox sense. When there are urgent, pressing needs for change, we are not inclined to look to the nonrational mind for leads. Therefore, while I narrate the following anecdotes of visionary experiences among leaders in unsophisticated tribal, preurban societies (and at the end, one or two from urban ones), I ask the reader to suspend the predilection for practical thinking-things-through and to give credence to the experiences of the nonrational.

Examples of Messianic Cults

In a comprehensive review of messianic myths and cults of most parts of the world, Lanternari[6] finds certain regularities that recur from culture to culture. These I will recount in order to provide some guidelines to help make sense of the narratives that follow. All appear to involve a belief that society will return to the conditions prevailing when it began: Its new millenium to come is based upon that of the Golden Age — *Endzeit* is based upon *Urzeit*, the end-time upon the primordial time. Cataclysms and catastrophes are the prelude to the end of the world, and the rising up of the dead is a consistent feature. Reversal of the existing social order is accompanied by the ejection of a foreign oppressor who is causing disruption of the culture's familiar ways. The regeneration of the world then introduces an age of abundance and happiness, ruled by a messiah whose redemptive action fulfills the people's hope to restore their tradition. The re-creator of the world is usually the personification of the historical national hero whose return has been long awaited; he is often the ancestral founder of the culture and the lineage of its leadership. In cases where the crisis is occasioned from the outside by the impact of an oppressor, this messiah saves his people by a militant struggle against the foreign influence and power; where it is from the inside by indigenous needs for reform, he saves by fostering more sophisticated ends, that is, spiritual and ethical values.

Similarly, in a study of the messianic cults occurring in India, Fuchs[7] has found such regularities of motifs and summarized them in over a dozen categories. The characteristic common features are that the society is intensely dissatisfied with its social and economic conditions; emotional unrest and hysterical symptoms, along with the abuse of drugs and alcohol, become prevalent; a charismatic leader rises and makes demands for the implicit faith and obedience of his followers; a test of their faith takes the form of a change in their way of life and destruction of their property; he rejects the established authority and issues a call to rebellion, often also threatening severe punishment of opponents and traitors. The ideology has elements reminiscent of the Golden Age and reflects a renewed interest in the society's tradition, thus restoring the pristine culture and rejecting its foreign counterpart. There is, however, a desire for heaven to bestow the aliens' goods and for society to adopt some of the traits of the superior culture. A mythology is developed envisioning renewal of the world through a catastrophe which is followed by the establishment of an earthly paradise and, hence, a New Golden Age.

Among these "crisis cults," as Weston LeBarre[8] has called the messianic phenomena accompanying the process of rapid acculturation, perhaps the most famous are the "cargo cults" of Melanesia.[9] At the end of the last century in Milne Bay, a prophet named Tokerau arose who proclaimed a cataclysmic series of events ushering in a new world era. This was to start amid the myth and ritual conditions of the New Year with its Feast of the Departed. As usual, the world would undergo upheaval and regeneration, ushered in by volcanic eruptions, earthquakes and floods, and unbelievers would be swept away. Winds changing to the southeast would transform and fill the earth with the spontaneous abundance of crops and fruits. This new era would be marked by the arrival of ships in which the deceased ancestors would come back to visit their families. After Tokerau, other prophets followed, foretelling the advent of ships bearing material goods deriving from the white man: tools, clothing, money, and other such objects of envy. Not only liberation and the abolition of slavery, but prosperity, well-being, and equality would be the gifts from the sea in these new times. The sense of these prophetic promises seems to be that ghosts, to these people, are white; therefore the white men bringing their extraordinary products on their ships must be from the spirit world, and their cargo the gifts of the dead.

In Polynesia, the corresponding cults of liberation[10] are particularly interesting for our present discussion in that their derivation from the New Year festivals is not unlike that of the Israelite messianic expectations springing out of the New Year rites of the ancient Near East. For at the turn of the year, in this myth and ritual tradition, the dead were believed to return and were given reverence, and a ritual combat was enacted with a military drama to protect the ordered world and establish an ideal era. In the new crisis cults, these elements developed into the larger picture of world regeneration and resurrection of the dead to live again in a new cosmic era. The old ritual combat now became the hope to war against the church and government of the western outsiders. These cults differed from those of other island societies in that their more belligerent aspect derived from the social conditions in which these peoples had developed military and political aristocracies, hierarchies that found their mythic expression in a supreme deity.

The disturbing impact of the white colonial powers upon these island people is paralleled by a similarly devastating effect upon Native Americans in the New World. The struggle of these societies to survive has most frequently met with disastrous failure and even their absorption and disappearance into the urban life of the white "dominant culture." Yet there is much to learn from the accounts of certain ones that responded to the new conditions with a strong revivification under prophetic leadership.

A remarkable visionary among Native Americans was Handsome Lake of the Seneca,[11] an Iroquois tribe, who became their reformer and prophet at the beginning of the nineteenth century. His people had suffered such a decay of their ways that they found themselves little more than a slum culture at the time. It seems to happen sometimes that a reformer falls into a condition as personally demoralized and ailing as that which his society is experiencing as a whole before he can embark on the visionary journey. Such was the case with Handsome Lake who was suffering so deeply from bereavement at the death of his niece that he had sunk into bitterness and depression. Compounding these was his shame at having committed a sacrilege: when in a state of drunkenness he had blurted out some of the sacred songs. So deeply ill did he become that he was thought to be dying. A coldness crept over his body until, in the course of it, only a single spot in his chest remained hot, and from this the warm vitality gradually returned to his trunk and limbs. In the midst of his deathlike coma, he was experiencing several visions. At the start, three angels gave him directives from the Creator telling how things must be among his people, naming the evils to be abolished. But this was only the beginning of grander things to come. Ecstatic states in shamans and prophets alike frequently provide occasion for ascent into the heavens where secret things are revealed. In such a trance Handsome Lake was taken by the Great Spirit on a Sky Journey as if he were entering his death. He traveled a bright road, which he found to be the Milky Way, and on it discovered he was following the tracks left by human souls in their death. As he beheld before him a brilliant light, the way divided into a wide path at the left leading to hell, the Land of the Punisher, and a path at the right ascending to heaven, the Land of the Creator. Then there appeared the frightening agency of world destruction, a so regularly occurring feature in prophetic experience. In the eastern sky Handsome Lake was shown two drops of fire, one red, one yellow, which threatened to ascend and spread death over the world in the Great Sickness. His mission was to prevent this catastrophe with the help of the three angels and the Great Spirit, supplemented by the reassuring presence of a large white object in the western sky that functioned to regulate the air. At this point, the task of throwing off the yoke of white dominance and oppression was framed curiously in the appearance of two foremost revolutionaries, Christ and George Washington, who were encouraging him to set about winning independence. Some ritual instructions were given as well to preserve the ceremonial traditions of his people, but more urgently a sacrifice should be made to avert the Great Sickness that would otherwise bring an end to the world.

Following his revelations, Handsome Lake took his high mission in too grandiose a spirit and became far too overzealous, persecuting witches and alcoholics sometimes to their death. In a third vision, then, the three angels set him on the right way once more, turning his attention to codifying his revelations and reviving certain ceremonies. There then being a need for new leadership and government for the Seneca, he appointed members of his family to office.

The outcome of these visionary revelations and their impact on the cult following was no small achievement: It was the revival of the Seneca nation into a new future. Adaptation to the larger society was also improved when a Quaker arrived to give advice on the issues of acculturation. The net effect is impressive, for the Seneca have remained a self-respecting people with some cohesion and with a special talent for steel work.

There are certain parallels between these visionary forms and those of the Native American Ghost Dance. In the latter part of the last century, a Paiute, John Wilson,[12] experienced revelations that led to his becoming a messianic prophet (his name, Wovoka, had implications of being the Son of God). His first visionary experiences came upon him characteristically after an illness and high fever, and a new cult was soon ordained. One account describes cosmic events: He saw an eclipse of the sun, and, like Handsome Lake, he took a journey to the Other World where he saw the Great Spirit and met Amerindians who had died and were forever young and happy. There followed then the fruits of his visions: the power to govern the elements — the rain and time itself; revelations of ethical instructions — he was enjoined, together with his followers, not to harm or fight and to do right at all times; in his vision of world regeneration, the dead would return to life, bearing gifts but, as usual, the white people would be carried away by a high wind; poverty, disease, and death were to be eliminated; and this Promised Land was to be only for the Amerindians.

Another account says of Wovoka that he led an uneventful life as a shaman until the coming of the Ghost Dance and the Peyote Ceremony. On this psychotropic substance, he had the customary celestial visions in which he was guided to the heavenly kingdom and its secrets were made known to him: He saw images of the life of Christ and his road from his "Ascent to the Moon." Wovoka was instructed to remain on this road the rest of his life. He beheld also the Abode of the Moon and the Sun and Fire, as well as the ancestral spirits. He was given directives for the layout of the sacred area for the "Big Moon" chants and ceremonials in which the role of Christ was transferred to the Peyote Spirit. From his many visions he was recognized as a healer, a clairvoyant, a composer of chants, and a prophet through whom the Great Spirit would speak. The ritual dance represented several renewals: the end of the familiar world and its regeneration, the return of the dead, and the revival of Amerindian society.

Evaluating Cultic Movements

In discussing these prophetic and messianic movements, the question that most naturally and most urgently comes to mind is whether their occurrence necessarily means that it is in the best interest of the people to follow them. Since they arise out of a mythic dimension, must this somehow imply that they are benign and for the general weal of the society? It must be emphatically stressed that by no means have these kinds of movement always been beneficial to the spiritual or material health of the community.

One might justifiably make the observation that the same hazards prevail over the outcome of prophetic cults as over the psychotic form of the renewal process. If the prophet is sufficiently paranoid, for example, he may become severely overbearing and tyrannical, punishing with death anyone who does not grant him allegiance.

An example of the disaster of despotism is found in the career of Kolaskin,[13] among the Native American Sanpoils in the last century. In the manner so common to prophets, he suffered a severe illness, finally succumbing to it and being pronounced dead; in wondrous fashion he then came to life during the preparations for his burial and sang a song newly created by him. He related visions that occurred during his death experience: While watching his own healing process in this state, he was instructed by the Creator to preach new reforms that would similarly heal the social body to which he belonged. A second visionary state concerned the usual world catastrophe motif, leading him to predict floods that later would destroy all of humanity except his own followers; in preparation for the event, he began work on building an ark. At this point, however, he became carried away with the sense of power and took the authority of judgment into his own hands, throwing into prison all who refused to obey him. This extreme and authoritarian rule inevitably caused rifts, which soon grew into feuds and open battles, until the government in turn came down on him in the same spirit and threw him into a federal penitentiary.

Another unfortunate result of prophetic cults may occur out of naivete when people are led into toilsome and fruitless ventures with seductive promises that are not fulfilled. Prophets have offered their followers the allure of a new city and new age in some faraway place toward which all would migrate only to end up experiencing the most painful of hard-won disillusionments.

The extraordinary concreteness with which the imagery of a new age may be taken is exemplified by a Brazilian tribe. In the fifteenth century A.D., the Tupi Guarani[14] migrated in several waves even to the west coast of the continent in search of the promised "Land without Evil." Their shamans persuaded their followers to stop work in their fields, since the harvests would come of their own accord and in abundance to each home. The shamans convinced them, too, that their enemies would surrender in the same spontaneous spirit. Consequently, they no longer spent their time in toilsome work but rather in ritual dances. In the sixteenth century, the Tupinambas similarly left their villages by the thousands to seek the "Land of Immortality and Perpetual Rest," trekking westward for nine years, their spirit being kept up by the performance of miracles by the shamans and by their fear of death and destruction at the imminent end of the world.

Many are the funny and sad incidences of prophets giving their people the hope of a new age in which their well-being would be supplied without labor. The faithful would thereupon lay down their hoes and plows and await the miracle, only to find that poverty and starvation were overtaking them. Another example of this was seen in the 1930s when one of the cargo cults of the Solomon Islanders[15] was entranced with the belief that a cataclysmic flood would eliminate the whites from among them. Members were instructed to work at building storehouses for the goods that would soon arrive by ship. Inasmuch as this event could supposedly only occur when they had run out of their own provisions, they were told to desist from their work in the fields to hasten the miracle. Governmental authorities put a stop to the rebellious movement by arresting its leaders.

Occasionally a prophet would come to grief at the hands of state authorities by being pronounced insane. This happened to one Bedward[16] in Jamaica half a century ago. He declared the vision, by now so familiar to us, of celestial journeys and of the end of the world; he was to be taken, like Elijah, to heaven and would then return to give judgment as to who should follow him there, and at this second coming the whole earth would be destroyed by fire. He called himself Christ Son of God. With the inevitable failure of his ascension and glorification, he was arrested and committed to an asylum as insane. How fine is the line of distinction between prophet and patient!

In evaluating the validity of visions and visionaries, it would seem, as I have mentioned, that the same principle might apply to the unfortunate collective movements as to the individuals in psychotic states. The fault in both may be said to lie in the misunderstanding of the symbolic nature of visionary images. The events promised may be valid as long as they are seen as belonging more rightly to the progress of the spiritual life of a people, not to the mundane level of outer reality; that is, they are appropriate to the imagery symbolic of psychic potentials more than to the literal depiction of outer events to come. The point brings us to the question of the functional significance of these visionary experiences.

Formulations of Revitalization Movements

The few brief illustrations cited here should give at least some impression of the universality of the phenomenon that in any part of the world the visionary state and the consequent crisis cult tend to accompany the process of acculturation. They constitute what A.F.C. Wallace has described as "revitalization movements" in rapid culture change. His model of these events is particularly useful to the present discussion in that he relates them to the extraordinarily altered states of consciousness that the prophetic leaders reach, and he sees in these the spawning ground of new myth and ritual forms.

As Wallace formulates it,[17] a set pattern of behavior emanates from the established cognitive structures and value systems of a culture, and becomes a "mazeway"; this is the sum of all the responses to its conditions that a society has learned through its problem-solving activity. As long as these ways are effective and constant, the culture's steady state prevails. When new conditions arise, due to the impact of foreign interventions or of indigenous changes, trouble may set in. If the old solutions do not handle the new problems, unrest and frank distress are felt throughout the society.

For example, in its original steady state, Handsome Lake's Seneca nation had offered certain avenues to men to fulfill their roles, experience their effectiveness, and feel the consequent self-esteem; they could become skilled hunters, warriors, or statesmen. Yet when the white invasion and containment deprived them of each of these opportunities, an acute loss of morale prevailed and something resembling a slum culture resulted.

Typically, the period of distress is marked by both cognitive and affective dissonance; the old world of meanings and values breaks down by no longer fitting the new conditions. The emotional stress of this disorientation is marked by symptoms of various kinds: psychosomatic, hysterical, or addictive (to alcohol or drugs). In this general unrest, certain individuals who are sensitive and unstable tend to experience profoundly altered states of consciousness. Those who have the ability to articulate and the charisma to convey their visions gather a following. For one to become a prophet, one must have a vision that offers what is needed for the times, and the new myth must be "received" by the people.

In this cult-forming history, Wallace sees a pattern in which a "hallucinatory" style of experiencing visions appeals first to an inner core of immediate associates who share them in much the same mode. Secondarily, the zeal is reflected in a larger following of enthusiastic converts of more hysterical makeup, who adopt in a dissociative mode a new second personality (and who may lose it as readily). The several phases of the process of rapid culture change are then formulated as follows:

1. a Steady State, as a period of moving equilibrium with only slow culture changes;

2. a Period of Increased Individual Stress, in which the equilibrium breaks down by a failure to provide satisfaction of needs; stress becomes intolerable and disillusion widespread, as the culture is perceived as disorganized and inadequate;

3. a Period of Cultural Distortion, as members seek to restore

some degree of personal equilibrium by socially dysfunctional expedients such as alcohol, drugs, breaches of mores, and violence;

4. the Period of Revitalization, made up of several components: the *formulation of the new code* that arises from the visionary revelations expressed by the prophet, a cultural "mazeway resynthesis" that is elevated to the status of the supernatural and which sets up a "goal culture"; its *communication* to a following attracted by its more highly organized system; this *organization* draws disciples of a variety of sorts, those who experience the resynthesis, those enthusiasts who are converted, and those opportunists who join as an expediency; an *adoption* sets in that tends to harden the code which goes increasingly nativistic and hostile to dissenters and to national enemies; a *cultural transformation* is brought about that brings an abatement of the symptoms of stress and dissonance and cultural distortions; finally with an ensuing *routinization* there is a shift in the movement from innovation to maintenance of the new cult and its code or political functions; and

5. the New Steady State is marked by a value structure that serves as the basis for new minor and slowly continuing changes; the record of the movement is enshrined in myth and ritual forms that divinize in greater or lesser degree the leaders and events of the new order.

Wallace prefers to regard a revitalization movement not as a mechanical interaction of social and cultural forces but as a cognitive information-processing and problem-solving process marked by creative discovery and invention. These may be seen as sudden changes in cultural *Gestalt* by deliberate and organized attempts to construct more satisfying cultures through the rapid acceptance of wide patterns of innovation. It is interesting to observe that while he emphasizes this cognitive and problem-solving work, he speaks of the visionary cult-founders as paranoid and their visions as hallucinatory! In this and in the observation of changes in *Gestalt* and wide patterns of innovation, I am reminded of Sullivan's description of the acute schizophrenic episode as a process "reorganizing whole masses of life experience."[18]

In the Jungian model,[19] this same picture of revitalization may be rephrased as an activation of the archetypal unconscious at a time when the previously prevailing structure of meanings and values begins to break down amid changing conditions that are presenting new problems. The conflict occurring at such a juncture constellates the opposites, and the old and the new, the familiar and the unfamiliar, become represented in the mythic expression of a clash and a resulting cataclysm. The archetypes are activated when the customary learned ways fail and "the instincts are in danger." That is, as long as custom is taking care of the fulfillment of existence, there is little need for the work of the myth-forming action of the psyche; the already-established myth takes care of most exigencies. But when conflict enters in with changing conditions and new problems, this automatic unfolding of life is disturbed and produces anxiety. The conflict of opposites is handled then at an archetypal level, and the renewal process sets in to form a new world view and to provide a new structure of meanings, values, and design of life.

Jung's concept of the unconscious psyche, ever since his formulations of it in *Symbols of Transformation* in 1912,[20] is that at its very deepest roots its energies divide into the instinctive and the culture-making aspects. The former go into action in prescribed typical patterns of behavior in response to typical situations; the latter go into symbol formations which are designed to convert and transform energies, to liberate them from the confines of pure instinct and set them in creative directions. The symbol is in this sense like an energy-transforming machine, so to speak, and culture is an aggregate of such devices to put these energies to work.

Lanternari, impressed by the psychologically revealing qualities of the messianic movements, makes the poignant statement that "There is probably no known religious phenomenon in which the dialectical interpretation of relationships between personality (the individual personality of the prophet) and culture (the social personality of the group) becomes more convincing than it does in messianic cults."[21] We may echo this appraisal and say that nowhere is the culture-forming aspect of the archetypal unconscious more explicitly demonstrated than in the renewal process, whether it be in individuals or in societies, in the culture clash of either.

The Imperative to Withdraw

A striking parallel in the prophetic and the psychotic manifestations of the visionary states lies in the imperative to withdraw. Lanternari points out that among all the indigenous messianic movements at the unsophisticated level, the cult following is impelled by its very nature to make its escape from society and the world "to establish a society and a world of its own beyond history, beyond reality, and beyond the necessity to fight to bring change and improvement."[22] This constitutes a "temporary evasion" from the world while awaiting the final redemption. The collective rituals in the form of possessions, trances, incantations, and visions, are the means for achieving this evasion in an exaltation. The purpose, Lanternari finds, is to perform the special function of making a positive contribution to the regeneration of the society as a whole by developing this foretaste of the sense of liberation and redemption; once the desire for these has been satisfied, the need for evasion dwindles.

The significance of the evasion and withdrawal appears to be the necessity to protect the operation of the archetypal psyche from intrusions by the ordinary world. The energies of the "high arousal state," whether in the individual or the society, are concentrated in depth away from, and protected from, the mundane concerns of the everyday life context. If they are given full sway, they do their work of steering the renewal process toward its conclusion and then, it is hoped, toward its later fulfillment in the world once more.

Healing of a society and healing of an individual do not differ greatly in their modes, it seems. The point calls to mind the original meaning of the word "therapy"; the Greek "therapeia" has the connotation of a "waiting upon," and "service to," of "attending" primarily the gods. The term was applied to treatment through the cult of Asklepios, the god of medicine, where it was primarily a ritual procedure in service to him; his temple was a place apart from the world for invoking the healing visitation of the god in dream, in the aloneness of incubation rites.

The Forty Days of Visions

A final observation I want to make is that in visionary experience, the period of time that appears to be customary for the "high arousal state" to run its course is six weeks, the familiar forty days. The mention of the number calls up well-known instances in history, most notably the visionary struggle of Jesus in his forty days in the wilderness. In China, Hung's death-like trance similarly lasted six weeks.

Hung's experience[23] is a beautiful illustration of the relation of culture change to visionary states. In the mid-nineteenth century he led the T'ai P'ing Rebellion and came close to overthrowing the ruling dynasty and becoming China's emperor. As a young man, he attempted to enter the field of politics but failed the imperial examinations.

Mortified at the humiliating defeat, he underwent a sever depression. A dream convinced him that his death was imminent, whereupon he sank into a stupor so deep that his family believed him to be in the throes of death. During this time, however, he in actuality was embarking upon a visionary journey which lasted the familiar six weeks. In this celestial adventure he was met by an old woman who washed him and removed his heart and other internal organs, replacing them with ones colored red, and then led him to an old man. This venerable figure elected him to the task of exterminating demons and recalling the Chinese people to their duty to him. Upon his recovery, Hung was somewhat changed, his manner now heartier and his presence weightier, more imposing. Six years went by before he succeeded in grasping the import of his visions; some Christian tracts put into his hands allowed him at last to find all the meanings falling into place. He took both the Bible and his revelations as guidelines for his new reform movement called the Great Peace, *T'ai P'ing*, the Chinese term for a new ideal order in a regenerated world. He called himself "Younger Brother of Jesus" and "Heavenly King," and the Christian doctrine for his new regime was set forth in the Trimetrical Classic; in it his visions are mentioned.

> He was received up into Heaven
> Where the affairs of Heaven
> Were clearly pointed out to him
> The Great God
> Personally instructed him
> Gave him codes and documents
> And communicated to him the true doctrine.

With a large following and sizable army, he set up a government in Nanking for several years, but the rebellion failed militarily in the end, being blocked by the western powers from advancing.

Another delightful and colorful account of a forty-day visionary state is found in the apocryphal Book of Esdras.[24] In preparation for his apocalyptic revelations of world regeneration, Esdras was instructed by the Lord to go out into the fields with five companions to commune with his God and record in books what was revealed to them. "Take with thee . . . these five which are ready to write swiftly; and come hither, and I shall light a candle of understanding in thine heart. . . . " With these five, he went out, taking many box trees to isolate themselves from the people for six weeks; the Lord gave instructions to say

Let no man therefore come unto me now, nor seek after me these forty days . . . And the next day, behold, a voice called me, saying, Esdras, open thy mouth, and behold, he reached me a full cup, which was full as it were with water, but the color of it was like fire. And I took it, and drank: and when I had drunk of it, my heart uttered understanding, and wisdom grew in my breast, for my spirit strengthened my memory . . . The Highest gave understanding unto the five men, and they wrote the wonderful visions of the night that were told . . . and they sat forty days, and they wrote in the day . . . .

Summary

From the foregoing accounts it is clear that when a culture is deeply shaken by changing conditions, and finds itself in need of a wholly revised orientation in order to integrate new, unfamiliar values and priorities, the psyche responds creatively through gifted individuals. Visionaries perceive the revelations of innovative myth and ritual forms that might render the meanings of the new state of affairs, and that might thus govern and channel the motivational energies to allow the next culture pattern to function as an integrated whole. Myth then serves the purpose both of affording a framework with which to integrate the new meanings, and also the dynamics needed to implement them.

The awesomeness and majesty of the cosmic events in vision are the measure of the power of the new forms in respect to the insufficiency of the prevailing modes of thought to take care of the task at hand. In these visionary processes, the world image appears almost invariably as the fulcrum of the great turns of history.

World Images in Turmoil and Transition

3

From many observations, a few of which have been elaborated in the foregoing accounts, it has become evident to me that visions of the end of the world and of its new beginning take an impressively central place in the major turning points in the development both of persons and of cultures. They may be said to concern the destruction and re-creation of the psyche's world image in the turmoils of drastic change.

Even though one may now live in an age of reason, science, and technology, and find the mentality of myth and vision a little distant, still when one finds oneself at the crossroads in matters of psychological development, the dreams that become constellated reveal a lively myth-making process. If an individual is fragile in makeup because of certain emotional circumstances, these archaic contents may become so activated as to overwhelm the field of awareness, resulting in what is commonly regarded as a "psychotic episode." This is a state, as Jung has succinctly put it, in which the dream takes the place of reality. An acute condition of this kind stirs up the deeper levels of the psyche in such a way as to provide an open window into those processes that transform its energies and motivations. On this account I have found the investigation of psychotic ideation to be a fruitful avenue toward gaining an understanding of the myth-making process. We can also see in it a picture of the intense struggle of persons to find their way into social maturation and trust of relationships.

After the preceding review of a variety of messianic movements, can it any longer sound unfamiliar to us when we hear persons who, in their visionary states of this overwhelming kind, have felt that they have a calling to be a savior of the nation against an enemy; that the world is in the balance between total annihilation and rescue; that major world powers are meeting in a final Armageddon at the world's center; that they feel themselves to have died and to be dwelling among the living dead; that they are beholding the creation of a New Heaven and a New Earth; that they envision their mission to bring about a new age in a heavenly city; or that they feel themselves being enthroned as king or queen of a new world order?[1]

Prophetic Visions and their Psychotic Counterparts

I have been impressed, therefore, with the similarities in the renewal processes shown in the visionary experience of prophets and of psychotic states. Culture change under acute stress is the concern of each, one serving the society, the other serving the personal emotional life. Yet there are, of course, important differences. It is my opinion that the psychic process is the same in each, but the qualities of personality through which the process is mediated are at variance. Prophets are talented, articulate, and charismatic. Individuals while psychotic become shattered by their visions, their myths are as fragmented as they are, and they find it hard to express their myths clearly or with the ardor of feeling.

Our cultural assumptions determine our habits of thought in regard to psychosis. Our traditions have undervalued the inner life in favor of the external, the objective, and the action-oriented effectiveness in relating to the outer world. However, a new cultural proclivity is setting in that holds the opposite view — an esteem for the inner, the personal, and the harmonious relation to our own center.

Our need obviously is for a psychological model that can take account of all the various dimensions of the psyche. It needs to indicate how the psyche goes about effecting its own growth through its own nonrational processes and the stressful turmoils that they involve. The item of first importance in this model is that it should take account of the ordering, organizing, and integrating processes percolating upwards from the unconscious toward the ego. This viewpoint would counter the prevailing assumption that order in the psyche is handled by the ego and imposed from above downwards. A corollary of this point would be that transformation is not effected only by the insights and consequent "controls" that the ego might gain, but that is takes place in symbolic modes below the surface, preparing the ego for new ways of emotional expression and living.

An Account of a Renewal Process

For an understanding of psychotic process in such a growth model, the chief difficulty is to discern how it is that new ingredients of development evolve from their representation in symbolic imagery in the lower, inner levels, into their full expression in emotional living in the upper, outer levels of the psyche. To provide the experiential feel of this train of events, I will give a brief account of an illustrative case.

Francesca was admitted in mid-December into a residence facility where the policy was to allow the psychosis to run its course without medication. She was a young Catholic woman in her late twenties who had been married seven years and had two young children. The occasion for her break was that she had fallen in love with Paolo, a friend of hers and her husband's. The day after revealing this to her spouse, she became psychotic. Also, in the recent weeks before, she had become involved with a woman friend in what she called "devil worship," implying black magic and witchcraft.

There was a clear repetition of family history in her romance: When her father had returned home from World War II unable to provide her mother with love, the mother had responded to this frustration by carrying on an extramarital affair and later became alcoholic, for which she, too, had to be hospitalized on several occasions. She had worked in a restaurant where she had met the man she married after divorcing her husband. Francesca became closely involved with Paolo, in the similar circumstance of a tryst in a restaurant, when she, like her mother, found her husband to be cool and passive. The recent death of her stepfather, of whom she was fond, left her feeling somehow guilty, redoubling the guilt she felt toward her children over her amorous involvement.

On admission to the residence, Francesca was concerned about dying. She felt pain and pulling sensations in her chest and arms; these seemed to her to represent her being drawn into four directions, as if on the arms of the cross. "This crucifixion is a kind of crossing over," she said in a punning wordplay — the allusion was to the facility's name, Diabasis, the Greek word for a "crossing over."

She was giving expression to her guilt and remorse by pounding her chest in a "mea culpa" manner; "I'm carrying my mother's burden," was her statement. She wanted to be held and stroked and to become a little girl again. "What a trip!" she declared, "I'm a little girl again, and Adam and Eve were my parents. Ha!"

During these first days she craved much holding and cuddling. On the third day she explained, "My body hurts. It feels empty and I need love. I'm filled with memories of my father and mother." It was on the occasion of this statement that she narrated the story of her mother's rejection, affair, and subsequent alcoholism and hospitalization, and of her own guilt toward her children. The next day, she was full of good humor and laughter that the staff found both mirthful and contagious; she was full of talk and affectionate expressions toward various members of the staff. drawing close and hugging. In fact she strongly identified with the Love Goddess. She spoke of fears of death and of some general cataclysm which would amount to a "rebirth of society." She was sure she had to die and be reborn. Her god, she said, was a plant that had withered but then grew new foliage. Her withdrawal began to lift during these days, and by the ninth day she was indeed experiencing the feeling of being reborn and was delighted with her new state of being. "There's a new me!" she declared, "I have new, reborn feelings!" and these she perceived as new little green shoots of the plant.

After the first week, most of her talk was quite coherent and her mood usually elevated. Her principal emphasis was upon getting affection from people and having an open reception from them, particularly the male members of the staff. In all this there was a good deal of showy, "phoney" expression of feeling and seductiveness that became somewhat aggravating to the staff.

In the third week, she expressed some feelings of being called to a special mission — "to make things all right for Jesus to be here on earth" — and she felt some identification with one of the great women mystics and with Joan of Arc.

At the end of the fourth week, she felt "God is within me — I feel the goodness of knowing this. I was the Devil [before]," She also had a sense of "The King and the Queen within me." After the fourth week, she remained clear of her psychotic condition, and she was ready for her discharge at the end of the eighth week.

The account of Francesca exemplifies the principle of the transformative process in the psychotic experience that when a new component of development is becoming activated and taking shape in the depths of the unconscious, it first appears in the form of a symbolic image of mythic cast. As she found her marriage becoming unfulfilling, Francesca naturally felt prompted to complement the relationship with another that promised to contain all the elements left out. The missing elements were encountered in projection outside, seemingly embodied in another man. With remarkable faithfulness to its meaning, she accounted for this liaison as an effort to reach her husband through the other man. The fault was only that the needed lovingness was appearing not within herself but was instead projected out in the form of Paolo. The guilt, one might say, came not only from the moral prohibition of infidelity but also from the intuition that this was not getting to the issue. One is reminded of the Greek expression for "sin" in a word that connotes "missing the mark."

There was no way ahead for her in this direction. Her recoil and guilt threw her into a profound regression and activation of the archetypal unconscious; as soon as this set in, an array of powerful images impressed themselves upon her that belonged to the typical sequence that I have come to call the "renewal process."[2] The intent of it is to reorganize the self, and in it the basic motivations that emanate from the center, the core of the personality, are transformed.

The elements of this process that are typical of most cases are present in her account. She found herself at the world center at the time of creation in Eden, as daughter of the primordial parents. She also was thrown back to the feeling of the beginning of her life as a little girl again, and wanted to be cuddled as a babe in arms. This return was accompanied by the experience of death by crucifixion, burial, and descent into hell or purgatory, and of possession by the Devil. A conflict of opposing cosmic forces was seen as a war, possibly "a war of the worlds," together with the sense of an impending upheaval of the world in an earthquake. She feared being turned into a man, which made her angry. She was finding herself exalted to the status of the Goddess of Love, and of a new Joan of Arc, or sainted mystic. She beheld the image of the royal couple, King and Queen, in herself. The death and descent led over into the experience of rebirth and starting life anew, with "new reborn feelings." Great things were happening for the world in the form of the "Coming of the Lord," which would by implication promise a new era, possibly the messianic one, judging by the choice of phrase from the prophetic scriptures. She felt herself specially chosen to prepare the way and make the world right for the messiah to come.

Now if all she needed at the beginning of this process was to learn to love more caringly and with more warmth, then why all the elaborate myth formation? At first glance, perhaps most of it would not seem to have much to do with the question of loving. Various schools of thought have different recommendations to make regarding the symbolic ideation: "It should not be allowed to go on," or "It may continue, but one should not give special attention to it," or "If her inner journey takes this form, she should be allowed to make of it what she will without interference from therapists." The policy of our facility was to relate to it with interest and caring, and to try to make sense of it with her and not suppress it by medication.

The historical evidence gives to the sequence of mythic imagery meaning in that the imagery follows the main lines of the great myth and ritual forms of antiquity, the New Year Festivals of renewal of king and kingdom that I have described extensively elsewhere.[3] The close parallels found in these ceremonials are what have led me to call this style of psychotic episode the "renewal process." The only satisfying conclusion that can be drawn is that when the psyche is in need of reorganization, these are its habitual ways of effecting it. They are its innate modes of instigating change. If it does not make sense to us and appears "bizarre," that is not the fault of the psyche or of nature but our own for not being able or willing to understand it.

To put it another way, when the values that one is to live by are in need of change, they cannot be altered fundamentally just by right thinking or right feeling. They undergo transformation in the foundations of the mental life; fundamental change is effected in the fundaments of the psyche.

In these terms, this young lady went through something like this: Her psychic center was activiated, and she died to her previous mode of existence and regressed back to childhood, there to begin over again to form and experience a new structure of values and meanings. Her values clashed in an array of opposites to form a new world image, that is, a new *Weltanschauung*. Among the opposites, she became acquainted with the contrasexual component. Meanwhile she identified with the archetype of woman, the female deity, but significantly in her aspect of the Love Goddess. The Goddess image, one might say, was the wellspring of her innate potential for lovingness, the personification of the Eros principle that had remained somewhat dormant in her through the years of her growth. The semidivine couple, King and Queen, were likewise personifications of her potential for the man-woman relationship. With her own new beginning in the image of rebirth, she was aware of many new feelings being generated. Along with this, she was filled with the atmosphere of a new age personified in the coming of the messiah, that is, her own new social and cultural set with which she would be reentering the world with her new start in life.

When put this way, can it really be said that this imagery is of little value? It would be if all the symbolic images were merely wish fulfillments or ego ideals. This is where the psychological model by which we gauge the meaning of these processes comes into play to determine our conclusions. If we say that it is not wishes but potentials that are locked in these symbolic expressions, then we regard them in an altogether different manner.

The difficulty in psychosis, again, is that of actually effecting the transformation of new ingredients of development. They first arise in mythic expression — in the state of potential; they then evolve into a full conscious capacity to bring them into play — in emotional living. Francesca's capacity for relationship began to appear in her identification with the Love Goddess archetype and her perception of the King and Queen images in her. The more conscious state of this capacity was registered in her rejoicing over her "newborn" or "reborn feelings," although these needed much conscientious effort and therapy to adapt them to an actual relationship. Certain confrontations by her therapist did in fact assist her in becoming aware of her actual feelings out of their background in the more diffuse waves of archetypal love; that is, the all-embracing love emanating from the mythic image of the Goddess.

The statements of her experience of new birth are accurate renderings of the meaning of her psychotic journey. The import of the entire progress through death, regression, and new birth customarily appears to be, as I have pointed out, the transformation of the self and the reorganization of the personality. In the images of the Goddess, God and Devil, and King and Queen, it is the central archetype that is the dynamic focus of the process, and its work usually seems to engender a new capacity for relationship as the Eros principle becomes activated.

To sum up and epitomize the nature of the transformation in the psychotic process, the basic principle on which it is founded is that all components of development come to their fullness in the personality by a gradual differentiation from their inchoate state in the archetypal unconscious, where they are first represented in affect-images.[4] When certain components are needed for further growth of the personality and have not been playing their part in it before, they become activated in these deepest levels of the psyche. If such a change requires a basically new orientation, a visionary state is induced and the renewal process is set in motion. When the new component makes its appearance in an affect-image, it is at this stage a mere potential awaiting actualization in emotional living; thereafter, a gradual process of differentiation through experience, trial and error, and modification must be undergone.

World Images in Turmoil

I have selected this case as an illustration of the role of the messianic calling and breakup of the world image during the psychotic visionary experience that transforms the self and activates the Eros principle. I will now attempt to present a glimpse of the morphology of the world image as it makes its appearance in two areas of experience, the personal and the cultural, indicating the close similarity of the symbolic theme in individual and in collective experience.

Persons in a deeply psychotic state tend to visualize the world in the form of a quadrated circle, or mandala. I first began to realize this during the initial psychotherapeutic interviews with a young woman patient.[5] She mentioned that she was at the middle of the world between opposing factions. When I provided drawing materials with color, she elaborated her visualization of the experience, as Figure 1 shows. Her divided self is at the center, and the stages of her disturbance are in concentric circles around it, moving outward with time. Six petals indicated her "mixed-up ideas," giving the design a lotus-like enclosure. Surrounding all she drew a band divided in a red and a blue segment; these represented the mother's and the father's halves of the world divided in the opposition of their political parties, one conservative, the other liberal. The whole was enclosed in a square with four gates (not all completed in the drawing but mentioned verbally). The entire design had the meaning of her inner experience, of the hospital and grounds, and of the world in its entirety, all compounded together in a single diagram.

Her second drawing, shown in Figure 2, concerned her experience of a rivalry of friendships in her adolescence. The fronds were drawn as she told the story, but without hesitation the conflict was put into a cosmic context. The triangle-shaped blossom was the sun, the crescent at the root of the plant was the moon, and the surrounding circle the world. She then explained that some people think of the world as square as well as round, so she added the four corners as designating the afterlife in its opposing aspects and colors.

During the ensuing weeks, the number of political parties wanting to dominate the world grew to four, each with its particular ideology and value system. The final drawing, at the end of a process of several drawings and six weeks' duration, can be seen in Figure 3 to be a clearly quadrated world. The story it depicts was that the four parties, located in the four directions and their continents, at first clashed in a violent Armageddon, so that all was dark and stormy, but they then reconciled, and with the new peace the sun shone brightly at the center and all factions learned to live sensibly together in harmony.

Another person in a deep and profoundly disturbed psychotic state similarly expressed his experience in cosmic imagery. He felt himself going through the death and rebirth of an initiation process (Figure 4). It began with a Dantesque descent into hell (as a triangle with a central point), and through purgatory (as a square enclosing the triangle with a central point), and then an ascent to heaven (as a pentagon still enclosing the triangle — now the central point was God, with whom he identified). This last image was a space-time diagram inasmuch as it enclosed the final stage in a circle marked as a clock, counting the quarters as three, six, nine, and twelve. The central point subsequently turned out to be an important element, being an axis that could convey him up and down between the head and the heart. A somewhat similar image followed (Figure 5), in which he humorously represented his purgatorial regression in a delightful space-time diagram called "back-a-clock," counting the hours backwards this time, twelve, nine, six, and three, with the sun at the center of the quadrants, presiding over the whole. Societal concerns followed in which his inflation prompted him to believe that he was the new messiah on behalf of the World Mission to establish a new ideal society of a united world of Our Lady of Fatima. He depicted this world (Figure 6) in the rosary of this sodality: in four quadrants each representing one of the four continents — the Pacific countries, Europe, Africa, and North America — each with its own color. Finally, in Figure 7, we find a remarkable example of the power of an altered state of consciousness to transform the world image into its archaic form. Even though he was an aviation navigator, expert in the exactitudes of the most modern cartography, in this visionary state he beheld the world as a sort of icon, consisting of four petals surrounding a central body, representing North and South America, the Atlantic

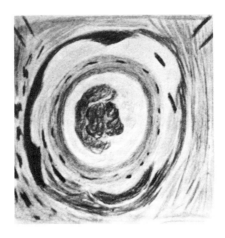

Figure 1. The Parent-Bound World

The client is in the center of the world in red and black, surrounded by father and husband, in green, and mother in orange. Concentric rings are in yellow, blue, and violet, and the six petals in as many colors. The enclosing ring is the world divided into the father's half in red, and mother's in blue. The grounds in green are intended to have four gates at the corners and a ring of traffic circulating counterclockwise in all colors.

Figure 2. The Adolescent World

The four plant fronds represent the client above on the right in yellow and green, a friend in blue on the left, and a second friend in orange and violet below on both sides being pulled toward each. The triangular blossom in gold is the sun, the crescent in yellow the moon as the root. The world the friends live in is round and grey, and that of the afterlife square and in four colors, blue, orange, green, and yellow.

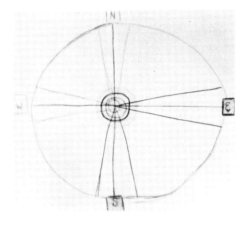

Figure 3. The World of Four Ideologies

The world is quadrated in four continents, parties, and colors which clash in war at the center, causing darkness. The sun emerges and makes the center bright as the four factions make their peace, shown as concentric rings in their colors, while a purple cross joins them at the center: the mother's party, the Republicans, and north are yellow; the father's party, the Democrats, and south are green; the husband's party, the Communists, and west are grey; the Socialists and east are red.

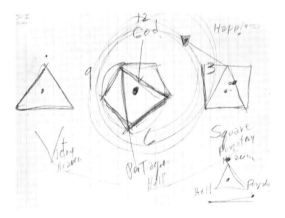

Figure 4. The Three Degrees of Initiation

The space-time diagram at the center indicates the three worlds of the inner journey: Hell the triangle, Purgatory the square, and Heaven the pentagon enclosed in a clock, with God at the center in each.

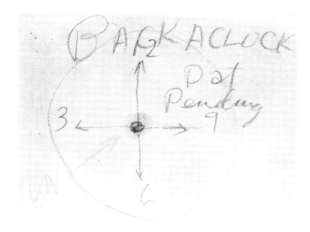

Figure 5. Back-a-clock
The space-time diagram signifies the client's world in regression. The sun, in yellow at the center, is surrounded by a cross of four hands in green as the four quarters of direction and of time.

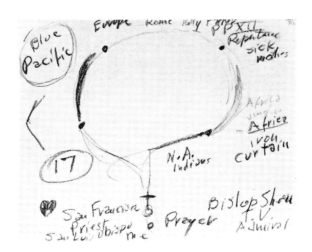

Figure 6. The World Mission Rosary
The quadrated world is composed of the peoples of four continents, colors, and creeds: the Pacific in blue, Europe in white, Africa in green, and North America in red. The cross is now below.

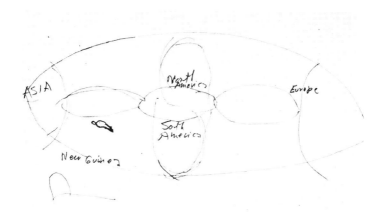

Figure 7. A Navigator's World Image
The map of the quadrated world has Central America at the center, surrounded by four ovals suggesting two lands and two seas; four continents are present in the entire oval.

Figure 8. The British World
The world is quadrated in four continents as the British Isles: north, solid green in a purple border; east, dotted green in purple border; south, light red outlines; west, dark red outlines. Centering is emphasized by a light red spiral, and a blue perimeter encloses the whole.

Figure 9. The Mesopotamian World
Babylon is at the center, the World Ocean encircling the round world. The quadration of the world is expressed by four pointed projections in the cardinal directions.

Cuneiform Tablet, ca. 600 B.C.

Figure 10. A Topocosmic City
The seat of the kings of the Sassanian Dynasty, the city is formed in the shape of the cosmos, contained in three concentric circular ramparts and quadrated doubly by eight avenues with gates in the cardinal directions. The ceremonial citadel occupies the center.

*Gur, near Firuzabad, Iran, dating probably from the
fourth century B.C. and known to Alexander.*

Figure 11. The Chinese World

The "Central Kingdom," Chung-kuo or China, is square with the image of the sun at the center and the "Four Seas" or Barbarian Lands extending in the four directions; the radiant dome of the sky encloses the whole.

Bronze Mirror, Han Dynasty, with "TLV pattern."

Figure 12. A Mexican Space-Time Diagram

The world is quadrated by plaques representing the previous four eras, the fifth and present one occupying the center and containing the image of the sun-god. The world is ringed by two serpents.

The Mexican Caldar Stone, Aztec.

and the Pacific, around an enlarged Central America: the idea of four continents still prevails, by his placing Europe and Asia at the right and left apices of an ovoid world.

The theme of four continents of a quadrated world again appears in Figure 8, the drawing of another young man in a deeply disturbed psychotic state. It shows a round world enclosed in a spiral, consisting of four "continents," this time the four British Isles, each in its own colors. The sun here is off to one side. It had for him the meaning of the ideal way of life for him and his wife, whose Latin background and style of family clan living upset him.

In similar vein, a young Latin American woman, not inclined to draw her imagery, gave clear verbal accounts of her vision of an Aztec world over which she believed her grandfather to preside as an autocratic emperor; she herself was queen. His four sons overthrew him and divided the Aztec world into quadrants to be governed by an ideal egalitarian regime.

These world images, I should emphasize, were created purely spontaneously and unbidden in interviews with me, drawn always during a line of lively chatter which articulated the flow of thought that went into them. Again and again the visionary mind's world is seen as round, either quadrated or squared, with a strong emphasis on what is at the center, and with the differentiation of four continents, races, colors, creeds, or political ideologies, each at the cardinal points of the compass.

World Images in Cultural Form

The visionary mind that appears in these altered states is archaic and ancient, but not primitive. It still carries the motifs of the age of great myth-making that I have called the Archaic Era of Incarnated Myth,[6] namely, the time of the highly energetic burgeoning of the mythic forms of the patriarchy in the Urban Revolution. At that time, the sacral kings were customarily viewed as the embodiment of the people and as the living center of the realm. The kingdom itself was conceived in the image of the world or the cosmos, and often built to show it in its quadrated, circular, or squared form.

Several examples of the iconography of these ancient cultures are represented here to give a glimpse of the world image as they visualized it.

Figure 9 shows a late Babylonian diagram of the world; the stone is chipped, making it a little difficult to discern that the ring of the perimeter is marked by triangular points in the four directions.

In Figure 10, the Iranian citadel of Gur near Firuzabad is constructed in concentric circles of ramparts and in avenues stretching out from the center in the cardinal directions, thus representing the mesocosm[7] in the likeness of the macrocosm.[8]

The Han mirror in Figure 11 portrays the Chinese world. The square is *Chung-kuo,* the Middle Kingdom, with the Son of Heaven at its center; four limbs of a cross stand for the "Four Seas," the barbarian lands awaiting assimilation into the ordered world of the empire. The dome of heaven encloses the whole.[9]

A space-time diagram is found in the Mexican Aztec Calendar Stone, Figure 12, in which the rectangular plaques in the four directions represent the four great world ages, the central area being the fifth and final one, presided over by the sun.[10] Two great serpents enclose the world (reminiscent of the theme in Figure 1 of the mother's and the father's halves of the world).

Other indications of the world pattern can be found in a variety of cultures. The Etruscan division into quadrants, each with its own color and characteristic metal, stood at the same time, like the Mexican, for the four great world ages.[11] Peru's capital city, Cuzco, was shaped into quadrants standing for the four segments of the empire in the four directions.[12] Comparably, the Egyptian hieroglyph for the word "world" was a circle divided into quadrants by a cross.[13] And in Ireland, the city of the Great King of Kings at Tara was at the center of the realm, flanked by four kingdoms.[14]

Cultural Ideologies in World Images

While the iconography of the world image is exciting to observe, so neatly following out the design of the archaic mythic cosmos, more significant still is the meaning attached to these symbolic forms: All these images of world or cosmos are expressions of certain kinds of cultural order and ideology.

The visualizations of the world image of the individuals with whom I worked likewise were expressions of order and ideology. As noted earlier, these people explained the meanings of the visualizations as they drew or verbalized them. Each was sensing momentous events under way to effect reforms of the world society and to produce a redeemed state and way of life through political or religious programs. Each saw him/her self in a key messianic role. In every case, these changes were to be brought about by cataclysimic clashes between opposing powers standing for socio-cultural or spiritual ideologies.

The question raised by these observations is, then, how is it that profound cultural renewals come to be represented in terms of the quadrated world image. What is it about this affect-image that is so powerfully dynamic in the process of change and transformation?

To begin with, it is evident that the world renewal that once took place on the collective level, in the great ceremonial festivals of the sacral kingships, has shifted over the centuries from its externalized form in myth and ritual traditions to its internalized counterpart in the spontaneous myth-making process of individuals. In the turbulent, disruptive visionary states of psychosis, however, the world renewal is still perceived as an external issue involving nations and religions. It is apparant to everyone except the person undergoing it that it is all taking place in the subjective arena. Indeed, what seems so public to the individual in this state is in fact among the most private and isolated experiences possible for humans to undergo. Yet the painful paradox remains that the issues these persons are grappling with are at the same time those that are troubling the collective society. Can it be that the problems and their resolutions in these visionary states represent in symbolic form those that the society also experiences?

What takes place in the quadrated world image, the mandala, has to do with transformation and integrative psychic processes within the individual, as Jung observed more than fifty years ago in his formulation of the individuation process.[15] Dreams and other visualizations of the affect-images tend to represent a psychic center that is superordinate to the ego and that takes the form of the quadrated circle, the mandala. When the self is engaged in the tremendously powerful process of reorganization, the phases of the changes are apparently governed by this dynamic center. It has its own way of bringing about the needed steps in growth and development that seem strange and unfamiliar to our rational consciousness, mostly for reasons of cultural bias, one that has pushed them back into unconsciousness through centuries of historical conditioning.

The Images of Self and World

Seen from this perspective, the world image represents both a selfhood and an internal culture. The issues appearing in the develop-ment of personality are at the same time the issues of cultural evolution.

Selfhood, after all, manifests itself through a way of life, a way of being in the world, arising out of a world view. This way amounts to a structure of meaning, a "belief system" and also a "value system." The image of self and of world is thus a kind of epitome in a symbol of that which will differentiate out and elaborate itself into all manner of specific concepts and feelings. One might compare this to the tiny acorn that contains, coded into it, all that is to become the gigantic oak. The life progress of a symbolic form is thus to be seen as an instance of nature's miraculous metamorphoses. Is it any more astounding to think of an entire subjective culture arising out of an affect-image than to conceive an entire human organism differen-tiating out of a microscopic sperm and ovum?

In this framework of organization of the psyche, when profound and acute reorganization of either the self or of the culture is required, the factors brought into play are the same in both. Sensitive persons who have the aptitude for visionary encounters with the archaic affect-images experience an activation of the world image. The oppo-sites are rent asunder, that is, opposing forces clash, and disorder vies with order. The previously predominating pattern is broken up, or at least such a catastrophe is threatened. There follows its transforma-tion in the image of world regeneration as the seed of a new culture form in mythic expression. This suggests that a transformed culture arises out of transformed persons.

Summary

To sum up, then, how the world image came to be what it is and to do what it does, evidence indicates that the mandala assumed its full form first as an image of the cosmos. This occurred at a juncture in cultural evolution when the mythic cosmic axis was projected out into the persons of sacral kings, and when the shape of the cosmos was concretized in the structure of the hieratic city kingdoms. At a slightly later turning point there took place, through the work of vi-sionary prophets and philosophers, the internalization of these images with the democratization of the kingly forms. Cosmic images then were recognized as expressions of an inner spiritual center and inner world. With this turn came an awareness of the selfhood of the individual as a wholeness to be realized by spiritual cultivation, expressed in the world image, centered and quadrated. Thus, the image embodies the affinity of the inner and outer worlds or cultures; each is an expression of the other's processes. The emotional aspect of the image occurs in the form of "peak experience,"[16] in which one feels intensely a oneness with all people and things in the world or cosmos. This emotion, needless to say, tends to be felt as an all-pervasive love for all beings. Great cultural transitions of earlier centuries have brought these discoveries to the fore in the world's consciousness.

Cultural Transitions   II

A Legacy of Pharaohs $\huge 4$

A mong the early centers of the Urban Revolution, the Egyptian is most generally familiar to us today; perhaps this is because the expression of its myth and ritual in its beautiful art forms — its pyramid paintings, its statuary, and its temples — have such a great appeal. When we contemplate these, it can easily escape our notice that at the beginning they all had to do with governance. When we see a statue of the falcon-headed Horus, do we recall that he and the pharaoh were one and the same? Or when we look at a painting of Osiris enthroned with crook and flail, do we remember he was the recently deceased pharaoh and now King of the Realm of the Departed? Do we know that the lovely Isis, "The Seat", was the personification of the throne? Indeed, an entire panoply of gods and goddesses had to do primarily with the royalty and the aesthetically balanced arrangement of the Dual Kingdom. Nor was Egypt at all exceptional in this, for myth and ritual in the cultures of that ancient world were expressions of the forms of social order and the monarchies that governed them.

On looking into the early urban culture of Ancient Egypt, one becomes impressed with the sense of sure order that suffuses through the whole pattern. Its model was the dependable regularity of the ebb and flood of the Nile, the very blood stream of its organism and source of its vitality. In this same spirit, the myth and ritual of its kingship in its evolution passed through an unusually clearly articulated sequence of developments from an absolute divine monarchy and collective moral order, and through states of gradual democratization of its royal prerogatives, to an outcome in which the sense of the moral responsibility of the individual emerged into clear expression.

In the early years of the Old Kingdom, the ceremonial governmental forms were permeated throughout with a sure conviction of the utter regularity in the order of the cosmos and its divine agencies. Only later did the realities of the actual subsequent history disappoint these expectations. For when things were prosperous, the pharaoh had only to govern his own daily activities with ceremonial rigor and the kingdom would find itself correspondingly well governed; he had only to strike a firm stance as victor in war and the campaigns would of themselves, almost by definition, be victorious. When, on the other hand, there occurred sorrowful times of disruption of this order, wise men and prophets held onto their faith enough to remind their rulers urgently that the reason for the troubles was their failure to sustain the divine plan in accord with their duty as kings. This habit of mystic ideation so intensely focused upon regularity could only lead to an ethical sense that would prove to be equally founded upon the sure rule of integrity. On the other hand, as the history unfolded it becomes evident to us that Egypt never reached the level of development that might envision the function of compassion among and between the people as a bonding principle giving society its cohesive force. Beneficient loving-kindness remained always in the hands of the king to give forth to his flock as their good shepherd.

The Sacral Kingship

Nonetheless, Egypt's history affords many observations that are of value to the theme under discussion. The first concerns the very beginning of this ceremonial kingship, from which emerges a striking picture of the genesis of myth and ritual forms. If one were to entertain the notion, as I once did, that the "higher" myths came into being by a gradual sophistication of folk beliefs, one would have to be brought to a radical revision of that supposition by the example of early Egypt. For here the mythic interrelations between Osiris, Isis, Seth, and Horus were established *de novo* at the start of the Urban Revolution (c. 3100 B.C.), and prevailed in their main outlines for the following three millenia, though with many modifications.[1] When the first pharaoh (of uncertain name) accomplished the military feat of uniting Upper and Lower Egypt, he proved himself a titan not only in war-making but in myth-making as well. For he created a justification for his universal rule by the explication of it in his Memphite Theology.[2] In it the several regional deities who had been worshipped in the nomes, or local city kingdoms, were brought into a new relation to each other by an act of creative innovation. We are left with the conclusion that this must have been the fruit of visionary work by this first pharaoh; it led Frankfort to recognize him as a creative genius.[3] Thus arose a mythology that was given to a populace by their new ruler, a development downward from the top rather than its rising from the folk upward.

In its essence, this theology was a successful formulation of the reconciling of opposite powers and realms. Seth, the king god of Upper Egypt, and Horus, that of Lower Egypt, were to "stop their quarreling" under this new regime conceived as the work of the nine principal deities, the Ennead. Horus was to wear the crown of both lands and be embodied in the ruling pharaoh. This dual kingship of the Two Lands was reflected not only in the double crown but in all the offices of government as well, each correspondingly dual. In another dimension, two kingships were established, that of Horus as ruler of the living and that of Osiris as chief of the realm of the dead. Each Horus king upon his death was ritually inducted into his enthronement over the realm of the ancestors through his transfiguration by which he "became an Osiris," while his son assumed the monarchy of the dual kingdom to become Horus.

The Center

The imagery of the center in Egypt's ceremonial is of particular moment for the purposes of the present investigation. The Pharaoh was clearly the embodiment of the governing center, enthroned upon a dais which symbolized the Primordial Mound, that first spot of land from which the whole earth spread into its extensity at the time of its creation by Atum. At his coronation, he released geese into their flight in the four directions, and shot arrows toward the cardinal points of the compass. His capital city, Memphis, standing as it did between the Two Lands, represented the midpoint of the earth. As well as in this form of centrality, he also embodied the entirety of the whole realm. So specifically was this expressed that his every move during the day was ceremonially portraying what was transpiring throughout the society, to such a degree that any ritual fault could engender ill fortune for its welfare.

The Giver of Life and Giver of Order

As the personification of the center and of the whole, the king was at the same time the Unique Man; in the earliest years of the Old Kingdom, the only individual to possess a soul which would live on into immortality through its transfiguration into an Osiris. In this aspect he was not only Giver of Order but Giver of Life as well. That is, both the order and organization of society emanated from his person, and also the life principle itself. He governed "in the embrace of his father, Osiris," indicated ritually by his wearing a gold stomacher representing the arms of his father.[4] The sense here was that the life-giving energy was provided from the underworld by the ancestors and channeled through their chief, Osiris, and thus into the person of Horus the King, from whom it radiated outwards throughout the realm of living beings.

The ideal of the Egyptian kingship was founded upon the concept of a "vital force," a "ka," which gave life and order to the kingdom, that is, to the whole world.[5] The king's *ka* was a composite of various deities representing the qualities of his rule. These divine components, as Wilson sums them up, combined into "a blend of sustenance and punishment."[6] Here again is an array of opposites reconciled in the personification of the center. How deeply the king's being was felt as a presence in the life of the people is expressed beautifully in a poem of counsel by a state official to his children,[7] urging them to worship him within their bodies and associate with him in their hearts:

> He is Perception which is in (men's) hearts,
>   and his eyes search out every body.
> He is Re, by whose beams one sees,
>   He is one who illumines the Two Lands
>   more than the sun disk.
> He is one who makes the land greener than
>   (does) a high Nile,
>   For he has filled the Two Lands with
>   strength and life.
> The nostrils are chilled when he inclines
>   toward rage,
>   (But) when he is merciful, (they) will
>   breathe the air.

The king's *ka*, his vital force, was the source of the Ka of all people, who in this fashion mystically participated in his being, as he did in theirs.

While the life-giving energies came from Osiris and the underworld through the king, those that provided the organizing principle of the moral order originated from the sky. While Osiris had as his attributes the waxing and waning qualities of the moon, the Nile, and the vegetation, Re — as the divinity of the sun — was characterized by his absolute regularity. Called the "Sun of Righteousness," he was the legendary author of the kingship and its first ruler in the time that was later looked upon as a Golden Age.[8] He thus personified the sure order of society and the organization of the realm, that is, all that became the collective moral tradition and law. All later prophetic calls for reforms in times of disorder had reference to Re as the originator and prototype of ethical rule. His daughter was Ma-at who personified right order, righteousness, right doing or truth, the implication being that truth is not so much something you think but what you do; there are repeated allusions to virtue as "doing the truth." There is a certain parallel here between Osiris's conveying vital force through the king's Ka and Ma-at's suffusing righteousness throughout the realm through the person of the king.

Visionary Experiences

As I have already mentioned, this entire system of symbolic expression in the myth and ritual of early Egyptian kingship appeared *de novo* when the first pharaoh through his conquests united Upper and Lower Egypt. The Memphite Theology was a brilliant product of visionary creation. How frequently the further stages in the changes and differentiations in the long history of Egyptian ceremonial were initiated through visionary experiences of rulers cannot be discerned from the records, though it cannot have been rare among a people so habitually occupied with their deities.

There is a dramatic passage that has come down to us from the fifteenth century B.C., telling of a visionary state in which the god made Thut-mose III his choice for the kingship when he was a young priest serving in the temple. This god was the ram-headed Amon, who was elevated to supremacy in the mythology of the monarchy in those times. Especially was this the work of Hatshepsut, the young prince's redoubtable aunt and stepmother, who was restoring the ritual centers after their devastation some while before at the hands of an Asian people, the Hyksos, who had captured the rule of Egypt for a century and a half. The young prince wrote[9]

> (The god Amon) — he is my father, and I am his son. He commanded to me that I should be upon his throne, while I was (still) a nestling. He begot me from the (*very*) *middle of* (his) heart (*and chose me for the kingship*) . . . .

As the young priest stood in the hall of the temple

> (*Amon-Re came forth from*) the glory of his horizon. He made heaven and earth festive with his beauty, and he began a great marvel . . . .

The god recognized him and stopped, while the young priest bowed to the ground; the god worked a marvel "remote from the faces of mankind and mysterious in the hearts of the gods."

> (He opened for) me the doors of heaven; he spread open for me the portals of its horizon. I flew up to the sky as a divine falcon, that I might see his mysterious form which is heaven, that I might adore his majesty . . . I saw the forms of being of the Horizon God on his mysterious ways in heaven.

Re then established him with the dual crowns and dignities of a god, with the uraeus serpent, the falcon, and the strength of the mighty bull.

> (He made me wear the Two Goddesses (the crowns); He made my kingship to endure like Re in heaven . . .

He was endowed by the god with victory and dominion over the foreign lands, to rouse terror and to extend the frontiers of the realm, that is, of the ordered world. In return, the pharaoh piously tended and provided for the god's temple. His reign was unusually long and prosperous, fifty-five years of rule being exceptional in those days. His innovative contribution to Egypt was his shifting of policy from a somewhat isolationist governmental housekeeping to an active and successful program of extending the bounds of empire into the countries toward the northeast, bringing in a wealth of revenues from them.

The Moral Order

In the long history of Egypt's thought and practice, of especial moment for the purpose of this discussion is the gradual democratization of kingly forms in a way that engendered the moral sense within the conscience of individuals. In the earliest years of the monarchy, the figure of Re presided over this sphere of the distinction between right and wrong, or as the language of that time put it, between "that which is loved" and "that which is hated."[10] His daughter Ma-at came into being out of an impressive "vision of the enduring state and its ever-functioning organization," being a "moral order of the world, identified with the rule of the Pharaoh."[11] This ethical order was solidly embedded in custom and tradition, a point stressed by a monarch of the end of the early period in his instructions to his son, Merikere.[12] With profound respect for the wisdom cultivated in the Old Kingdom, he tells his son that for the wise man, "Truth (Ma-at) comes to him well-brewed, after the manner of the ancestors. Imitate thy fathers, thy ancestors, . . . for lo, their words abide in writing. Open, that thou mayest read and imitate knowledge." What a striking statement of the nonindividual, collective form of virtue: to imitate the fathers, and even to imitate knowledge!

Righteousness and justice were to be entirely according to the ancestors, the product of their work, as the Pharaoh Ptah-hotep of the Fifth Dynasty saw it.[13] For him, government was to be conducted in the spirit of kindliness and wisdom, virtues that begin with the family relationships and reach out from there into the official relations of the state. The king was embued with the effective forces — the virtues — of righteousness and justice derived from Re and personified in Ma-at, and conveyed through his person to the realm.

A Time of Troubles

By contrast, we come now to a dramatic display of the opposite effects of the individuality that had been lodged in the kingship. The Old Kingdom was brought to its demise and a Time of Troubles ensued, when the aristocracy began to lay claim to its right to exert independently the kind of power and dominance that had been strictly the prerogative of kings. The central authority of the kingship lost its hold and the realm became instead a loosely coordinated group of feudal states under autonomous rule that was often irresponsible. The sure order of Ma-at began to disintegrate and men lost their confidence in the blessings issuing from the king's transformation at his death. As Breasted points out,[14] on the one hand, an attitude of skepticism prevailed in those years representing an abandonment of the erstwhile acquiescence to authority and tradition so characteristic of the Old Kingdom, and thus a loss of stability; on the other hand, this resulted in a gradual growth of the recognition of the individual's power to believe or not believe, as a conscious choice. This, then, was a step backward in social order but forward in self-awareness and personal initiative. The individual was emerging as a moral force, with a sense of conscience as the ultimate authority.

Prophets and Reformers

The role of prophets and philosophers became vividly active in evil times when the kingship was weak and decadent. It was not certain that they spoke from experiences of visions that might create new myths, but they did function as wardens and keepers of myth and ritual traditions, and they urged their rulers to resume a fidelity to the ancestral ideal of kingship for which they were responsible.

With the prevailing sense of disillusion in regard to the absoluteness of the divine kingship, the normative functions of society were disintegrating. These conditions of distress and dissonance were characteristic for the rise of prophets who would speak out against the ills of the times and envision the advent of one who would by divine election restore the ideal of righteous rule. One of these was Ipu-wer,[15] who specified the abuses of the social order and proclaimed the advent of the true king.

> WHY REALLY, the ways (are not) guarded roads . . . Ah, would that it were the end of men, no conception, no . . . birth! Then the earth would cease from noise, without wrangling! . . .
> WHY REALLY, grain has perished on every side . . . . Everybody says: "There is nothing!" The storehouse is stripped bare; its keeper is stretched out on the ground . . . Ah, would that I had raised my voice at that time — it might have saved me from the suffering in which I am! . . .
> BEHOLD NOW, it has come to a point where the land is despoiled of the kingship by a few irresponsible men . . . .
> BEHOLD, not an office in its (proper) place, like a stampeded herd which has no herdsman . . . .

The text has lacunae at this point, but the theme shifts wistfully to the true pharaoh who should represent the much needed ideal of the kingship in the image of the good shepherd.

It shall come that he brings coolness upon the heart. Men shall say: "He is the herdsman of all men. Evil is not in his heart. Though his herds may be small, still he has spent the day caring for them." . . . Would that he might perceive their character from the (very) first generation! Then he would smite down evil; he would stretch forth the arm against it; he would destroy the seed thereof and the inheritance . . . (But) there is no pilot in their hour. Where is he today? Is he then sleeping? Behold, the glory thereof cannot be seen . . . .

He then reiterates that authority, perception, and justice are the attributes of kingship, yet that the present pharaoh seems to prefer to let confusion and contention reign instead, both by his action and his lying.

Another example of prophetism comes from a Middle Kingdom text that relates in retrospect the story of a sage of the Fourth Dynasty (roughly five centuries earlier): He had foretold the downfall of the Old Kingdom and the consequent social chaos. Of greatest significance had been his declaration that the remedy must lie in the return of the quality of the first creation and its ideal conditions, as established by the sun-god, Re, who personified the ordering of society. Then, he had expressed the hope that a new ruler would arise who would, as a king of messianic savior, reorder the realm. The sovereign now bids the sage, Neferti (or Nefer-rohu), to speak forth not of the past but of future events, and he replies in writing:[16]

Reconstruct, O my heart, (how) thou bewailest this land in which thou didst begin! To be silent is *repression*. Behold, there is something about which men speak as terrifying, for behold, the great man is a thing passed away (in the land) where thou didst begin. BE NOT LAX: BEHOLD, it is before thy face! Mayest thou rise up against what is before thee, for, behold, although great men are concerned with the land, what has been done is as what is not done. Re must begin the foundation (of the earth over again). The land is completely perished . . . .
How is this land? The sun disc is covered over . . . .
This land is helter-skelter . . . . The face is deaf, for silence *confronts*. I show thee the land topsy-turvy . . . .
He separates himself (from) mankind.

After these and many such portrayals of the evils of the times, the vision of an ideal king then is proclaimed, that is, Ameni (Amen-em-het) of the Middle Kingdom, for whom this is written:

(THEN) IT IS THAT A KING WILL COME, BELONGING TO THE

SOUTH, Ameni, the triumphant, his name . . .
REJOICE, ye people of his time! The son of a man will make his
name forever and ever.

The evil and rebellious will be silenced, enemies will fall to his
sword, his wrath will descend upon rebels and the treacherous:

The uraeus-serpent which is on his brow still for him the
treacherous of heart . . . .
And justice will come into its place, while wrong-doing is *driven*
out. Rejoice, he who may behold (this) and who may be in the service
of the king!

Breasted has emphasized how respectfully the pharaohs of later
dynasties, after some centuries had passed, alluded to the sayings of
these early prophets to substantiate their claim to be faithful
upholders of the ideal of the kingship.

These prophetic admonitions resulted in a renewed hope for
social order to be upheld by just kings, and the pessimism of the early
Feudal Age gave way to a new effort among the official class to apply
this recently developed sense of conscience to their functions. Egypt
became ready to revivify its kingship in the person of this
Amenemhet,[17] first Pharaoh of the Middle Kingdom, the one who in
these instructions to his vizier quoted the prophets. He advocated a
program of social justice and kindness as evidence that the king loved
his people with the religious conviction that these moral ideals were
the decree of the god.

Democratization

A Time of Troubles like that of the Feudal Age (the First Interme-
diate Period) may lead either to prophetic calls for a faithful return to
the tried and trusted ways of the tradition established by the
ancestors, or else to a visionary creation of new myth and ritual forms.
The latter, while it may draw upon the ideals set forth in the Urzeit
of the cult founders, still transforms them to meet the fresh challenges
of cultural conditions when these have changed too radically to allow
the restoration of long-standing custom. Toynbee's formulation of the
innovative work of a creative proletariat giving rise to a new religious
cult led him to the conception of a new "Osirian Church" emerging
out of the Egyptian Time of Troubles.[18] Frankfort dispelled this notion

with cutting criticism, based upon information coming increasingly to light after Toynbee's time; he found no evidence of such an Osirian Church.[19] Clearly, Egypt went the other way of restoration. With the establishment of the Middle Kingdom, the ideal of kingship personified in the figure of Re was renewed, giving rise to an impressive social regeneration and consequent fresh power and dominance of the state.

Of note for our present discussion, though, it appears that another train of events was taking place, one that proved to be of greater psychological import, that did indeed involve the Osirian motif and did affect the life of the common man. This development was the gradual democratization of kingly forms concerning the afterlife.[20] Egypt's myth and ritual consisted of two major species, its kingship and its mortuary cult; one might see these as the traditions of Horus and of Osiris, the living king and the deceased king. The former heritage, as we have noted, was restored to its old strength following the model attributed to Re as its founder. The latter heritage, on the other hand, went through striking changes. The concept that had prevailed at the start, according to which the king as Unique Man was the only true individual with an immortal soul and with the sole prerogative of becoming Osiris at his death, was somewhat short-lived. It was not long before courtiers and high officials of the realm chose to be buried in tombs close to that of their royal master in the hope of accompanying him on his journey into the next world. This was the beginning of an outward and downward dissemination of the royal prerogative, and it soon entailed not only the mortuary privileges but, hand in hand with them, also the increase of power of the high officials relative to their king's.

In the Feudal Age, these developments reached their extreme in both these aspects. Mortuary customs showed the officials were no longer huddling about the royal tombs to be brought along on their king's journey; rather, they were housed at death in their own magnificent tombs, independently in their own provinces, and were buried with the rituals, derived from the kingship, of becoming each one an Osiris. Along with this, their power grew to be so autonomous that the central authority lost its supremacy and the realm became a scattered assortment of feudal states. Egypt became replete with great individuals.

The term "democratization" not only applies to this dissemination of royal prerogatives but also to developments that went much further in the direction of human equality. The last judgment that had assessed the king's righteousness and justice on the threshold of his transfiguration was now shared by all. The coffin texts of this age, reflecting the pattern of the former pyramid texts and containing prayers once used on behalf of the kings only, were now written for not only the official but also the middle class. They began to declare a new equality: "Re says all men are equally responsible at the judgment," for "I have made every man like his brother."[21] Breasted concludes[22] that this new awareness of moral responsibility in respect to the last judgment had a powerful influence for righteousness in Egyptian life.

In this mortuary theology, Osiris, always the favorite of the common people, did in fact take the ascendancy, though not in the sense of establishing a new cult or "church" as a distinct religious grouping. The mythic worlds of monarchs and of commoners became intermingled. As Breasted notes,[23] the celestial figure of Re now became depicted as traveling in his solar barque through the underworld domain of Osiris, and at the same time Osiris became increasingly solarized and presided over the last judgment, formerly the function of Re. Being justified at the weighing of souls before the throne, at one time a requirement for the king alone, now was everyone's concern. Providing only that a deceased individual had the funds to pay for this Egyptian way of death, any soul could now become an Osiris. All social distinctions were now said to be levelled according to the creator's intention at the beginning of time, so that all men found themselves on the same plane of moral responsibility, all equal before the law.

What could be a more clear representation of the psychological meaning of democracy! Long before it had any connotation of representative government or of any right to vote, it had the significance of a species of consciousness marked by a sense of social responsibility. Equality meant not the right for all to share in privileges of wealth and prosperity so much as the answerability of all individuals concerning questions of the well-being of society, that is, of each other.

This kind of consciousness clearly began in the archetypal myth and ritual framework in which the psychic center was personified in a sacral king who presided over the welfare of his people with a paternalistic and benign caring. He was a superfather of a superclan, whose duty was to love the subjects for whom he was responsible, and toward these ends was, at the start, the sole carrier of the principles of righteousness and justice. His annual rites of renewal at the New

Year Festival, with his combat against the forces of disruption and chaos, were measures to preserve his potency as Giver of Order and Giver of Life so that the people might flourish. The democratization of this functioning of the archetypal center amounted to its realization within the psyche of each member of the society. Order and life were everyone's business, and the moral consciousness and conscience were born in all.

Akhnaton, a Visionary King

The most unusual and colorful visionary among pharaohs was, of course, Akhnaton (fourteenth century B.C.), who proclaimed the final culmination of the prophetic development in the image of the "Sun of Righteousness." His short reign of theological, mythological, and social reform became a brief flowering of a new vision of monotheistic, ethical, and rational order arising out of his adoration of an all-embracing divinity, Aton, the disk of the sun in whom he found all that was good and beautiful in creation. His ardor was so excessive that he closed out all manifestations of worship of other deities. Since the consequent unemployment rate among priests and attendants of the numerous temples to other deities rose sharply, and long-accustomed and much-loved faiths were forbidden, the reforms were soon rejected by the entire realm and the king found himself isolated with his own predilections. The kingdom inevitably returned to its old ways, yet this did amount to a first attempt in the Near East at such a vision. It only needed to await its time for a fuller historical readiness in the slower evolution of cultures elsewhere.

A veritable anomaly among pharaohs, Akhnaton's sixteen-year rule defied all tradition and temporarily revolutionized the myth and ritual forms. He has been called a prophet of nature and human life, conceiving a great moral order of a new kind, his soul being moved chiefly by the emotions.[24]

Many hymns in adoration of Aton have come down to us, replete with joyous emotion evoked by beauty in nature and human nature. As Breasted puts it,[25] "All this discloses a discernment of the universal presence of God in nature, a mystic conviction of the recognition of that presence in all creatures," showing Akhnaton to be a "God-intoxicated man." He was a visionary who did indeed perceive the quality of love with a poet's eye. A prayer of his exults in this: "May my eyes be satisfied daily with beholding him, when he dawns in this house of Aton and fills it with his own self by his beams, beauteous in love, and lays them upon me in satisfying love for ever and ever."[26] In his rapture he identified this light with love, also with beauty, indicating God's presence. However, mystic though he was, entranced with the love and beauty in the divine and finding that all creatures are embued with them, he did not reach the perception of this love as a bonding force among members of the society. Rather, he still remained in the tradition of kingship as the mediating agency through which the people received these blessings. He thus saw his role in the same terms as those proclaimed by the former prophets of the Feudal Age, already mentioned, that is, as "valiant herdsman" and "shepherd of men," reflecting thus the demeanor of his Aton with his "fatherly solicitude for all creatures" — as he said, "Father and Mother of all that thou has made."[27]

Summary

In summation of ancient Egypt's history, it must unfortunately be recognized that although its two millenia of experience revealed many tendencies toward a new consciousness of social responsibility, still the strongly conservative nature of the people prevented these from attaining fruition. Wilson,[28] writing several decades later than Breasted and basing his conclusions on an enlarged accumulation of data, pronounced a somewhat negative judgment on the eventualities of Egypt's history. He felt that the idea of social justice did not survive the restoration of political stability and prosperity in the Middle Kingdom's later years, in which the Pharaoh's high prerogatives were returned to him. A sense of national insecurity in the later part of the second millenium B.C., "effectively ended any advocacy of rights of the individual, and forced every citizen into submissive acceptance of the transcendant rights of the state."[29] The familiar outcome was the resigned conclusion that surrender and obedience would be rewarded in the afterlife.

I would suggest that if it had not been that the heavy hand of tradition and authority prevailed so strongly, and if a more radical transformation of the order of Egyptian society had been proposed by its prophets, there might have been some appearance of the theme of world destruction and regeneration in their vision. The closest they came to this was their appeal for a return to the spirit of the *Urzeit*, the time of the beginning of the creation and its Golden Age.

The outstanding observation gleaned from this Egyptian history, then, is the picture of a strong evolutionary trend concerning individuality. From the early forms in which this individuality was lodged in the kingship at the center of the world and the summit of the hierarchy, there tended to take place a step by step dissemination of it outward and downward to the common people. It looked for a while as if the ordinary citizen would assume the responsibility for the welfare of his society and of his afterlife. Only the restitution of authoritarian rule from the top, combined with the acquiesence of the people to a life of obedience, thwarted this possibility. I would hazard the conjecture that if the principle of loving brotherhood had been realized, this history might have gone differently. Perhaps it was all too early in the evolutionary unfolding of the psyche for that to happen. It was instead the fortunate lot of China to introduce this principle onto the stage of history.

Sages and Sons of Heaven 5

W hen one reads deeply into the ancient classics of China so as to absorb the atmosphere of its world outlook, one loses gradually any sense of boundary between the world mastery of the accomplished monarch and the self-mastery of the accomplished sage.[1] This philosophy was at every point addressing itself to the question of how to govern and was speaking to the ruling class. Yet the principles that applied to right governing equally pertained to right living. The good ruler was a man with high achievement in both; and a sage, while master of himself, was by the same token accomplished in leading the people. The classics concerned themselves equally with inner and outer governance, and at times the reader is left wondering whether the author is speaking about one or the other, for each became an aspect of the other. This system of thought thus affords one of the clearest instances of the internalization of the sacral kingship, whose attributes then become those of the "sincere man" or "true man," the person of integrity and wholeness.

Magical interrelations and *participation mystique* between the world of human society and the world of nature have been a general presupposition wherever there has been sacral kingship. It is fair to say that nowhere has that outlook subsisted through the later differentiations of mythic philosophy for so long and in such a highly evolved and explicit expression as it has in China. There the ideal of wisdom led toward the harmonious interpenetration of the vital forces of nature with those of man, the effects of which were to be felt in both the human and natural spheres.

The World View

The entire way of thought in ancient China was founded upon a world view entirely different from that of the West in which, as Needham has pointed out,[2] the world was created and controlled by a divine power external to it and legislating its ways. As a scientist strongly motivated to achieve an understanding of the evolutionary process, particularly in human history, Needham so clearly recognized the value of the insights developed in the Far East that he gave decades of labor to record it in full in what might be called a "Summa Scientifica" of Chinese thought. What particularly fascinated him was the Chinese concept of the cosmos as a "self-contained, self-organizing organism." He summed it up in what is by now an often quoted phrasing:[3] "The harmonious cooperation of all beings arose, not from the orders of a superior authority external to themselves, but from the fact that they were all parts in a hierarchy of wholes forming a cosmic pattern, and what they obeyed were the internal dictates of their own natures."

Chinese thinkers never conceived of a conscious act of creation, but rather "A process bringing the universe from initial simplicity and disorder to its present state of complexity and order is conceived of in purely naturalistic terms," as Bodde puts it.[4]

The source from which this organic cosmos received its character is seen in the special regard given to ancestors in this tradition. The rites of divination and sacrifice were given in early times to the "Ti," the royal ancestral spirits. The community of the *Ti* dwelt in "T'ien," in "Heaven," thus endowing that region with the quality of a living presence known as "T'ien-Ti." More specifically, the earliest historically known dynasty of the Bronze Age, the Yin or Shang, venerated a supreme ancestor who personified the realm of the *Ti* and was known as 'Shang-Ti," the "Highest *Ti*" (a term used in translation for the western "God").[5] The ensuing Chou Dynasty held *T'ien* as their supreme being and merged the two concepts in such a fashion that this Heaven was possessed of heart and will that presided over the affairs of the world of nature and of men.[6]

The Sacral Kingship

On the earthly plane, the corresponding personification of the governing presence of the ordered world, that is, of the kingdom, was the figure that the Chou culture termed the Son of Heaven, *T'ien-tse*. Like Heaven, *T'ien*, he was not in any sense an autocratic ruler but rather a suzerain presiding over a confederation of overlords who held a degree of autonomy that increased over the centuries. In other words, the state was organized in the image of the cosmos whose component parts operated according to their own inner laws. The early pictographs for Heaven and the Son of Heaven revealed their close affiliation: for *T'ien*, and   for the *T'ien-tse*, each representing the idea of the Great Man, one presiding over free space, the other with feet firmly planted on the earth.[7] The form that later evolved for the word "king" was   for *Wang*, containing the meaning that this figure stood as a center at the cosmic axis uniting in harmony Heaven, Man, and Earth.[8] His centrality was again indicated in his identification with the Pole Star, that point around which the planets and constellations are ordered and revolve; the king had only to sit on his throne facing the south with the Pole Star at his back and be at one with himself, in a right relation to his own nature, and the kingdom around him would find itself duly ordered in harmony.[9]

The office of Son of Heaven was conferred upon a dynasty by the "Mandate of Heaven," a concept introduced by the Chou to justify their wresting the rulership from the Shang. A king held his position only for the welfare of the people and only so long as he served the public good. It was viewed as a characteristic of the cosmos that all is constantly in process of change; and in keeping with this flux, the virtue of a dynasty begins with ascent but soon declines and finally becomes exhausted; at this point Heaven wills an overthrow and grants the mandate to a leader more endowed with virtue and able to overthrow the decadent rule.[10]

The virtue belonging to a dynasty does not, of course, merely refer to a moral goodness but to the original sense of the term, with its root in the Latin "vir," a strength or force. In typical Chinese fashion, a kind of cosmology of such virtues served as a framework for the legendary five Sage Kings of antiquity: Each was a proponent of a certain virtue, identified with one of the five elements and five colors, initiating aspects of Chinese culture each of which acted as a power that spread through and filled the kingdom, that is, the world.

The Center

In Chou times the king served a ceremonial office, ultimately derived from the role of shamans and rainmakers, and requiring him to perform as master of ritual. At its center, his capital city contained on one side, a Temple of the Ancestors, dedicated to Heaven, and on the other its feminine counterpart, an Altar of the Earth on a mound representing it. The former was the place of the *Fong* sacrifice celebrating the king's success, the latter of the *Shan* sacrifice which involved the Queen and her retinue in rites of fertility, with a barbarian as victim.[11] The monarch performed the ceremonial first tillage, a seasonal custom persisting until our century. He was regarded as the Unique Man, Keeper of the Great Peace (*T'ai-P'ing*) in which the various components of the realm lived in ordered harmony. The only allowable wars were those conducted against the barbarian tribes and motivated by the cosmocratic function of enlarging the bounds of the civilized world of the kingdom; these tribes were known as the Four Seas, schematically envisioned as occupying regions extending in the four cardinal directions, as already noted in Plate 11.

Another particularly impressive ceremonial center was the Hall of Light, the *Ming T'ang*, whose mandala design of circle and square was patterned after the cosmos. "Square below, round above," designating Earth and Heaven, it was surrounded by a wall with gates in the four directions and outside that a Jade Ring Moat. The round top was used as an observatory to keep track of the movements of the heavens, while its square base consisted of five or nine rooms, a ceremonial room at the center surrounded by chapels, representing the months of the year and the corresponding areas of the realm. The king officiated in it as a sort of master of space and of time, making periodic circulations of the regions of the kingdom symbolically betokened by the rooms.[12] Legend had it that the first ruler, Huang-Ti, in remote antiquity actually made the journey into the outer bounds of the realm in the four directions, and that later successors diminished the ceremonial circulation by going to the four gates of the capital city as an effigy of the realm, and finally only by this circulation in the *Ming T'ang*.[13] Here the lords and barons of the realm gathered annually from the four directions for the great ceremony renewing their fealty and the solidarity of the confederation.

A Time of Troubles

All that has been described in this account amounts only to the ideal of the form and practice of the Chinese kingship. In actual historical practice, things did not go according to design. For China entered upon a Time of Troubles in a Feudal Age, much like that of Egypt, in which the individuality embodied in the Son of Heaven as the Unique Man was arrogated by the nobility to the detriment of benevolent responsibility. After five centuries of increasingly weakening rulership, the Chou Dynasty was becoming decadent and impotent, amounting to only a theoretically governing power. In actuality, the petty kings and overlords were quite autonomous and were using their liberty to fight among themselves and enrich themselves by enlarging their territories and their firm autocracies. To fill both their armies and their coffers they were bullying a populace acutely suffering under this unbridled oppression and predation. Fields for tillage were laid bare, villages laid waste, and the people hungry and miserable in their defenselessness. The consequent crying need for some consideration for the welfare of the people became the impetus to a flowering of reflective thought in the brilliance of China's "Age of the Hundred Philosophers," again not unlike the appearance of prophetic wise men in Egypt amid similar conditions, although far more impressive than they in their insights.

The Great Philosopher-Reformers

Following upon the excessive exercise of the power mode of political life there set in an intense activation of its opposite, giving rise to an awareness of the receptive principle and the Eros mode of living in the world. The time was ripe for the natural sequence of change, with visionary experiences leading to new myth and ritual forms. Yet in ancient China the expected "crisis cult" found a more subtle expression, and its "revitalization movement" was couched in reflective, cognitive philosophy rather than religious fervor. The explorations into the question of how to live in society and how to govern the people represented one of the earliest, if not the first, among attempts to grasp the significance of universal love and compassion as the bonding principle in the cohesion of society.

The two most influential ways of thought in that new age were those represented by Confucius and by Lao-tse, and their chief spokesmen, Meng-tse (Mencius) and Chuang-tse, respectively. They based their views upon the same fundamentals, the Way of Heaven and the Way of Nature, the Tao, upon which all right order of the human and natural worlds depended. The difference between the two systems was, in essence, over the matter of propriety as against naturalness: For Confucianists there was a correct way established by the wisdom of the sage kings; for Taoists, correctness was beginning of confusion and the only healthy guideline was the Way of Nature in which the Tao was manifest. As the former say it, only if one governs oneself is one fit to govern the people; on the other hand, the latter held that if as a sage one governs oneself, one has no need to do any governing, for then the people would find themselves spontaneously abiding in the Way of Nature. In this spirit the Confucianists venerated the ancestral sages of the distant past for establishing the proper ways of good governing, holding Yao and Shun as especially dear to them; on their part the Taoists equally venerated the ancients, particularly the ultimate royal ancestor, Huang-Ti, for setting the example of nongoverning and letting alone.

Confucius: Human-Heartedness and Democracy

In the context of cultural crisis, the figure of Confucius takes on a particularly significant cast. It has become customary to think of him as the proponent of a somewhat Victorian style of propriety, with correctness of demeanor and manner that prevailed subsequently among Chinese aristocracy until our century. While that is in part true, the actual import of his *Analects* was far more profound, revolutionary, and essential to the well-being of the people.

During his lifetime, Confucius lived the role of wise teacher of a few disciples and held no official governmental post of any high degree. Nevertheless, the messianic role of restoring the ideal of kingship was a calling that he entertained to some extent himself and that was granted him in retrospect by later generations. When he was invited to take office in the state of Lu, he declined but added the poignant comment, "Certainly he did not call me for nothing. If anyone were to use me, might I not make a new Chou here in the east?" "He dreamed, in other words," says Creel,[14] "of setting up a new dynasty that would rival the former glories of the sadly declined Chou empire." In the time of the full flowering of the philosophic age in the Han dynasty three centuries after his death, he was so venerated that he was pronounced founder of a dynasty, receiving the Mandate of Heaven to rule the whole empire of the Middle Kingdom, only, however, in the ideal sense as monarch without actual government or throne. It was said that his was a messianic reign achieving the longed-for *T'ai-P'ing*, the Great Peace.[15] After another century, this was further amplified in the declaration that he was more than a king but a superhuman living god, whose *Spring and Autumn Annals* were regarded as setting forth the political ideals for the rule of the Han Dynasty and its program for the Great Unification.[16]

The office of *Wang*, the Son of Heaven, was envisioned in these Annals as a quite spiritual function which would be filled by a savior king ruling by "magical, moral force alone." This true king to come was "looked forward to with messianic fervor," for in his time Goodness was to prevail and become universal within a single generation.[17] In all this messianic idealization we find the characteristic flavor of a "revitalization movement," born out of times of crisis in Confucius's day.

What, then, was this "Goodness" that was to prevail? In the vision that Confucius set forth in his teachings, we find it centering upon a predominant quality comparable to that of the *Tao* in Lao-tse. It was *Jen*, an archetypal dynamism, a "mystic entity identical sometimes to the *Tao* of the Quietists," according to Waley, a "sublime moral attitude" that represents a display of "human qualities at their highest."[18] Thus, it was a sort of transcendental perfection accomplished only by heroes and perfected only in the Divine Sage, who in consequence was regarded as almost a demigod.[19] What is this superb spiritual entity and quality that makes for ideal kingship? It is best translated as "human-heartedness" or "compassion," that which prompts one to love others, to care for their welfare.[20] This is the compensatory principle proffered as the alternative to the strong-handed and overbearing rule of petty princes of the times. Speaking to the topic of *Jen* (often translated as "perfect virtue") Confucius emphasized respect and love for others: behavior toward everyone as if receiving a great guest; employing anyone as if assisting at a great ceremony; and doing to others as one would wish them to do to oneself.[21] The paternal benevolence of a ruler he defined as "to love all men."[22] He maintained that personal spiritual fulfilment requires one's consideration of others: "The man of *jen* is one who, desirous to sustain himself, develops others."[23] Dai points out that the written ideogram, *jen*, implies two persons in relation to each other, and that while it originally indicated the kindliness of a ruler to his subject, in the course of time it became "the way two human beings would naturally feel toward each other, if their Heaven-given nature had been properly developed, that is, to love each other."[24]

The specific functions effecting this principle of *jen* were two others which were extensions of it into more explicit expression: *chung*, conscientiousness toward others, and *shu*, altruism.[25] These constituted the mode of good social cohesion, which were framed as paternal benevolence of the prince toward his subject, and fibial loyalty of the latter to his overlord. In personal relationships Confucius was the first to formulate the Golden Rule in its negative as well as positive expression: not doing unto others that which you would not have them do to you, as well as doing unto others what you would have them do to you.[26] These expressions are so familiar to us, and so associated with Christian piety, that we are apt to find it hard to imagine that these pious thoughts could amount to startingly revolutionary principles in the concept of government and social reform. We have to remind ourselves that, indeed, these were new expressions in the world at the time and could well have sounded totally alien to the ears of those in power. In fact, Confucius did encounter some such response, since he went from court to court attempting to instruct the princes in right government but was not successful in having his principles adopted or himself appointed to the necessary posts to bring their execution into practice.

Creel's assessment of Confucius's aims[27] is that he wished to make changes so sweeping that little would remain of the feudal order. He spelled out full-blown proposals of truly democratic principles, in the sense of equal opportunity, which have been characteristic of China's political practices ever since. Particularly revolutionary was his view that equal worth may be found in persons of all classes and that even the barbarians were to be accepted and assimilated on these terms. The people were not to be considered the means for the state's ends, but the other way, the ends for which the state served. The Master said that his Way was pervaded by a single principle, the vision of a cooperative world made up of relatively free agents not dominated by coercion; the kingdom could be no better than the individuals composing it, so all starts with the individual person. Confucius thought of the whole society as one great family, which has an order and a discipline without the motivation of fear, only a desire to cooperate in carrying out shared purposes. "Within the Four Seas, all men are brothers," the Master said, and when asked about virtue, he said, "It is to love all men," and about knowledge, he said, "It is to know all men."[28]

Can one call such a reform movement religious? There is no question that it has that quality and that the term "philosophy" conveys too much the sense of the cognitive to describe these classics. The "attitudes" to be cultivated contain more than meets the eye, for they are the main motif in the development from early royal ritual to the later ethical living.[29] They were called *"jung,"* a term stemming from the ritualists who represented the ancient religious traditions and practices, and having the implication of adopting a particular appearance in the face of certain situations. Each rite required its appropriate attitude or emotional stance, whether reverence, eagerness, grief, joy, or other. Confucius made a study of such attitudes as applied to correct ways in living in society, unfortunately translated as "propriety" but actually intending more depth than that word carries for us. Thus, the ancient auguristic-sacrificial manner developed further now into the ethical sense in the individual and, as Waley phrases it,[30] it was seen that "Man, no longer a pale shadow of the ancestors, has within himself all the attributes that formerly made the cult of the *Ti* Kings the supreme end of tribal cult." In Confucius's thought, the companionpiece to *jen*, human-heartedness, was *yi*, righteousness or rightdoing, with specific reference to the proper ritual or ceremonial behavior.

Mencius: Inner Kingship and Inner World

The principle of *jen* was further elaborated by Confucius's great explicator, Mencius, a couple of centuries after him. Mencius understood *jen* as a compassion that was innate, unlearned, a natural endowment in persons that was not produced by culture but protected by it.[31] It leads to a selfless state in which any distinction between oneself and others, or oneself and the universe, disappears. This line of thought led Mencius to a perception that the macrocosm is reflected in the microcosm, inasmuch as this selflessness led to an identification of self with the universe as a whole: Thus, "the myriad things (the whole universe) are complete within us."[32] There results from this view a sublime concept of spiritual development: By the practice of *yi*, right doing, there evolves the natural endowment of *jen*, lovingness, and the outcome is the Great Morale (or Passion Nature) which emerges from the very center of one's being.[33] This today we would recognize as a formulation of the work of the archetype of the Self, the very center of one's being; accordingly, Mencius taught that indeed this Great Morale represented the fulfillment of the development of one's original nature (the law of one's being). Through this evolution of one's selfhood "All men can become Yao and Shun,"[34] that is, a sage king. The "sageliness within," emphasized by

Confucius, had its counterpart in "kingliness without," which Mencius formulated as the "Kingly Way," and which was entirely the effect of the king's practice of love, that is, compassion and altruism.[35]

What is important about Mencius's doctrine, that *jen* is an innate and not an acquired quality, is from the psychological point of view not only the implication of the essential goodness of man; it is also the recognition that the foundation of one's being gives rise to these energies that drive toward fulfillment. That is, it arises from what we would call the archetypal psyche with its ancestral heritage. He stresses an insight that is especially noteworthy, that the means by which such innate drives enter into cultural experience is by first projecting them out into external figures, those of ceremonial kingship or of myth and legend. As already mentioned, Yao and Shun were for the Confucianists the exemplary representatives of the sacral kingship; they personified the ideal of that function of rulership. Then in the course of history and cultural maturation these qualities become recognized in their internalized form once more and may be achieved by anyone who attempts spiritual cultivation: "Any man can become Yao and Shun." What can be a more fitting expression of the function of myth and ritual in the evolution of culture, specifically in the development of the qualities of love and compassion? The Kingly Way, the Royal *Tao*, is principally that of lovingness.

Mencius's psychological perceptiveness extended even further in his analysis of the means by which such drives find their way into practice. He recognized that the family is the first model for living in society, and that the parent figures are the first bearers of the relations to authority. He taught that the attitudes between father and son, paternal benevolence and filial piety, were the first schooling for the growing individual in what was to become his relation to the ruling prince. There was thus a hierarchy of fathers: *Ti*, the ultimate father as the ancestral Heaven; the Son of Heaven, the sacral king; the regional prince, the father of his people; and the paterfamilias. The loving quality of loyalty and benevolence that flowed up and down this ladder of authority is what held society together. It is on account of this whole framework of thought that the Confucian classics are addressed to the *shih*, "Knights of the Way," the *Tao*, the counterparts of the "Knights of the Chariot," the warriors; they were cultivated gentlemen dedicated to the way of Heaven. The term *ch'un-tse* means "sons of the king," thus sons of the Son of Heaven, familiar to us in the translation "Superior Man," the individual accomplished in learning and virtue, living by the Middle Way.[36]

Later Confucians

One of the most beautiful among the classics is *The Doctrine of the Golden Mean*, literally, "The Center of Equilibrium and Harmony."[37] This center of balance between the opposite stirrings of emotions is the "great root" from which grow all the human actions in the world; the harmony is the *Tao* or Way to experience emotions in their due proportion. For our present discussion, one sequence of thought stands out among the many rich insights. Spiritual cultivation, Tse-sse says, is required to bring one to enlightenment and perfection, or more accurately, to a state of "sincerity" with enlightenment. The term implies completeness and being true to oneself, guileless and authentic. Now a qualification is added that is in keeping with all that we have been finding in this literature. We are told, "One cannot perfect oneself while disregarding the perfection of others";[38] that is, we can develop our nature only through human relationships. This we might call the first appearance of a psychology of interpersonal relationships. Only with sincerity can we fully develop to the utmost our own nature, and thereby that of others and of the things of the world. Thus, by following this Way, we "assist the transforming and nourishing operations of Heaven and Earth."[39] This follows the Confucian method which is, through the extension of love, to elevate the mind above the usual distinctions between self and others.

The cosmic implication of emotional and spiritual cultivation was carried further in the Han times by Tung Chung-Shu.[40] Heaven, he said, has its own feelings of joy and anger, its own mind which experiences sadness and pleasure, analogous to those of man. Man, a replica or duplicate of Heaven, is at one with it. The great triad, Heaven, Earth, and Man, constitutes the origin of all things: Heaven gives birth, Earth gives nourishment, and Man brings to perfection. The ancients, he said, formed the character for "king," *Wang*, by drawing three horizontal lines for this triad and a vertical line through the center joining these three principles: "Occupying the center of Heaven, earth, and man, passing through and joining all three — is he not a king who can do this?"[41] Man shares four temperaments and passions with Heaven and its seasons: "The spirit of spring is loving, of autumn, stern, of summer, joyous, and of winter, sad";[42] if he holds these deeply within, not allowing them out recklessly, then he may be called the equal of Heaven. Indeed, without man's culture-making the world would be unfinished and the universe suffer imperfection. For man continues Heaven's work, beyond what it can do, through his *jen*, his human-heartedness, and this is the work of the great exemplary sage kings.[43] This Goodness, the basic stuff of which man is made, needed these kings to bring it into effect, as a continuation of nature, not a reversal. In all this teaching we find, then, a truly evolutionistic framework for the role of man in the creation; it is man who has the moral consciousness and lovingness to perfect it beyond the capacity of Heaven (in striking contrast to the Christian *Agape* as solely God-given, to be discussed below).

Mo-Tse: Universal Love

An active reformer in matters of government and war was Mo-tse, who was the first to set himself in opposition to the prevailing Confucian way of thought.[44] Speaking in a manner that sounded almost like a prechristian Christian, he advocated what he called *chien-ai*, universal love, a concept coming close to the notion of the brotherhood of man. He objected to the formulation of love put forth by Mencius, that love follows along the lines of the relations between father and son or prince and subject; such clan ethics are discriminatory and punishable by Heaven. *Chien-ai* is love among all one's fellow beings, and Heaven rewards it. It seems, however, that he was what we might call a thinking type, and love for him was a merely logical conclusion as the best way for people to get on well together in society. It lacks the mystical cosmology and mythic cast of the *jen* of the Confucianists. However, he went about teaching the princes in their courts that taking the initiative in offensive war was to invite only ills for themselves and the people, and that the most they should do with arms was to protect their kingdoms; toward this end, he made a study of the methods of defensive warfare. The Taoist Chuang-tse made fun of Mo-tse's followers, painting them humorously as a raggedy crew of eccentrics going about the courts of the empire to preach peace. We might say this was like a counterculture move by conscientious objectors opposing the abuses of the Establishment! The doctrine of *chien-ai* did not make a profound impact or blossom into a future in the mainstream of Chinese thought, perhaps largely because his writings were lost in the burning of the books by Chin-shih Huang-ti.

Taoists: The Way of Nature

The Taoists represented a protest movement of much greater consequence than Mo-tse's. For anyone who has lived in China, it is evident that Taoism speaks for the way of life of the people and for their prevailing outlook and world view.[45] The Confucianists' thought was focused upon the government providing benefits from above to the people below, and was addressed to the aristocracy, the officials and ruling classes. Democratization of the kingship was explicitly expressed as the opportunity of every fulfilled individual to become a sage equal to the ancestral sage Kings, a Yao or Shun. In this school of thought, the image of the center still resided at the peak of government structure in the Son of Heaven, and the benevolence and virtue of the sage king spread out to the people. The teaching of the Taoists, on the other hand, emphasized the way for the people to develop their own natures in such fashion that they would find no need for being governed from the top of the social structure. This was written from the experience of nonofficials and for them; it provided a concept of democracy as a spontaneous tendency of the people, who when fulfilling their nature tend naturally to live harmoniously in society. In this spirit, the Taoists extolled the legendary original founder of their culture, Huang-ti, as an exemplar of the Taoist way. The image of the Center therefore resided within the individual, who had only to live in the One, holding to the Light, and then social relations and human-heartedness would take care of themselves.

Advocating the Way of Nature, with roguish irony and humor the Taoists set this Way over against the precepts of the Confucianists, who, as they saw it, talked too much, especially about virtue. These, they said, cut things up by their definitions, thereby missing the feeling for the whole and getting out of touch with the One, the center.[46] Where the Doctrine of the Golden Mean was to cleave to the Equilibrium between the opposites, Chuang-tse[47] maintained that by dwelling at the center, one transcended the opposites. The essence of the Tao was that by living in that state the opposites ceased to be opposed: Only the One is abiding and the rest is all change. Thus, one should forget all the distinctions between right and wrong, beautiful and ugly, and discard "knowledge" which cuts things up into distinctions, because such opposites are in a state of endless flux moving in a revolving circle about the center. [48] Mystical knowing is "wu-hsin," nonknowledge or no-mind: "Nothing is better than to use the Light."[49] Thus, Chuang-tse's recommendation is, "Let us joy in the realm of the infinite and stay there, and experience the One, which is undifferentiable."[50]

As we read the early Taoists, we find little encouragement of love and kindness except perhaps in its negative — the more we talk of it, the more likely it is that it is not happening: "After the Tao is lost, then arises the doctrine of kindness,/After kindness is lost then . . . justice,/After justice is lost, then . . . ritual./Now ritual is the thinning out of loyalty and honesty of heart, and the beginning of chaos."[51]

However, we should not be misled about the presence of caring in the Taoist Way, for to dwell in the One is to enjoy full recognition of one's deep interrelatedness with one's fellow beings: "Banish wisdom, discard knowledge,/And the people shall profit a hundred-fold;/Banish 'love,' discard 'justice,'/And the people shall recover love of their kin."[52] The prince has only to dwell in the Tao and the relations within family and state of themselves become harmonious. As Waley paraphrases it,[53] "If we stop looking for 'persons of superior morality' . . . to put in power, there will be no more jealousies among the people, etc." He points out that slipping into *wu-yu*, desirelessness, and *wu-wei*, nonactivity, is a way acquired in "trance," that is, in meditation, and he speaks of the Taoist school of thought as quietism.

Chuang-tse quipped that if you find an expert in matters of government do not let him near the capital city, but just leave the people alone to live out the tenor of their lives in the Way of Nature and they will dwell in harmony and prosper.[54] The fulfilled *chen-jen*, the True Man, knows what is of Heaven and what is of Man, cheerfully accepting life as it is and not leading the heart astray from the Tao; in contrast to Tung Chung-shu, he warns that such a man should not supplement the natural by the human means. Only by being free in mind and calm in demeanor can he wage war and not lose the affection of the people. He spreads his blessing on all the people, yet does not do so through any conscious effort to love them.[55] In all this, we observe that Taoism is still addressing itself to the acute problems of the times, to the suffering of the populace under the tyranny of predatory overlords who oppress them.

Speaking to the Confucians, Chuang-tse argued that the doctrine of *jen* and *yi*, human-heartedness and duty, can only create confusion, as does also any concept of "right and wrong." Such virtue only evaporates into desire for fame, and all the "learning" and "knowledge" only into competitive conscientiousness, until such men only crush each other. If, before one's own integrity becomes an influence, one forces the preachings of charity and duty on men and rules of conduct on wicked persons, one only makes them hate him, and so he becomes a messenger of evil. More important is to love one's self; only "who loves the world as he loves himself may be entrusted with the government of the world."⁵⁶

An equally important Taoist answer to the plight of the Chinese populace described at the start of this discussion concerns the "Receptive," another aspect of the compensation to the current excesses of dominance and power. The teachings of Lao-tse are too well known to need much elaboration here, except to highlight some of his explications of this receptive principle. The highest good is like water in seeking the lowliest places. Hence valleys are the image of living nearest the Tao. The passive, receptive, female element alone has access to the Tao. The poetic stanza praising the Valley Spirit is generally familiar: It is the Mysterious Female, which never dies, which is the base from which Heaven and Earth sprang, and which is always within us to be drawn upon, never running dry.⁵⁷ We should note here that a cosmological comment is not left as a statement about the objective world itself but is linked with the inner world. Today we would put it that the archetypal feminine is the root and source of our world image, providing us with a means of apprehending the nature of the outer world in terms of the Receptive.

When a king lives and rules according to the Way of Nature, the *Tao*, the Receptive becomes his mode. He adopts the stance of *wu-wei*, nonassertion or nonstriving, and thus practices a noninterfering and letting be, in response to which the people thrive by taking care of their own affairs. By the law of "reversal," this *wu-wei* becomes highly effective: "The sage puts himself in the background, but is always to the fore," and thus "Is it not just because he does not strive for any personal end that all his personal ends are fulfilled?"⁵⁸ The effectiveness of this mode of the *Tao* is the result of the power of its accompanying *Teh*, a virtue in the sense of a dynamic force. By it, social order is not imposed from above the people but evoked from within the members, a noteworthy observation that we shall continue to consider.

The Taoist way of democratizing the kingly forms was therefore in terms of recapturing the natural democratic propensities inherent in human nature. The Way of Nature signifies the manner in which the entire cosmos operates, that is, as an organism in which the component parts function cooperatively according to their own inner being. As Heaven does not regulate everything from its supreme position yet has its own heart and will, so the sagely king does not command the affairs of the realm but creates a presiding presence that allows the people to fulfill their own lives according to their own natures.

In this spirit, Lieh-tse could say, "Only when there is perfection of each individual and each attends to his self and stops thinking about benefitting the state, can the state become sound."[59]

The I Ching: Active and Receptive Principles

Further testimony to the correspondence between the nature of man and that of the cosmos is found in that treasure trove of ancient Chinese wisdom, the *I Ching*, which reflects both Confucian and Taoist thought. Wilhelm explains[60] the sense of the book as a "complete image of heaven and earth, a microcosm of all possible relationships," enabling us to calculate their movements in every situation, for man has innate capacities that resemble heaven and earth. An early commentary (the *Shuo Kua*)[61] says of the first hexagram of pure Yang (male) lines, called "The Creative," that as the sign of Heaven and of the kingship "The Creative brings about rulership": "The Creative is heaven, therefore it is called the Father./ The Receptive is the earth, therefore it is called the Mother"; these are the essence of the first and second hexagrams.

In the comments on the first, "The Creative,"[62] is an account of the fulfillment of man; whether it leads to the kingship or to the status of the sage is a matter of equal choice; one accomplishes his mission outwardly, the other inwardly, and both have a pervading influence on the life of the realm. Wilhelm tells us, "In relation to the universe, the hexagram expresses the strong, creative action of the Deity. In relation to the human world, it denotes the creative action of the holy man or sage, of the ruler or leader of men, who through his power awakens and develops their higher nature." The movement of the lines describes a progress from his hidden power at first, through his gradual appearance in his chosen field and his recognition, and to the point where a free choice can enter in: "A twofold possibility is presented to the great man: he can soar to the heights and play an important part in the world, or he can withdraw in solitude and develop himself. He can go the way of the hero or that of the holy sage who seeks seclusion. There is no general law to say which of the two is the right way." He thus chooses according to the inner law of his being. This expresses beautifully the full equation of the outer and the internalized kingship, of that which belongs to governance and that which pertains to spiritual cultivation.

In the second hexagram, "The Receptive,"[63] we find further links between the Receptive principle and that of human-heartedness, through the concept of devotion.

It tells us, "The attribute of the hexagram is devotion; its image is earth. It is the perfect complement of *The Creative* (the pure Yang) — the complement, not the opposite, for the Receptive does not combat the Creative but completes it." Then, in regard to the questions we are dealing with, it says, "As applied to human affairs, the principle of this complementary relationship is found not only in the relation between man and woman, but also in that between prince and minister and between father and son." In respect to the issue of imposed order and evoked order, we read, "The attribute of devotion defines the place occupied by this primal power in relation to the Creative. For the Receptive must be activated and led by the Creative." The Creative connotes the spiritual in potential, the Receptive the actual in spatial reality; the Creative begets, and the Receptive brings to birth. In human affairs, then, what is implied is "action in conformity with the situation," that is, knowing "how to meet fate with an attitude of acceptance," thus letting oneself be guided. The genius of the Receptive lies in its realism, in taking into account the actualities of any situation and learning from them what is demanded of oneself. According to this, nature's own spontaneous order is evoked in contrast to any man-made order.

The most eloquent expression of government by quiescence and the Receptive, and by "sageliness within and kingliness without," is in Waley's renderings of Lao-tse's tenth chapter:

> Can you keep the unquiet physical soul from
>   straying,
>   hold fast to the (One) and never quit it?
> Can you, when concentrating your breath,
>   make it soft like that of a little child?
> Can you wipe and cleanse your vision of the
>   Mystery
>   till all is without blur?
> Can you love the people and rule the land,
>   yet remain unknown?
> Can you in opening and shutting the heavenly
>   gates
>   play always the female part?
> Can your mind penetrate every corner of the land,
>   but you yourself never interfere?
> Be chief among them, but do not manage them.
> This is called the Mysterious Power (*teh*)

World Regeneration

Although these early centuries were times of turbulence and societal upheaval, the ritual themes of death and rebirth or of world regeneration found no expression except in Taoism, and even there only in its esoteric tradition. The *chiao* is such a rite, derived from the late Han period and still practiced today. It is performed once every few years to renew the cosmos by cleansing it of all faultiness produced by the dark forces during the intervening time and by strengthening the bright *yang* influences. The priest wields a sword endowed with magical efficacy to fight the legions of malevolent agencies and lock them out, calling upon the benevolent spirit armies and other major powers of the universe to render their assistance in this "cosmic combat." Crowned and robed like a royal figure, the priest establishes a sacred center marked out by a space-time diagram upon which he performs a ritual dance. By deep concentration he envisions in his mind a mandala and gathers to himself certain cosmic agencies in pairs of opposites; these marry and give birth to a divine child called the "red infant." By this ceremonial "the spirits are restoring the cosmos to its pristine vigor of life, *Yang*, and blessing," that is, re-creating the health of the world's original condition by a "return to the beginnings." At the same time, the priest's body undergoes a similar transformation that can then be conveyed to members of the community in the manner of shamanic healing. In this colorful ceremonial the outlines of the ubiquitous renewal process stand out clearly.

In the more exoteric traditions there is an idea that I find suggestive of the function of world regeneration; that is the concept of rebellion framed in terms of the withdrawal of the Mandate of Heaven and its bestowal on a hero and the new dynasty he creates. These dramatic transitions marked the radical turning points in the development of Chinese culture. This expression of change is less drastic than the motifs of world destruction and re-creation found in many other cultures, perhaps on account of the fundamental and enduring trait of remaining faithful to tradition. Impacts from outside or from within were assimilated in the spirit of evolution rather than revolution.

Summary

In China, then, the visionary proposals offered by its classical philosophers were profoundly radical in their democratic spirit and psychological perceptiveness. Among these, the recognition of human-hearted caring as a bonding force in social cohesion was utterly revolutionary and had the distinction of being the earliest appearance of this concept in history. It was paralleled by the correspondingly sophisticated insights of Buddhist thought and practice of the same period.

Kingship and Compassion   6

As we look into the evolution of the kingship in India, we begin to get the impression that the maturation of a culture requires many centuries of unbroken continuity before it can attain the degree of wisdom that can envision a social order of brotherhood and democratized kingly forms. To Egypt's social reformers and prophets, the early Pyramid Age was already viewed as long gone in remote antiquity, while to the Chinese philosophers, the era of the founding sage kings belonged to a hoary past of more than a millenium before. So also in India, the Buddhist perceptions concerning Universal Kings and Enlightened Ones were born out of nearly a millenium of cultural experience and spiritual reflections.

An intriguing question appears in the closeness of the lives of Confucius and Gautama the Buddha in time, their births being only a decade apart. One might well ask if there was some transmission of the new doctrine of human-heartedness and compassion from one to the other. Today we are finding overwhelming evidence of migrations of traders and explorers by sea as well as by land over great distances in that first millenium B.C.; might such adventurers have carried new knowledge and ideas between India and China? I find no special reason to try to account for the simultaneity of these new teachings by such means, since each sprang out of the rich and specific heritage of its culture. Even though it might sound untenable to the hard-core materialist, it might be more plausible to conceive of some sort of *zeitgeist* leading these two ancient civilizations to quite parallel developments in their spiritual evolution. Better yet, I think, is the proposition that it is in the nature of the psyche to follow the pattern of this sequence in the development of the images concerned with social order.

The Sacral Kingship

India's kingship was an office that became increasingly sacralized over the centuries.[1] Having its mythic model in the kingship of the gods, after the Buddha's time under the Mauryan Dynasty kings were called "Beloved of the Gods," Great King and Savior, and with the Kushan Empire were called "Son of Heaven," or Devaputra, "Son of the Gods." Only still later were they regarded as divine in themselves.

The first king-god of earliest Vedic culture was Varuna, the Sky, whose role was to uphold *rita*, comparable to the Egyptian Ma-at, and representing right order or the right way, authority, and righteousness; Varuna was the king as *gopa*, herdsman, comparable to the concepts of the Good Shepherd. In time the role of King of the Gods was taken over by Indra, elected out of their assembly in time of war as their leader, a mytholgem that reflects the social order of the human community in which the assembly of elders elected such a chief in times of crisis.[2] Indra was *vispati*, guardian and herdsman of the people, and protector of the helpless of the lower castes under the heel of the overbearing ruling class. An alternative mythic theory of kingship was that Indra was given his appointment as king by his father, Prajapati, when the gods sacrificed to him, conveying the meaning that this office was conferred upon a ruler by divine sanction.

Yet there was more divinity in the person of the king than these myths suggest, even in the Vedic times. *The Lawbook of Manu*[3] states in a stanza of verse that the person of the king is composed of eight eternal particles, being eight deities (including Varuna and Indra), who guard the points of the compass. "Hence," it says, "the king surpasses all other beings in splendour," and then, "He is a great god in human form."

At his inauguration a king underwent a series of rites, each to accomplish a certain aspect of his transformation from his state as an ordinary prince to that of a sacral personage and Universal monarch with attributes of divinity. The main ceremony (the *rajasuya*)[4] put him in the mythic role of Indra,the king god, in subduing the four quarters of space, and of Vishnu, the Sustainer, in taking the three giant steps that measured out the realms of sky, air, and earth; three arrows given into his hand emphasized the same. His anointing, as usual, was the means of conveying the sacrality of his royal nature. The three realms thus mastered, he then (in the *sakamedhah*)[5] established his earthly dominions in the familiar form of the fourfold world image with his place at the center; he sacrificed to the god of each of the four directions and of the midpoint. The victory of order over chaos was expressed in a ritual combat in which he took the part again of Indra in his great mythic victory by hurling his thunderblot, the *vajra*, to destroy the demon enemy, Vritra, this time representing the weapon by a token only (by throwing the "ghee," a ritual butter).

The nature of enthronement as a ceremonial transformation was dramatized in a particularly interesting manner in a consecration rite representing the king's rebirth (the *abhishekaniya*)[6] in very explicit terms. In his annointing with the life-giving waters he was called "child of the waters of the best of mothers." The birth process itself was designated by a series of investitures; the first garment called "the inner caul (the amnion) of knighthood," the second "the outer caul (the chorion) of knighthood," and the third a mantle bestowed with the declaration, "Thou art the womb of knighthood!" causing him to be delivered in birth. He was then given the customary bow by which he again overcame the demonic Vritra.

Two curious ceremonies of an antiquity deriving from very ancient Indo-Aryan origins were also part of these complex proceedings. Quite strange to our ears is the account of the famous Horse Sacrifice (the *asvamedhah*),[7] in which the bounds of the royal domains were measured out by the wanderings of a stallion, a creature of great sanctity among this people who had conquered India chiefly by means of their swift chariots. Since in their tradition, spreading all the way from India to Ireland, the land was personified in the queen and its rule in the wedlock with her, this became ritually dramatized in the sacrifice of the stallion and the removal of his genitals so that the queen might copulate with them in a Sacred Marriage. Equally venerable was an ancient rite (the *vejapeya*)[8] in which the king established his position at the cosmic center by sitting upon a carriage wheel atop a high post; his rotating on it gave him mastery over the three realms, while a chariot race around him endowed him with victory. This turning of the wheel remained not only a recurrent motif in Indian kingship, but as we shall see shortly, became one of the renowned attributes of the Buddha in his "turning of the wheel of the Law."

What it means for a sacral king to have divine attributes and the consequent responsibilities is eloquently detailed in a poem[9] that has the tone of many of the prophetic outcries against the corruption of the kingly ideal and for the advent of the saving righteous ruler. The Four Guardian Kings are addressed by Brahma when questioning him how it is that a king, though born of man, can be called divine. The answer is given that by the authority of the gods he enters his mother's womb, ordained by them. He is created as son of all the gods to put a stop to unrighteousness and prevent evil deeds, thus to establish all beings in well-doing and show them the way to heaven. The king is mother and father to those who do good. When the king disregards evil the gods grow angry in their palaces, for if he does not do his duty he ruins his kingdom; the harsh winds blow, rains fall out of season, stars and planets become unpropitious, the vegetation goes awry with grain, flowers, fruits, and seed not ripening, so that famine prevails. When such disasters occur, the gods pronounce the king unrighteous and he "will not for long anger the gods;/From the wrath of the gods his kingdom will perish."

The most colorful representation of the ideal of kingship was the figure of the *Chakravartin*,[10] the Wheel King, a universal monarch. Such a ruler was born with the thirty-two signs of the Great Man, the paragon of kingship, recognized in certain bodily features. He was also possessed of the seven royal treasures, among which were the wheel, elephant, horse, and other features. Only one so born merited a burial in a *stupa*, a cairn that represented the cosmos, with round dome and square structure below as Heaven and Earth, and containing in its midst a column designating the great Mount Meru standing at the central cosmic axis.[11]

A Time of Troubles

At the end of the sixth century B.C., the times were marked by signs of dissatisfaction and escapism. These were most probably due to the gradual disintegration of the old tribal structures giving way to small regional kingdoms and republics. In consequence, the traditional ethnic ties providing a sense of security were being lost and uneasiness was mounting, and the people were oppressed by rulers.[12]

We have seen that the imaginal mind has a propensity to recast the story of a visionary cult founder into myth as a culture hero who carries the evolution of the sacral kingship a step forward. The legendary life of Gautama Sakyamuni the Buddha presents us with one of the most classical instances of this development that can be found in history.

The Buddha: Birth and Early Life as a Sacral King

Gautama came of a small hill tribe in northern India, of the family of its chieftain. He chose a life of renunciation; legend, however, soon glorified his royal station and imposed upon his life story a clearly archetypal and florid myth form. I am going to present this legendary account at some length not merely because of its poetic colorfulness and hyperbole but because I wish to bring into high relief, in order to demonstrate the internalization of the kingship ideology, the many indications of the doctrine that the role of the Universal Monarch and the role of the Enlightened One were equated.

Many of the signs accompanying his birth, and his rebirth in his renunciation, were attributes of the royal ideology. In a mythic vein appropriate to the kingship associated with sky powers, the legends told of his lineage, the Sakyas, as being born of the Race of the Sun. Their first founding ancestor was Son of Mani, a Son of the Sun,[13] and was born of an egg heated by the sun. Another rendering[14] gave an account of a succession of kings tracing the descent from the first founding king of the warrior caste, the Kshatrya, down to this Sage of the Sakyas. Like many other royal lineages claiming to be Sons of the Sun, there are narratives concerning the practice of Royal Brother-Sister Marriage: The sons of the Sakyas' ancestral king Okkaka wedded their sisters to keep the lineage pure, but left their eldest sister to marry another king, Kola. The thirty-two sons of the Koliya married their cousins, the thirty-two Sakya girls, and ever after the Koliyas and Sakyas intermarried in unbroken line according to the rules of cross-cousin marriage in the exogamous clan system.

Gautama is said[15] to have chosen himself the time and place of his birth while residing in one of the heavens, selecting that district where universal monarchs, enlightened ones, and great disciples were born. The Buddha came of what may be called a virgin birth. This was, of course, a common feature of the myths of great founding kings in various cultures of antiquity. His mother Maya came to her spouse the king, at the time of the midsummer festival in Kapilavastu to ask that she might take vows: "O Lord of men, make me not an object of desire . . . Be there nought unmeritorious to thee, O king . . . ." She then had a dream in which four kings lifted her and bore her to the great sal-tree in the Himalayas, and their queens bathed her, robed her, and adorned her in heavenly garments. They laid her upon a divine bed in a golden mansion on a silver mountain. The Buddha took the form of a white elephant on a golden mountain, and descending from it alighted on the silver mountain. Holding a white lotus in his silver trunk, and trumpeting as he entered the mansion, he circumambulated three times the bed on his right, smote her right flank and entered her womb.

At the birth that followed this conception, various ceremonial acts were performed which belonged to the coronation of sacral kings and which indicated universal dominion. When the signs of the advent of a great man appeared, Maya took herself to the Lumbini grove, and grasping a branch of a great sal-tree was delivered while still standing. Four great divinities received him in a golden net and presented him to his mother. When four Great Kings received him on a ceremonial antelope robe, he surveyed the six directions — the four quarters, the nadir, and the zenith — and took seven steps toward the north. While one of the divinities held a white parasol over him, another a fan, and others some further royal regalia, he stopped at the seventh step and raising his lordly voice declared, "I am the chief of the world" and roared his lion roar.

There followed an episode[16] closely similar to the gospel account of recognition of the young messiah by Simeon after the nativity, and again indicating the equation of the sacral king with the Enlightened One, just as in China, of the Son of Heaven with the Sage. The elderly sage Asita from the Himalaya beheld the young child endowed with the thirty-two marks of a great man and breathed a solemn utterance, "Marvelous verily is this person that has appeared in the world," whereupon he made the ritual circumambulation around him. Of the thirty-two marks, he proclaimed that such a man has two possible careers and no other: "If he dwells in a house, he will become a king, a universal monarch . . . . But if he goes forth from a house to a houseless life, he will become a Tathagata, loudly proclaimed, a fully enlightened Buddha." He announced that this boy would without doubt attain complete and supreme enlightenment, turn the supreme Wheel of the Doctrine and teach the doctrine for the welfare and happiness of the world.

The boy's father, however, being a man of mundane affairs, made every effort to have his son live the worldly life and take the way of a universal monarch. The young prince was raised as a candidate for the throne in sumptuous surroundings in three palaces, with a splendid retinue, a most elaborate court life, and many diverting entertainments. Warned by Brahmins that his son would renounce the world upon receiving four signs — an old man, a sick man, a corpse, and an ascetic — his father had guards posted at the gates of the four quarters of the palace enclosure to prevent this occurrence. When it came time to be presented to the nobles as heir apparent and to take a wife from among the Koliyas, he qualified himself by a series of tests according to the royal custom, among them the drawing of a bow with which he shook the land with a noise like thunder. This thunder image, so widespread among the attributes of the sacral kingship, is a theme that we will see recurring in the long evolutionary history from the uses of violence to those of nonviolence.

Upon the occasion of his taking an excursion in his chariot outside the bounds of the palace precincts, the young prince did encounter the four signs, that is, representations of human sorrows. These impressed him emotionally with the force of a revelation and a vocation, setting him upon his path to seek the meaning of suffering, and marking the turning point from the life of a prince destined for the office of Great King to that of renunciation. On the night of the birth of his son he quit the palace; the timing suggests the equivalence of the two forms of rebirth, that of giving birth and that of inward regeneration. A touching episode[17] relates that a girl's love for him became the occasion for his realization of the meaning of true happiness, that which arises from the extinguishing of desire. Upon hearing her murmur a little verse of admiration, he felt aversion in his heart for lusts and thought, "When the fire of passion is extinguished, it is happy . . . . She has taught me a good lesson . . . . Even today I must reject and renounce the household life, and go forth from the world to seek Nirvana." Thereupon, the tempter, Mara, demon of worldly aspirations, came unsuccessfully to tempt him, warning him not to depart but accept in seven days' time the universal rulership, for the jewel-wheel of the empire would appear to him at that time; this was to be an announcement of the will of the gods comparable to the bestowing of the Mandate of Heaven upon a new Son of Heaven in China.

The young Guatama then took to the forest to practice austerities. Realizing eventually these customary ascetic modes to be futile, he took his seat under the Bodhi Tree in deep meditation, contemplating the causes of suffering and liberation from them. In four weeks' time he took the part of victor in the Cosmic Conflict against the "armies" of darkness, that is, of desire and passion, led by Mara.[18] Here, it is to be noted well, the classical ritual combat of kingly ceremony has become an internal struggle. The royal victor here seemed a veritable earthshaker, for after stroking with his right hand his head and couch, he smote the earth so that it roared and sounded forth a terrible sound. The mighty army of Mara became alarmed, dispersed, and melted away.

The motif of the world center as the beginning point of creation appears now, comparable to the position of the throne of Egypt on the Primordial Mound. For later legend assigned to this spot the Diamond Throne, or Thunderbolt Throne, situated at the center of the cosmos appearing at the start of its creation, represented by a round slab of stone with a lotus enclosing a ring of *vajras*, or thunderbolts. Here the Great One achieved his supreme enlightenment and Buddhahood, that is, the state of awakened consciousness.

From this experience came the Buddha's triumphal realization of the Four Noble Truths concerning the nature and causes of suffering from desire and attachment, and the liberation from them through the Eightfold Path, the Middle Way. His first sermon to his five disciples was followed by a rapid spread of his doctrine.

From Sacral King to Enlightened One

The theme of royalty is emphasized in texts that tell of signs at the birth of the Buddha with the thirty-two marks of a Great Man already mentioned. These signs imply that such a great individual is elected from birth to be either a Great King in the traditional governmental role, or its equivalent, and Enlightened One in the function of spiritual leadership.[19] He was therefore destined from birth to have the choice between these alternatives, the career of a Chakravartin, a universal monarch with the divinely endowed power of the sacral kingship in the socio-political arena, or the equally universal sway of an Enlightened One over the realm of the spirit, both serving with utmost excellence the welfare of the people and the advancement of the culture. As at birth, so upon his death certain signs were reserved for the designation of a Great Man. The stupa already spoken of, the reliquary shaped in the form of a three dimensional mandala or world-image, was a monument that was exclusively the privilege of such a unique individual, whether Chakravartin or Enlightened One. The wheel is also an attribute to both, that of the king designating his universal rule, the other to be found in the Buddha's "turning the wheel of the law," the Dharma.

In this myth and ritual imagery we catch a glimpse of the process of metamorphosis as the ceremonial of the sacral kingship emerged from its external political expression in government to its internal spiritual realization as the means of achieving a new form of higher consciousness. In this spirit the description of the Chakravartin in the Ambattha-Sutta gives the picture that he "dwells in complete ascendancy over the wide earth from sea to sea, ruling it in righteousness without the need of baton or of sword. But if he go forth from the household life into the houseless state, then he will become a Buddha who removes the veil from the eyes of the world."[20] Or similarly in another text we are told "As Wheel King he would hold sway over the entire world with courage and righteousness, leading all other kings, or as Enlightened One his wisdom would illumine the whole world and pervade it with his all-embracing love."[21] It is interesting to observe that in the later Tantric form of Buddhism, as Conze has pointed out, the ceremony of initiation "derives from the ancient Indian ritual of the (abhisheka) inauguration of a Crown Prince. In theory, a Crown Prince was, through that ceremony, transformed into a world ruler. Similarly in this case, the water of Knowledge is supposed to enable the devotee to become a spiritual world ruler, i.e., a Buddha."

Compassion

Prominent among the Buddha's teachings are the fruits of enlightenment: clarity as to the error of separateness, and its remedy in the cultivation of compassion. The nature of external appearance leads one mistakenly to perceive a separateness of subject and object and of self and other, as if there were a distinction of one soul from another. The Buddha proclaimed a doctrine of "no-self" of "no-soul,"[22] a view very difficult for western minds to grasp or assent to. Implied is the principle that however much we may strive to establish a sense of individuality in our development of personality, there turns out to be in the end no such individual being. This is so because, with the true wisdom attained in spiritual cultivation, a state is reached in which it is realized that the Oneness of all being is the sole reality, all the rest being merely mistaken habits of mind. Here there is no self-realization, only no-self realization!

Arising out of this experience of the One, there emanates an upwelling of compassion for one's fellow beings.[23] This takes primarily the form of pity and sympathy for all those still lost in the illusion occasioned by desire, craving, and attachment. But further, since oneness implies no special selection of objects for this feeling, a compassion for all beings takes precedence over love for individuals. This all-embracing love for everyone and everything in the cosmos is an archetypal emotion characteristic of deeply altered states of consciousness; it leaves an open question about the more everyday conscious feeling for persons.

Added to this universal compassion, however, is a more personal brand of feeling called friendliness.[24] This approaches more clearly the concept of a love between members of the community that then becomes the dynamic that holds society together by giving it cohesiveness. In regard to this societal dimension,the entire doctrine with its Four Noble Truths, Eightfold Path, and the Ways of Righteousness, is advocated as means for kings to rule wisely and to create a prosperous kingdom. The concept of kingship is that the monarchs do not rule by divine right but by social contract,[25] to be responsible to the needs of the people. It must be observed, of course, that the complete adherence to the Way was considered fully realizable only in communities of monks living apart from the world — the wider community benefits secondarily.

In the Buddha's doctrine, the first of the four cardinal virtues is this friendliness of person to person and to all beings. Under the heading of Right Mindfulness, these states of mind are set over against their opposites, the prevalence of friendliness, compassion, joy, and equanimity causing a diminishment of ill-will, vexation, aversion,and repugnance, respectively. The first extends an unlimited universal love to all beings.[26]

> As a mother cares for her son,
> Her only son, all her days
> So towards all things living
> A man's mind should be all-embracing.
> Friendliness for the whole world,
> All-embracing, he should raise in his mind,
> Above, below, and across,
> Unhindered, free from hate and ill-will . . .

A society is envisioned in which each respects the personality of each, thus setting up a closely woven fabric of warm, mutual caring.

Basham sums up the doctrine of friendliness this way:[27]

> Mindfulness of friendliness is among the daily
> exercises of the monk, and can also be practiced
> by the layman; as he detaches himself in

imagination from his own body, and as though
looking down on himself, pervades himself with
friendliness directed toward himself, for it is
impossible to feel true friendliness or love
for others unless, in the best sense of the
term, one feels it for oneself; then he proceeds
in imagination to send waves of friendliness
in every direction, to reach every being in
every corner of the world . . . the waves of
friendliness constantly poured out by many
thousands of meditating monks have a very
positive effect on the welfare of the world.

Noninjury and nonviolence, *ahimsa*, are emphasized constantly in the teachings, coupled with compassion:[28]

The monk Gautama has given up injury to life,
he has lost all inclination to do it; he has
laid aside the cudgel and the sword, and he
lives modestly, full of mercy, desiring in
compassion the welfare of all things living.

So also returning good for evil is often advocated:[29]

Conquer anger by love, evil by good;
Conquer the miser with liberality, and the liar
with truth.

And again:[30]

Never in this world is hate
    Appeased by hatred;
It is only appeased by love —
    This is an eternal law.

As we have already noted in regard to the rather similar admonitions of Confucius, these views have become so familiar to us after twenty-five hundred years that they seem not remarkable. In their own day they were utterly revolutionary.

On Governance

The Buddha was in no sense confining his teachings to the

concerns of the individual quest for spiritual cultivation. Like the prophets and philosophers of Egypt and China, he was one who in Times of Troubles spoke out as a reformer and advocate of good government, calling for restoration of the ideal of the kingship. He is said to have been disturbed by the inhumanities that prevailed in government in his time, by which the people were being oppressed and exploited, tortured, persecuted, and impoverished by excessive taxation.[31]

In consequence the Buddha set forth his "Ten Duties of the King":[32] generosity, high moral character, sacrificing for the general good, honesty and integrity, kindness and gentleness, austerity, freedom from ill-will, nonviolence and noninjury, forbearance, and finally, nonopposition to the will of the people. Again these reach our ears as perhaps somewhat tame and benign, even self-evident virtues, but among the circumstances of the time they must have sounded like a welcome alleviation of painful oppressions of the people.

That these words were not wasted on only a handful of disciples but did in fact introduce a revitalization movement in society, is borne out by the events attending the founding of the Mauryan Dynasty two centuries later. Asoka, once he had established dominion over the greater part of India by his wars, renounced his violent ways of conquest and adopted the Dharma of the Buddha. In his edicts carved in stone in various borderlands of his realm, he announced the policies of this reformed style of governance. Though self-consciously pious in tone, they did set the mood of benevolent and paternal caring.

The Second Edict says,[33] "All men are my children. Just as I seek the welfare and happiness of my own children in this world and the next, I seek the same for all men." To the unconquered people of the borders he pleads that "they should expect only happiness from me, not misery; . . . that . . . I will forgive them for offenses . . . ; that they should be induced by my example to practice Dharma; etc."

World Regeneration

It is striking that with all the atmosphere in the Buddhist teachings of a deep transformation of consciousness and of the cultural expression of it, there is no mention of impending world destruction and regeneration. The *kalpas*, those world ages or cosmic aeons, are a different matter, for they are of long duration, not immediate as in the usual visions of prophets cited in chapters two and three. I have the impression that the difference is to be accounted for by the degree of sophistication. In a cultural phase in which the consciousness is not highly differentiated, the image of change is portrayed as a literal annihilation of the familiar world and its regeneration. In the subtly evolved mentality in the India of the Buddha, on the other hand, spiritual practices such as meditation had already begun at least a thousand years before (as suggested by the representations of the Horned God of the Indus civilization sitting in the yogic posture of meditation). Under such conditions the experience of the newly transformed world image takes the form of world destruction of a more interior nature — that is, of recognizing the illusory character of one's way of perceiving the world, which is then to be dissolved and replaced by one which sees all phenomena as the creation of one's own thought-forms, and in consequence envisions the perfected world image as a mandala.

Summary

In sum, it becomes clear that in India, as in China, occurred the equating of sageliness with kingliness, of the Enlightened One with the Universal Monarch. This recognition that the kingly forms belonged to the inner man was accompanied by the vision of love and compassion as bonding forces making for the cohesion of society on a universal scale. The recptive principle was given full reconition. The Judeo-Christian history reveals a similar evolution of the ideal of the sacral kingship into its internalized form along with a doctrine of love, *agape.*

Agape and Anointed Ones

7

The histories narrated so far have made it evident that many centuries of continuous development are required for the maturation of a culture to the level at which its paragons of the spirit are considered the equals of its heroes of rulership, and compassion found as worthy as dominance for providing the cohesive force for the ordering of society. The ancient Near East affords a dramatic instance of the point in the negative, of cultures that did not reach such sophistication. There is a sad irony in this picture, since the cultural transformation in the Urban Revolution apparently found its first impetus in that part of the world, according to the archeological evidence.

Mesopotamia had none of the stability enjoyed in the Nile Valley. Its geographical conditions of floods, droughts, and other natural disasters gave its inhabitants a cosmological outlook that expected no sure predictable order, but rather a certain capriciousness in its deities. Its city kingdoms and empires reflected this flux in never-ending series of manmade catastrophes through their taste for warmaking, conquest, and destruction of one another.

The turbulent cultural soil of the ancient Near East was not nourishing for an untroubled cultivation of spiritual insights. What occurred instead was a sequence of bloody and destructive conquests of one people by another, with the dominance moving step by step northward, the Sumerians giving way to the Accadians, and these to the Assyrians. In the northwesterly area, in Anatolia, the Hittite empire did not have a long life, and in the western region, in Syria, the Canaanite culture was overrun by the Israelites moving in from their exodus from Egypt and nomadic life in the desert.

In all this sequence of violent political upheavals, however, there was a more quiet passing on of rich cultural heritage. The Canaanite city kingdoms fashioned their myth and ritual forms of governance after the model of those that had been evolved in Mesopotamia. In turn, the Israelites took these over and developed them further with the character of their particular religious genius.

The Sacral Kingship of Israel

One of the great gifts bequeathed to us by the ancient Judeo-Christian literature is its documentation phase by phase of the evolution of the ideal of kingship from its governmental aspect to its spiritual equivalent.[1] Having its forerunner in a covenant between a tribal confederation and its divine overlord, the sacral kingship began with David. During the prophetic periods the future hope for the savior king gradually turned into the concept of a purely spiritual leadership. In the figure of Jesus as the Anointed One, the Christ, the Awaited One was given a fully embodied personification and a "New Covenant" of revoutionary character with a concept of a purely inward Kingdom of God, superceding the "Old Covenant" and the Davidic kingdom.

In its preurban, pastoral and nomadic culture, the people of Israel were bound together as a nation that found its definition in a covenant with its god, Yahweh. He it was whom they viewed as having delivered them miraculously from their bondage in Egypt, where they had been "Habiru," a population of Hebrew outsiders not belonging to the culture of that highly structured kingdom. After their Exodus, they became an autonomous nation in their own right as a confederation of their twelve tribes. Even in their Promised Land among the Canaanites, they were again outsiders inasmuch as the culture surrounding them was like the other ones of the ancient Near East, urban in economy and style of social structure and kingship. The Israelites as they emerged from the desert were hostile to the cities of Canaan and destroyed them. They came to their full consciousness of being a nation only gradually during the two centuries following their arrival (1200 to 1000 B.C.).

The Israelites' confederation found the meaning of its existence in its covenant contract with its god Yahweh as its overlord,[2] Moses being viewed as the founder both of this relationship and of the nationhood of the people. The agreement took the form of a treaty following the model of a traditional formulary prevalent in the Near East of the time, by which a subject people subscribed to the obligations laid down by the king, thus formulating the relations of vassal to suzerain. Documents of this kind have come to light from the Hittite culture of the centuries just preceding. Briefly, such a covenant consisted of six elements: a preamble with the suzerains's identity; a historical introduction recounting the relations up to the time; the basis of the future relations in unstinting loyalty; the treaty regulations forbidding any other loyalties or independent sovereignty; an invocation of divine powers to witness; and various blessings and curses as the consequences of obedience or disobedience. The second book of Moses, Exodus, was the Book of the Covenant, (specifically, chapters 20 to 25), and the written covenant itself resided in its Ark and was deposited in the sanctuary at Shechem, where it was read at regular intervals. All this was again according to the prevailing customs.

With the advent of David at the turn of the millenium, Israel embarked upon a wholly new course in which he became the founder of an urban-style kingship. This profound change was born of a Time of Troubles. The strong and prosperous nation of the Philistines in the southwest of Palestine was overwhelming and scattering the tribes, even causing a confirmation of utter disaster for them by capturing the Ark of the Covenant at Shiloh and thus robbing the federation of its most holy testimony of its very existence. Through his prowess, David rescued Israel, restored its Ark, and transformed the culture from its tribal ways to ones more in keeping with the times.

It is pertinent for our present discussion to observe the way in which David's innovations fitted into the pattern of the acute culture change of that period. The context was one of extreme crisis, with total annihilation of the nation being all but concluded, and with the shocking realization that the Ark, the very heart of the cult of Yahweh, was gone from them, perhaps forever. Just when it appeared there was nothing left to rally around, David's victory became the occasion to inaugurate a new cult form that accomplished the transition into Israel's Urban Revolution. Buying the city of the Jebusites, Jerusalem, and making it his headquarters, he adopted its form of the sacral kingship and royal cultus, "after the order of Mechizedek," its king.[3]

This creative move rendered David not only one of Israel's most highly esteemed heroes but also a cult founder in its great revitalization movement, equal in stature to Moses who had fulfilled that function two and a half centuries earlier. The new cult brought Israel's myth and ritual into line with the prevailing urban culture of the Near East of that time,[4] save only that in its practice it was constantly reiterated that "Yahweh is Israel's true king," leaving David as only his vice-regent.

The borrowing of the cult was so complete that even some of the hymns that had been addressed to Baal, Canaan's royal thundergod, were tranferred to the worship of Yahweh, most notably in Psalm 29:[5] "The Voice of Yahweh soundeth over the waters;/ The most glorious God hath thundered forth,/ . . .The Voice of Yahweh is full of power;/ . . .Yahweh doth shatter the cedars of Lebanon . . . ." There is a growing trend among scholars of recent decades to recognize in the "royal psalms" the spoken part of the typical enthronement rites of the New Year Festival characteristic of the sacral kingships of the day.[6]

I have reviewed the evidence for these cult practices in my previous work on the sacral kingship, *Roots of Renewal*,[7] and will here only mention its highlights. The fall festival consisted of enthronement rites of renewal of the kingship and the kingdom, a drama rehearsing the cosmic combat between the order of the realm and the "Kings of the Nations," representing the forces of death, darkness, and chaos;[8] a victory reenacting the creation; the reenthronement of the royal victor; the rebirth of the king from the "Womb of the Dawn";[9] a questionable hint of a sacred marriage; the reading of the Tablets of Destiny to determine the fate for the coming year; and a reaffirmation of the convenant. There were accompanying ritual processions with music and dance, in which David is said to have danced in an ecstasy before the Ark.[10]

As vice-regent, David's role was to enact the part of Yahweh in these rites. He was not considered a deity, yet he had certain divine attributes as an "elohim," and was son by adoption of his divine father, and his servant; the royal oracle for the occasion of enthronement known as the 2nd Psalm quotes the decree of Yahweh:[11] "Thou art My Son;/ This day have I begotten thee./ Ask of me, and I will make/ The nations thine inheritance." The well-being of the realm depended utterly upon the king's moral and physical wholeness, specifically upon his exhibiting the righteousness and justice that were his charge.

The ever-present theme of centrality is clear in the imagery of the enthronement. The concept of a mountain of the gods was transferred from the Canaanite Mt. Zaphon in the north to that of Mt. Zion occupying a position of high spiritual potency at the midpoint of the great round of the world encircled by the cosmic sea above and below; from these oceans Yahweh could release the life-giving waters through the windows already familiar as those opened by the Canaanite Baal to nourish the earth. The locus of the throne was conceived as a central cosmic axis at which the waters of the heavens and the abyss were brought into relation.

It has been observed that in this transition accomplished by David, the image of Yahweh grew from that of a tribal overlord to that of a supreme being, a cosmic creator and head of the world's divine powers.[12] A psalm (82) says of him, "God taketh his stand in the divine assembly;/ Amidst the gods he pronounceth judgment." His "righteousness and justice" set the keynote for the moral order of the world, springing out of his kingdom, and in contrast, the "Kings of the Nations" represented the threat of death and disorder pitted against his reign, then to be defeated ritually in the sacred cosmic combat.[13] These changes in myth reflected those taking place in the rising grandeur of the realm. Under this new governance, Israel prospered. Particularly under the rule of David's son, Solomon, when Israel was finding itself at the favorable position of the crossroads among the trade routes and their commerce, the royal city was aggrandized and a new temple and palace were erected to house the King of Kings and his vice-regent. However, with these changes, the proponents of the tribal cult of nomadic tradition were unhappy and disapproving, still holding to deep loyalties to the older tribal Yahweh. The result was a split into two kingdoms, that of the north, still carrying the name of Israel, seceding from Judah and its royal cultus.

A Time of Troubles: The Early Prophets

During the ensuing centuries the monarchy became decadent and at the same time the power of Assyria was becoming a gigantic threat looming over the realm, and the security of this little state was in peril. A painful discrepancy was felt between its tiny dimensions and the immensity of its mission in the world. Out of the distress rose visions of the royal figure who would replicate "Yahweh's saving action" on behalf of his "chosen people." It was clear from the start, to the prophets who gave voice to these hopes, that the only recourse in the face of the danger was for Israel to hold to its perfect obedience to the god of the covenant, and its wisdom to live by it. In the eighth century, a series of prophets and the schools of their following began the visionary work of forming an image of an "Anointed of the Lord," a "Messiah" of the house and lineage of David who would restore the ideal of his kingship. Amos[14] declared that a political downfall was only their god's way of wakening the people of Israel to a realization of the error of their ways and hence to repentance, the necessary prerequisite to their salvation. This laid forth the pattern of the "future hope" followed for many centuries, to culminate in the concept of the "Days of the Messiah." Hosea[15] introduced the theme of the troublous "birthpangs of the Messiah" out of which Israel's new life would be brought into being, and depicted the tender image of God in his loving-kindness and compassion, wooing the nation as a lover entices a maiden to betrothal.

Some of the loftiest poetry of all religious literature is to be found in the Book of Isaiah,[16] the first thirty-nine chapters of which were also written in the eighth century B.C.. These visions conceived a limited form of the Messiah, as a scion of the house of David who would restore the ideal of his kingship with its righteousness, justice, and peace as its foundation, holding to the contract of homage and fealty to their Lord and his covenant. In this began the true messianic hope that would prevail for many centuries. Throughout, Isaiah gave it form by following the themes derived directly out of the enthronement rites of the New Year Festival; there would come one born from the Womb of the Dawn, tender as the dew, a new light born out of the darkness, bringing the dawn of a new day of Yahweh's saving action, and names of power and virtue being given him. It is probable that all this was implying a reference to the actual birth of a new prince of the royal house from its queen.

Troubled Times: The Later Prophets

With the occurrence of the much-feared Babylonian Captivity and the Exile of the sixth century, the destruction and ensuing restoration of Israel were perceived in terms of the familiar ritual combat of the enthronement rites.[17] In them, the enemy prevailed at first, but was overcome by the saving intervention of Yahweh. With the Restoration there was a veritable return to the beginnings, and a new order was to be established with a revival of the covenant pact.

During this time, the visionary experience of the prophets was making a gradual distinction between the ideal and the real in kingship,[18] and the democratization and internalization of the kingly forms were being clearly articulated. As in the case of Egypt and of China, the moral responsibility that had resided solely in collective form in the person of the king now was seen as the obligation of every person. Jeremiah[19] gave eloquent testimony to this transformation when he spoke of the Law, the terms demanded of the people by their divine overlord in the convenant, as being now "written in the hearts" of the populace.

As we have come now to expect, the motif of world regeneration made its appearance among the other evidences of profound changes in the consciousness of the culture. The writer of the third and last section of the Book of Isaiah[20] drew upon the enthronement festival motifs to express the new spiritual order of the future. The Lord would bring about a second creation, a New Heaven and a New Earth, with a New Jerusalem, a city of paradise, at its center and highest point. There would be a New Covenant of an age in which, here again, the Lord says, "I shall write my Law in their inward parts." That is, the moral order would be the business of every man and woman, not merely the king's, representing thus an individual consciousness rather than the former purely collective *participation mystique*.[21] In keeping with these changes in consciousness the concept of the long-awaited messiah became increasingly spiritualized, so that now it was envisioned that a priestly prince would arise from the lineage of David, a shepherd of the people but only one among them, first among equals.

Most noteworthy among the writings of the sixth century are the four "Servant Songs" found in the second section of the Book of Isaiah, but by the hand of one referred to as Trito-Isaiah[22] (i.e., otherwise the author of the third section). These verses of great beauty depict a figure who suffered and redeemed through his pains. It has been suggested by scholars[23] that this servant was the image of the people of Israel viewed as a social organism, a collective individual who would die and be resurrected. Herein is the first mention in the bible of resurrection from death. Others have been struck with the royal ideology in the dying and suffering king motif. Yet the consensus grows in the direction of seeing in this figure the account of an actual prophet with a spiritual task for which he was persecuted and gave his life. The songs borrow motifs from the enthronement festival.[24] The first is the "royal initiation oracle"; the second, the thanksgiving for the elected king, hence for "My Servant, Israel"; the third, a psalm of lamentation; finally, the fourth is a deeply moving narration of the suffering vicariously undertaken to redeem. In Mowinckel's formulation, the sufferer is endowed with royal rank as the reward for his righteousness, a fine instance of the democratization of the royal ideology.

Times of Danger: The Apocryphal Books

Several hundred years later, Israel found itself in a Time of Troubles of a new sort. A couple of centuries after Alexander had marched with his conquering armies through the entire Near East and had introduced the new era of hellenization of those civilizations, Israel was feeling the danger of dissolution of its unique tradition and way of life and belief. A couple of generations before this time, the Maccabees had brought a spirit of renewed strength and confidence by overthrowing the hellenic rule of Egypt, and for a while it had seemed at last that Jewish sovereignty and self-respect had been firmly reestablished. Yet in the middle and latter years of the second century B.C., the Hasmonian rulership became increasingly corrupt and Israel's spiritual identity was once more in danger of perishing.[25]

As long as Israel in that interval had been feeling triumphant in its newly restored state there had been little, in sacred writings, of messianic deliverance. However, as hopes were waning and the demoralization of the national religious spirit was making itself felt, visionary figures made their appearance in the land, introducing a new variant in the royal ideology called the Son of Man, and also a new motif in visionary experience that was to become a prevalent theme for some centuries, that of ecstatic journeys into the heavens.

Enoch's Journey into Paradise

A grand expression of these was the First Book of Enoch,[26] composed by a group of visionary prophets of the middle part of the second century B.C. A great cosmic drama was introduced, as might be expected, by a state of fear and trembling in troublous times — omens would appear, and there would be astonishment, anguish, turmoil, and woe. The classical expression, reiterated again and again in the apocalyptic books, depicted the upheaval in the image of terror:[27] "And all shall be smitten with fear,/ And the Watchers [angels] shall quake/ And great fear and trembling shall seize them unto the ends of the earth . . . / And the hills shall be made low,/ And shall melt like wax before the flame./ And earth shall be wholly rent asunder, . . . " The turmoil ushered in an age of transition and renewal, with phenomena known as "the birthpangs of the Messiah."

One should be forewarned that, in reading these visions, one must let oneself drift into a more than usually permissive frame of mind in regard to the mythic narrative. One must remind oneself at every turn that the events recounted are not to be taken in the sense of the mundane actuality but in that of another species of "reality", which is the psychic or symbolic. Otherwise one's rational mind will feel itself somewhat outraged at the extravagance of the events being described and foretold.

Enoch, the text recounts,[28] one day was caught up in the spirit and carried by a whirlwind to the end of the heavens, a distance that was believed ordinarily to take a year and a half's journey underground. His encounter there with the Lord of Spirits, with members of the heavenly host, and with the elect (the deceased righteous ones), revealed to him the "secrets of the creation." The entire experience may then be regarded as a species of shamanic cosmic journey of an exceptionally high order.

Lifted up "on the chariots of the spirit," Enoch found himself in paradise, that is, in the Eden that had been removed from earth and translated into heaven. There the great souls who had proven themselves righteous and wise had been taken up bodily from this earth and miraculously transported in the flesh to this region "where the dwellings of the righteous" were. In this paradise he found that this Heavenly Community were dwelling in the Garden of Righteousness; in it were the Tree of Knowledge and the Tree of Life, as in Eden, and the Fountain of Rigtheousness, the Springs of Wisdom, and the River of Life. Here shone in all its radiance the Invisible City of the Heavenly Jerusalem. In the presence of the Lord of Spirits in the highest heaven, he was told that since he was born to righteousness all would walk in his ways and that with him would be their dwelling places. By this divine affirmation, Enoch was elected to the position of guide and pattern of righteousness, a true leader of souls, a psycho-pomp.

The Myth of the Son of Man

Such is the background leading up to the vision that concerns us in this discussion, that of the appearance of the Son of Man.[29] Enoch heard the Lord of Spirits reveal what he had in store for the future: "On that day Mine Elect One shall sit on the throne of glory/ And shall try their works,/ And their places of rest shall be innumerable . . ./ And I will transform the heaven and make it an eternal blessing and light:/ And I will transform the earth and make it a blessing:/ And I will cause mine elect ones to dwell upon it. . . . " This becomes the prelude to Enoch's first vision of the Son of Man:[30]

> And there I saw One who had a head of days,
> And His head was white like wool,
> And with Him was another being whose countenance
>   had the appearance of a man,
> And his face was full of graciousness,
>   like one of the holy angels.

Enoch asked an angel, who was showing him the hidden secret things, about the Son of Man, who he was and whence he came, and was told, "This is the Son of Man who hath righteousness . . . and who revealeth all the treasures of that which is hidden," and who shall "put down the kings and mighty ones from their seats/ And the strong ones from their thrones."

In recounting the myth of the Son of Man, I am going to piece it together from the various fragments of it found in several of the apocryphal books. The reason for this becomes evident when one reads these scriptures, for they follow no orderly narrative sequence; these are recordings of visions that appeared piecemeal and helter-skelter. In this they are faithful to the character of altered states of consciousness, in which typically the images come and go without linear design. These are known as the "pseudepigrapha" of the first century B.C. and the first century A.D., so called because they were assigned to historical figures of note whose names would endow them with a greater sense of validity and therefore acceptance. These are the apocalyptic books of Enoch, of Baruch, and of Esdras. The image of the Son of Man had been first prefigured in the Book of Daniel in the second century B.C.

This myth of the Son of Man belonged to the growing tradition of eschatology that promised hopes of salvation for Israel in the context of a complete tranformation of the world. The essence of eschatology is captured in the phrase of Barnabas,[31] "Behold, I make the last things like the first," showing it therefore to belong to the mythological motif of the two golden ages, that of the beginning and that of the end of time, *Urzeit und Endzeit.*

Like the mythological names "Adam" and "Anthropos," the "Son of Man" conveys the meaning of "the man" as a representation of the prototype or archetype of mankind, its *eidos.*[32] He was considered to be hidden at the first from the time of the creation "under the wings of the Lord of Spirits," as a secret being hidden in an invisible land at the end of the heavens.

The Son of Man was envisioned making his entry upon the world stage appearing from the sea:[33] "There arose a violent wind from the sea,/ And stirred all its waves. And I beheld and lo!/ As it were the form of a man/ And I beheld and lo!/ This man flew with the clouds of heaven."

Great and terrible was his arrival, for all that he looked upon trembled, while the impact of his voice melted all before him like wax. The imagery is reminiscent of the epiphany of Yahweh in the voice of the thunder in Psalm 29, already cited. A like image was evoked when from the summit of the cloud there came "as it were the likeness of great lightning," the divine being mainfesting himself to save his people. This tradition of the appearance of the Son of Man had been recorded in the visions of Daniel at the early part of the second century B.C.:[34] "I saw in the night visions, and behold, one like the Son of Man came with the clouds of heaven and came to the Ancient of Days. . . . "

The motif of storm and war led now to the appearance of the enemy. The hosts of Satan rose up to vie with him:[35] "There was gathered together from the four winds of heaven an innumerable multitude of men to make war against the Man that came up out of the sea." Fearsome was the response, for the Man's glance melted all like fire, and his sword became "drunk with the blood of the enemies of God," while the rod of chastisement issued from his mouth with the spewing of a stream of sparks.

Having proved himself victor against the forces of evil, the Son of Man was enthroned at the world's center on the Holy Mount Zion,[36] next to the throne of glory of the Lord of Spirits. From this seventh of the marvelous mountains seen by Enoch in his visions, the Son of Man exercised dominion over the world.

The way was thus prepared for the momentous new event in the world's history, the resurrection of the dead.[37] In this drama the elect, who had heretofore been living as a "heavenly community" of great spirits in the paradise at the far end of heaven, now made their return. These were the righteous souls that were brought back through the person of the Son of Man as intermediary, even all the souls being contained in him. In the new state of the world, these elect and the living and the angels all mingled together, being now all alike.

Hard upon the Resurrection followed now the Day of Judgment.[38]

In this original form, however, it concerned not the fate of souls after death but the more cosmic judgment upon the representatives of evil. There was judgment upon the stars which were fallen angels and which had refused to follow their allotted regular courses in the heavens; they were cast into the "place of condemnation" with flames of fire in the burning chasm of Gehenna. Condemned to destruction were Nephilim and his followers, the fallen angels who consorted with the daughters of men and brought lust into the world, with the arts and crafts of the casting of metals for weapons and warfare.

The Victory, Enthronement, Resurrection, and Judgment being thus accomplished, the Kingdom of the Son of Man would be established.[39] This was to be the sublime Interim Kingdom, to be of four hundred years' duration in a superterrestrial and transfigured earth that no longer would know troubles, sorrow, toil, or hardship; in it the good would be a thousand-fold, men having a thousand children and the vines a thousand branches. Here the Lord proclaimed, "Winds shall go forth from before me to bring each morning the fragrance of aromatic fruits; the closing of day distilling the dew of health." The people would banquet upon the flesh of the mythical monsters, the female serpent Leviathan who dwelled in the sea, and the male bull Behemoth who inhabited the wilderness (an image suggestive to the Yin-Yang opposites).

Surprisingly enough, this idyllic picture served only as a prelude to the final Age of the World to Come.[40] Here we encounter what may be considered one of history's grandest images of world destruction and regeneration. For in these visions there would take place a massive fiery obliteration of all of creation. Even the Son of Man himself would perish.[41]

> My Servant the Messiah shall be revealed . . . and shall rejoice the survivors four hundred years. And it shall be, after these years, that My Servant the Messiah shall die and all in whom there is breath. Then shall the world be turned into the primeval silence seven days, like as at the first beginnings.

There is here portrayed the most complete transformation possible, the entire cosmos being resorbed through fire back into the state of chaos and darkness of the time before creation. The profound seven-day hush would preside over all, conveying the very image of black nothingness.

Out of this dark void now would break forth a burst of light and form with bright images of a new age:[42] "Behold, I make a New Heaven and a New Earth and make all things new." In this way, a triumphant rebirth of creation was announced, in a new beginning and a new aeon. Paradise would return from heaven and a New Zion on the Holy Mount of Paradise, a New Jerusalem as a heavenly city hidden heretofore among the secrets of heaven. Here the Son of Man would sit enthroned as the King of Paradise at the right hand of the Lord of Spirits.

In this new age the elect would rise up to eternal life, light, and blessedness,[43] and "all the elect shall shine like the brightness of fire." They would be clothed in the garments of life, the Law now written on their hearts, and would live in righteousness, wisdom, and peace; they would shine for untold ages, as a generation of light. Enoch, when he beheld in his visions the throne, described a fountain of righeousness which was inexhaustible; and around it, many fountains of wisdom, out of which the thirsty drank and were filled with wisdom.

The meaning is clear, that the elect in the new age would share the divine attributes of wisdom, righteousness, and compassion, formerly contained solely in the godhead and in his representative, the sacral king.

These visions of the Son of Man and the wonders of the heavenly spaces tend to appear to us of today's mentality as grand hyperbole and phantasmagoria, even as promising little that has to do with the "real world." Yet we must bear in mind that these images concerned and expressed the very heart of the Jewish society's way of religious experience. It is real myth, grandiose and colorful, made of visionary material that must be assigned accordingly to the "real world" of the psyche and its emotional motivations.

The outer events of the political scene of Israel provided the conditions and the impetus for the formation of these images. The anxiety and stress of threatening times gave rise to the visionary states that produced these inner dramas of high poetic quality and intensely powerful affective charge. These portrayed the affect-images that were arousing new motivations and providing new guidelines toward the national survival of Judaism as a religion, and thus of this people as a culture. For it is one of the miracles of history that with their intense religious inspiration and devotion they have remained a people, against the threat of annihilation and the fact of foreign domination and even dispersion.[44] Another of the wonders of history is that these visions provided the soil out of which grew the new Christian religious form centered upon the theme of the Son of Man and spreading its culture to the far ends of the world.

The Christ as Sacral King

The life and work of Jesus, we must recall, occurred in another of Israel's times of troubles, this time in the turmoil of resentment of Roman rule and the hostilities against it; only a few decades later, these would result in the destruction of the temple in Jerusalem once more, and the heroic resistance of the Zealots at Masada. For the purposes of our present investigation, I will select certain features of his role as a radical reformer. Together with his baptism, his initiatory trials were undergone in his forty-day visionary experience in the wilderness, where in his "temptations" the motivations of power and dominance were confronted and put down, to be followed shortly later by a new doctrine of loving relationships as the hallmark of a redeemed world society. Of this he proclaimed himself to be the head, but only in a certain sense.

Quite explicitly, the gospel writers who recorded the life and teaching of Jesus brought into high relief his role as spiritual king of a purely inward Kingdom of God. As the "Christ" he was the "Messiah"; both terms carried the meaning, "The Anointed One," that is, the king anointed of God and belonging to "the house and lineage of David," Israel's founding king. This new kingdom found its definition in the concept of a "New Covenant" (testament) growing out of and superceding the "Old Covenant" of tribal days, thus placing itself at the culmination of the long sequence of forms of the ideal of the sacral kingship.

It has been observed[45] that Jesus, in selecting from the various traditions current at the time the form that would best express his awareness of his mission, took principally the motifs belonging to the image of the Son of Man. In referring to his calling he preferred to use this title and to avoid the customary titles of the Messiah unless they were compatible with this identity. Of course, this does not imply that he felt himself to be enacting the whole of the myth of that figure in all its variety of aspects during his lifetime. It was pertaining to his resurrected state that the spiritual kingdom of the end days, the enthronement next to the Almighty in his judgment seat, and the transformation of the world were his avowed concern. The records make it clear that he expected those events to follow shortly. We are thus led by the gospel writers to think of the visions of Jesus as being filled with the mythic images of the world destruction and regeneration recounted in the writings of Enoch and other prevailing oral traditions of the day. We are left to conjecture to what extent Jesus' spiritual wisdom allowed him to take the program of these visions as concrete events of the near future, or to see them as mythic statements portraying the spiritual renewal that he was effecting.

However, Jesus developed a new conception of the role of this Son of Man in combining it with that of the Suffering Servant as established in the Servant Songs of Isaiah. Scholars have pointed out[46] that nowhere did the previous messianic expectation make any mention of a suffering death, and similarly it is nowhere to be found in the accounts of the destiny of the Son of Man. This calling to undergo rejection and suffer a redemptive death and resurrection had its origin entirely in the image of the Servant Songs.[47] The first and second of these became an expression of his spiritual kingship, the third and fourth, of his unique role of sacrifical victim and redeemer, as the supreme model of giving one's very life out of love for one's fellow beings. These were taken by him to be the program of his mission.

Agape and the Social Organism

In his teaching, likewise, Jesus conceived an equally new mission to proclaim a gospel of love that was theretofore unkown to Judaism. In the messianic expectations there had been no mention of a society based on the love of the members one for another. Mercy and loving-kindness were seen as attributes of God as a loving father, but men were to live by the Law, upholding the righteousness and justice that at the first were personified in the Davidic king. In the visions of the Second Book of Enoch[48] began the first appearance of injunctions to live in humility, gentleness, mercy and compassion, but according to recent scholarship these were written in the beginning years of the Christian era.

In numbering the injunction to live in loving-relationships as the second of the two essential commandments comprising Jesus' new version of the Law[49] — the first to love God, the second, to love one's neighbor as oneself — Jesus elevated the place of this *agape* to a supereme level. This was meant as more than a way for individuals to lead a spiritually good life; it was represented as a network of relationships binding the community of the faithful. That is, it was perceived as a bonding principle for the cohesion of society.

In the metaphorical expression, "I am the vine, you are the branches,"[50] we find a poignant transformation of the ancient image of the nation, Israel, as an integral living form embodied in the person of the Davidic king. There the society had been seen as an organism, as a collective individual whose integrity and health depended on those of the king at its heart.[51] Here the society of the Kingdom of God was now portrayed equally as a collective organism finding its spiritual life similarly embodied in the image of Christ the King. Paul slightly later extended this concept to the image of the collective "Body of Christ"[52] in which the society of believers were "members one of another," that is, component parts of the social body as an organism. He emphasized that individuals did not merely join up into this fellowship but must be initiated into it by a baptism "into the death of Christ."[53] Knowing as we do now of the role of secret doctrines, of mysteries, and of gnostic thinking in the atmosphere of Paul's thought, it has become increasingly clear that this rite was no mere formality of acceptance into the church. It involved ritually dying from the life of separate individuality, and through a visionary experience being born in a second birth, a "resurrection," into this new consciousness, consisting of a life of oneness with the totality.[54]

This new social organism was conceived as bound together not by simple caring and affection, but by a new kind of love, *agape*.[55] The term is not easy to grasp and is apt to be misconstrued as merely a universal love for all beings. While that is assuredly meant as the outcome, its nature is not only that. It is conceived not as a capacity for loving that evolves and differentiates through the maturing and developing of an individual's capacities for caring through life experience. It is defined as solely God-given, an endowment through grace alone. When in the writings of John it is said, "God is love," the intent is to render the meaning that "God is *agape*" of this kind, or the other way, the understanding that this *agape* is what God is. It signifies that when such a feeling of profound caring is sweeping through one's emotions, yielding an experience of oneness with the other, this is a manifestation of the divine.

So much was this new consciousness sacralized that Christian believers have regarded Jesus — as this incarnated Son of Man, this *eidos* and acme of mankind — to be divine. As the Christ, he has been said to be the "Only Begotten Son of God," yet the phrase derives from the already ancient enthronement oracle found in the Royal Psalm (2), by which the Davidic King was declared to be son by adoption of his divine father, Yahweh, who proclaims, "Thou art my son;/ This day have I begotten thee." The Davidic kings, in other words, were each pronounced "Son of God." Jesus inherited this title of sonship as an Anointed One in this lineage of David, as king in the inward and spiritual sense only. Paul gave clear expression to the principle of democratization and internalization of this heritage:[56] "God sent forth his Son, . . . that we might receive the adoption of sons. And because ye are sons, God hath sent forth the Spirit of his Son into your hearts . . . Wherefore thou art no more a servant [bound to the law], but a son; and if a son, then an heir to God through Christ." Paul thus perceived this indwelling divine spirit in the individual believer as the "Christ within" by which all baptized persons were to share in the numinosity of this archetypal royal entity endowed with the new *agape*.

Summary

In terms of the evolutionistic framework that is under scrutiny in our present investigation, the bonding principle that operates through a society held together by this *agape* derives from a long-time differentiation of an archetypal entity. The image of God in the early scriptures was that of a benevolent overlord and father, with attributes of justice and righteousness gradually turning into mercy and compassion, spiced with a wrath that insistently held his people to their obedience. As King of Kings he presided over the world, enthroned at the cosmic axial center. His vice-regent, the Davidic King, at the phase of the Urban Revolution, personified this divine governing presence in the human sphere, ritually located at its center and similarly endowed with the emotional attributes of benevolence toward the people. In the Christian phase of this development, and in keeping with the democratization of the kingly forms, the individual inherited this role of compassion, now emanating from a center not in the governing city but within the soul. This history implies that the psychic image of the center, the central archetype, is the source from which the capacity for universal love derives.

We turn now to a concept and practice of love of a different kind, one that is derived from the relation of man and woman as clearly as the one derived from God in the Christian doctrine, yet similarly becoming a force in the regeneration of society.

Quests and a
Kingdom of the Heart

8

I n the French Provence of the twelfth century an extraordinary
cultural phenomenon took place on the stage of world history,
the cult of "courtoisie." It has been written about from many
points of view, some filled with admiration and some with a slighting
skepticism as to its value and authenticity, and wholly different conclusions have been drawn concerning what really happened. One can
only conclude that it was so enigmatic in suggestiveness and import
that it acts as a field of possibilities attracting projections from the
psyche of each observer. At the risk of adding one more among these
subjective expositions of bias, my point of view in the present investigation is that much can be learned from the epoch concerning
the evolution of Eros and of the reverence for the feminine. It is the
era of the Arthurian Romances and of Courtly Love, in which the
formidable pyramid structure of the feudal society was crumbling and
giving way to new individuality.

In the historical background, stimulating both the romances and
the culture, was a rivalry between the dynasties of Northern and
Southern France. It was slightly more than two and a half centuries
after the unification of Europe in Charlemagne's Holy Roman Empire
and its demise by its partitioning into separate kingdoms. The Capetian kings of the north bore the tradition and heritage of the old
empire, while the newly rising Angevin kings of the south were gaining a power that led them to ambitious aspirations toward a new
empire that would include England. The Plantagenet Count of Anjou,
Henry, bearing the titles of Duke of Normandy and owner of Aquitaine and Brittany, was powerful enough to have as his aim the throne
of England. Only recently, Bretons and Normans had joined forces
under William in the conquest of England, and there was a stirring in

the Celtic soul with a dream of reuniting its peoples under a rule that represented its age old tradition.

Present scholarship is offering strong evidence[1] that in this dream is to be found the explanation accounting for the sudden burgeoning of these romances at that particular juncture in history, even though the older forms of the legends had been current and well enough known for a long time. In that explanation the motives are called political, but for the purposes of the present discussion I would suggest that the term should be taken to imply theories of governance. In the ferment of social change, the evolution of the ideal of kingship and of its myth and ritual expression accounts for the new impetus on a level underlying the political.

Two Cultures in France

Added to these political strains, then, were those arising out of deep-seated cultural proclivities.[2] That of the north bore a stern patriarchal cast, a warrior culture, appearing to those of the south as rude, uncouth, ill-bred, and cold. Their women were regarded as chattels to be won for title, property, and wealth. Their poetic expression is found in the *chansons de geste*, epitomized in the *Chanson de Roland*,[3] filled with the theorics of war-making and the technology of battle, and with loyalties to chiefs in the strictly organized hierarchy of the feudal social structure. The Capetian kings, powerful leaders in the crusades, were descended from Charlemagne and held him as their charismatic culture hero.

The more genteel culture of the south, on the other hand, was greatly influenced by the women of its ruling families. Eleanor of Aquitaine in particular was among its leading figures; once married to the French King Louis and accompanying him to the Holy Land in one of the Crusades, she divorced him, relinquishing the French throne for that of England as Queen of Henry II's Angevin Empire. Her daughter Marie de France commissioned the poet Chretian de Troyes to compose the first of the Arthurian Romances.

In contrast to the north, this culture was warm and cultivated, emphasizing the graciousness of *courtoisie* and gentility, with high reverence for woman and the love experience. Its culture hero was Arthur, whose legend sprang from Brythonic origin in the British Isles and Brittany, and spread throughout the Celtic world of the twelfth and thirteenth centuries. Its Angevin kings were in need of justification for their claim to the English throne and hence they fostered for political ends this identification with the Celtic tradition. Its literary epics of Arthur and the Grail were very different in tone from the *chansons de geste*. While they tell enough of the process of battle, they emphasize chiefly the refinement of knightly valor and the episodes are predominantly suffused with the mystery of magical events and with the interpenetration of this world and the other world of the dead.

The Courtly Culture and Fine Amour

In this atmosphere, the feudal system that had been giving firm structure to European society was becoming undermined and a new class of free men and women was evolving to displace it. In the courtly culture,[4] young knights and ladies were carefully schooled in the refinements of the relations between men and women. Knights looked to their ladies for inspiration to perfect both their love and their valor, and to temper their passions with the gentleness of restraint. To the lady of his choice the knight pledged his service and his *"triuwe,"* a troth in which he offered his fealty to her as his *"domina,"* his mistress. In this *"fine amour,"* a lover was inspired to ennoblement in beneficence, valor, and worth, and his lady was refined by qualities of prudence, mercy, and grace.[5] The aim was toward the perfection of character of fulfilled man and woman. Since marriage was looked upon as a contract arranged by church and state in the framework of the feudal system for property and title, having little to do with the motivations of attraction, the courtly love was an exchange of fidelity outside of marriage. "Romantic" love as a social and literary form had its origins here in its noble expression through *"les romans,"* the Arthurian Romances.

In the zest for this new way, a veritable explosion of literary production filled the courts with poetry and music. Early the *"trouveres"* composed *"lais"* to the ladies of their love, the leading exponent being Guillaume de Poitiers at the start of the century, inaugurating a literary *genre* that would prevail for many decades.[6] The grand expression came with the Arthurian epics, first commissioned, as already mentioned, by Marie de France, in which Chretien was to explicate and exemplify the new courtly love and way of life of genteel knights and ladies for their edification and education. Their popularity led to a burgeoning and flowering of this new literary form, spreading rapidly throughout the courts of Celtic Europe. An immensely energetic surge of creative innovation led to infinite variations on the basic themes, all giving expression to the requirements of fashioning the culture of the day, combining and recombining ancient Irish and Welsh deities, mythic events, and ritual procedures into ever fresh narratives.

A typical piece of Chretien's edification of courtly ways is found in the *Knight of the Cart*.[7] When Arthur's company is gathered a stranger appears, does combat with Kay, and abducts the Queen. Gawain and Lancelot ride off in hot pursuit, but the latter loses his mount in a skirmish. Not to be held back and hard pressed by his love for the Queen and his frantic drive to restore her to the court, he agrees to mount a trundle driven by a dwarf and used for the transport of criminals through the streets for their shame by public derision. This acceptance of degradation of his knightly demeanor with only the slightest hesitation is a measure of his devotion to his lady. By many adventures and trials, including the crossing of the perilous sword bridge, and by once gaining access to the castle of the lord of the dead and liberating the many captives incarcerated there, he wins the release of Guinevere. Upon his return to the court, expecting the grateful greeting of the Queen, he is met instead with derisive scorn from her. Her explanation for her contempt is that he failed in his courtly behavior toward her by entertaining a few moments of hesitation in the face of his humiliation in mounting the cart. This somewhat overly delicate preciosity of the point conveyed through this narrative is characteristic of the manner of courtly indoctrination.

The Image of Woman

In the background of the courtly attitude to woman lay a long historical tradition.[8] The ancient Celtic image of the feminine was revived in the myth form that had belonged to a society that not only was matrilineal but that had held woman in considerable reverence. She had had the solar attributes of brilliance and radiance of beauty too overpowering to look upon, since the sun had been a goddess before the advent of the patriarchal society and myth imposed by the impact of the Roman colonization. This goddess had been supreme and her priestess possessed of absolute power. In the social structure, woman was correspondingly independent and intolerant of any submission to man or to husband (as the heroine Deirdre demonstrated by her defiance to the death). Her children belonged to the tribe and so were not dependent upon her maternal ministrations, and, as is the habit among tribal cultures generally, the mother's brother carried the responsibility of monitoring the rearing of the nephew and overseeing his instruction in the ways of the tribe. She kept her own property, and if this was greater than that of the husband, she had more power than he to make decisions. If she were not pleased with her man she had the right to dismiss him by the ceremonial act of putting his armor outside the door. The requirements of love were given their full due: A woman had the privilege of giving the favors of her love to another man, and the husband could take a second woman into the household on a yearly contractual basis. With her strong nature she demonstrated qualities of will and initiative expressed in the mythic images of solar virgin goddesses; the term "virgin" was not meant at that time in the sense of chastity but as the original root of the word signifies, of *"vir"* (*vis*) *and "ergon,"* that is, energy and force.[9] These deities were endowed with creative and life-giving properties. All these societal and mythic expressions depicted woman in the fullness of her glory, and are to us absolutely necessary for the understanding of the uncanny awe in which the lady of courtly love and of the Arthurian romances was held.

To us of today who read and reflect upon the Arthurian romances outside of their historical context, they seem to give a strong impression of a doubtful morality in spite of the extolling of love as a supreme spiritual experience. Andreas Capelannus,[10] whom one might call a somewhat salty and humorous theoretician of the ways of courtly love, and who based his admonitions on the work of Ovid, was quite clear that this style of relationship should not only remain private and clandestine but even be guarded by the craftiest deception in respect to the spouse. And, of course, Lancelot, the most stellar of knights and most trusted by Arthur, was obsessed with a mutual and overpowering infatuation with Guinevere, who was not only wife to his supreme liege lord and king but even personified the sovereignty and the realm itself. Similarly, Tristan, loved and trusted by his uncle the king, was caught in the spell of a mutual love with Iseult the Queen. In both cases, the episodes of the story entailed the most cunning devices of deception and intrigue. These themes of lovers' trysts and subterfuges, in apparently flagrant abuse of fealty to one's liege lord, to whom one owed the utmost loyalty, were immensely popular at the time, as attested by the bewildering profusion of variations and innovations in such number as to fill many volumes. One cannot read these without a sense of deep puzzlement at the relish in these surreptitious and risky adventures propelled by the most intense desire.

Opposing Loyalties

However, things become quite clear when one is able to consider the meanings of these exploits in their own context of the cultural transition of the time.[11] They were designed to express the elevation of personal love relations above the formal feudal loyalties of the social system. An entire alternative ethic was being established, pitted against the traditional mores of church and state.

We can perceive in this a certain symmetry of mutually opposed obligations. A lady to whom one gave one's love was elevated to the position of "domina," mistress, in the sense of her being a female master, a "liege lady" to whom one owed a fealty fully as binding as that demanded by one's liege lord or suzerain. The trivial implication of the term "mistress" today is utterly different, with its somewhat degrading connotation of sexual convenience and illicit ownership. The passion of love was taken seriously, given its full due, and honored as the chief ingredient in the process of spiritual fulfillment of a knight and of a lady.

Honor in matters concerning one's lover almost necessarily involved dishonor in respect to one's lord, and vice versa. In their symmetry, two ethical systems stood side by side with their demands for fidelity and honor, and one lived thus in an exquisite tension between them. Yet the symmetry was out of balance due to the historical necessity of the time, and the scales were tipped in favor of love and freedom. The contraries were in collision. On one hand was an intensely personal and private code of honor in respect to a knight's love experience with his mistress or a lady's with her master, kept carefully clandestine to protect it against interference from the world. On the other hand was a public and political code of honor in respect to the requirements of feudal duty and the marital bond, all of which put one's reputation in the world at stake.

A closer look at the tribulations of Tristan and Iseult[12] can tell us more of the psychology of this trend in history. King Mark has a significant relation to Tristan in that he is his mother's brother, suggestive of the role of mentor, so prevalent among tribal societies instructing the youth in the ways of the culture and presiding over his initiation rites. Iseult the Queen personifies the Sovereignty and the realm, and her golden image derives from the ancient Irish sun goddess and divine Lady of the Orchard.[13] According to old Celtic customs of kingship, to love and possess the queen is to inherit the kingdom, and Tristan is heir apparent to the throne. The new courtly culture, by the same token, perceived the inner, spiritual significance of these ritual motifs. Hence, if Tristan is to reach fulfillment of the spiritual kingship of the soul, he must do the same, that is, love and possess his liege lady over against the constraints of his feudal obligations to Mark. Visibly, to win honor in his love of her he must court dishonor as the leading knight in the king's service; the barons explicitly declare this condemnation, thus putting them in a villainous role in the framework of the courtly ethic. Loyalty to one devotion is equivalent to disloyalty to the other, and the spice in the story that gives it poignancy is this exquisitely painful tension between opposite requirements. The tale's popular appeal is, then, that it epitomizes the growing pains of a new age in the twelfth century, its task being the winning of the spiritual quest of the individual over against his entrapment in the collective obligations that were in process of crumbling. The lovers' kingdom is of the heart rather than the state.

The imagery of the center achieved through this quest of love is beautifully expressed in the sojourn of the lovers in hiding in the Forest of Broceliand, safely sheltered from the intrusions of their public context. Here (in Gottfried's account) they dwell in "The Grotto for People in Love,"[14] a structure of mandala-like shape, with a golden and jewelled crown at the crest of its dome. For the practices of love, it houses a circular crystalline bed at the center, dedicated to the Goddess of Love; the theme is reminiscent of a Celtic mythologem, the crystal palace of the Queen of the Isle of Fairies with its crystal chamber in which the rays of the sun converge.[15]

Essentially, the drama is a tragedy, for though Tristan attempts to obey both requirements, those of the "real," outer world prevail over those of the inner and lead to the failure of both. Tristan must forego his passion; he marries another Iseult belonging to the mundane world, and without the magic of the spell of love, becomes impotent; finally, wounded in battle he is met by the first Iseult only at his death. One is left with the conclusion that tragedy comes from the irreconcilability of two fates, demands rising from the quest for fulfillment in the two domains, inner and outer, spiritual and mundane, private and public, magical and prosaic.

If we of the twentieth century are puzzled by the appeal that the Tristan saga held for that time, we have only to learn that Iseult bore all the attributes and powers of the ancient Celtic Goddess of the Sun and of the Orchard. Markale[16] points out that the later forms of the legend, in blaming the plight on a love potion, only were falsifying the original, in which Iseult quite consciously compelled Tristan to love. She became the model of the lady of courtly love and acted in the spirit of his "domina," his absolute mistress. As fairy or divine personage, she used the magical power of the *"geis,"*[17] a binding constraint with the force of a taboo that can brush aside all previous rulings and obligations. In this and two other legends, those of Diarmaid and of Deirdre,[18] love itself is to be freed once more from the current legal and obligatory shackles to recapture its fullness. Hence, Tristan is portrayed as transformed from his former awkward and impoverished self into a new state of being, skillful, wise, and free.[19] The tragedy arises from the circumstance that the price paid for his metamorphosis is his breaking all links with the past and his transgression of the existing prohibitions in the rebellious obedience to a different law; hence the retribution that society visits upon him.

The issue at stake was the possibility of a new cultural form offering a place for the love experience, to replace the one in which the whole organization of the society found itself threatened by the isolated experience of two lovers who were sufficient unto themselves, and who in this spirit set up their own world governed by the heart.[20]

Arthur and the Celtic Kingship

These questions of the structure of the *ethos* and *eidos* of society become expressed in Arthur's mode of government. The type of the kingship in early Celtic culture[21] on which it is based is best found in Ireland's. Here the customs and ceremonials remained undiluted by the Roman occupation that contaminated so deeply the cultures of the Gauls. The Irish King of Kings dwelling at the fabled Tara was supreme but did not exactly rule; he was a ceremonial figure on whom the health and well-being of the entire society depended. As in other parts of the ancient world, the Irish king occupied the position of the center of a quadrated world. [22] A "district" in their language denoted a "fifth," signifying that Tara was the central kingdom nestled at the midpoint surrounded by four lesser ones, a configuration that was a replica of the shape of the cosmos. This king held his office by common consent, one that could be inherited by any of the stronger members of his family for four generations only. His role was entirely to serve the will of the various lesser kings under him as their spokesman and executive. At his inauguration he obtained his royal status by marrying the land in the person of his queen who personified it, as an incarnation of the goddess called "the Sovereignty." This sacred marriage was the principal act in the enthronement rites, accompanied by certain trials by ordeal, and by his standing upon the Stone of Fail, which uttered a cry in the presence of the true king.

The Arthur of the twelfth-century epics was such a king. In this role, he had little to do with the Arthur of actual history; that Arthur had been a warrior chief heading a band of horsemen and other militia in the struggle to rid the land of Saxon invaders in the sixth century.[23] His success in war and in holding his Celtic society intact and in security for twenty-two years made him a great British hero, as the author of a Celtic golden age of peace and prosperity. The Arthurian Cycle of six and seven centuries later addressed the questions of the day and its courtly culture. He still bore the marks of Celtic tradition, a ruler without absolute authority yet with the charisma of a spiritual head and center of the realm, his position utterly dependent upon the grace of the Queen.

Society and the Individual

Arthur's kingship was the perfect mythic expression of rulership without personal authority but with profound respect for higher law. This was an issue of the time that had been expressed, only a little more than a decade before the commissioning of Chretian to compose his romances, by John of Salisbury. His *Policraticus*[24] gave voice to the attitudes of the clerks at a turning point in European culture, comprising the gradual dissolution of the feudal system and growth of the urban emancipation and independence of a class of knights on the rise. The text dealt with the conflict of interests of *"populus"* and *"universitas,"* that is, of the people and the structure, persons and laws, or more generally speaking, the individual and the society. The new mythic legends were designed to articulate the necessary compromise between these for the healing of community.

We are once more, then, witnessing in this history the emergence of a new species of individuality and the problem of its relation to the needs of the whole. That is, these courtly romances supported the role of the great individual in bringing to society its much needed redemption from a decaying collective structure.[25] So Arthur's reign was designed to strike a balance between the inner stability and order of knightly governance and the individualism of the knights and their adventures. His marriage to the Sovereignty as Queen was his tie to the law of the land, the society's tradition, following the custom of Celtic kings from before the time of the Indo-European patriarchial order.

Grail Questers and Vision Quests

The evolution of the concept of the Grail was an innovative adaptation of a mythic theme of a magic cauldron and of a cup of sovereignty.[26] When in the tales Arthur's Round Table is fully established, and peace and order are achieved and fulfilled by an enlightened rule, the question arises, "What next?" An emissary of the Grail appears with a calling for the knights to leave the security of the company of the Round Table and embark upon the quest of the Grail. Promptly, they abandon Arthur's court to tend its own maintenance, and they set forth each one alone on a way according to his own prompting. The Grail Castle is in the wilderness, at once nowhere and anywhere, now appearing and now disappearing, a magic place governed by the wounded Fisher King, maimed because of an illicit love, causing the desolation of its kingdom as a Wasteland. It has many affinities with the character of the realm of the dead. Only the truest and more perfect of knights, accomplished in the refinement of love, valor, and *courtoisie* could achieve the quest and, healing the wounded king and unspelling the land, be inaugurated as its next king. As cauldron, the grail was derived from ancient legends of such a vessel that could nourish without end, heal, or restore the dead to life: as cup, it derived from a golden vessel that was offered to a hero to convey the kingship, at the hands of a maiden who represented the sovereignty.

In the background of the concept of the grail castle were the events of ancient Irish lore.[27] A king at Tara was Nuadu, a navigator and fisherman, who suffered the misfortune of a wound in the thigh, necessitating the fashioning of a silver leg. Being thus unwhole, he could no longer serve in his office and withdrew to an underground castle from which he could lend his influence in the affairs of the kingdom. The god Bran is another form of the same figure, also wounded in the leg in one of the Battles of Magtured (Maytura). There is a suggestion that these battles were the mythic expression of annual ritual combats[28] between the ancestors of the Irish, the Tuatha De, and the monstrous Fomorians who descended from the god of the dead and dwelt in a tower of glass with the deceased; at seasonal festivals there was an abduction of a woman in the fall and her restoration in the spring. To win her was to win the sovereignty.

The basic thematic pattern of the grail stories may be summarized briefly, at the expense of the enjoyment and mystery of the drama when properly narrated.[29] A Loathly Damsel appears unexpectedly at the court and pronounces a challenge to the quest. Each quester sets forth in search of the grail castle, never knowing the way. To the worthy, the way leads to an invitation to the castle, and the quester beholds a wondrous procession in which maidens bear a grail and a bleeding lance; the grail may feed the assembled company magically. The host reveals himself as the Fisher King who has been kept alive by the ministrations of the grail after being maimed long ago by the Dolorous Stroke, causing the sad plight of the Wasteland. The fate of the land awaits the hero who is wise enough to ask the vital question that could unspell the land. The versions vary, but if the knight is sufficiently accomplished in perfection he asks the question and thus heals both king and kingdom. He may then succeed to the kingship.

These motifs are rewoven in the twelfth and thirteenth centuries from the "Matter of Britain," a store of myths and legends that may be faintly traced back through the *conteurs* of Brittany to their origin in Wales, and then behind Wales to the more ancient Irish myth and ritual of the first centuries A.D. In the latter, the health of the kingdom depends on that of the king and reflects it; when he is maimed, the land is crippled and unfertile. The Loathly Damsel is one and the same with the lovely grail maiden, as the Sovereignty, and her ugliness represents the sickness of the land; a hero who gives her his love transforms her into her radiant self and the land blooms once more. The grail derives from a number of magic cauldrons or cups of ancient lore,[30] ones which may feed a company magically, heal the ailing or wounded, bring the dead to life, tell the truth or speak wisdom, or record the names of kings about to be. The bleeding lance derives from the spear of Lug, a thunder weapon of such intense heat that it has to be kept seething in a cauldron of water, and of such destructive power that it could blast the whole kingdom out of existence. Lug was maimed by a wound in the thigh; Lug, Bran, and Nuadu each were counted as Ireland's first king and were the prototype of the maimed Fisher King causing the plight of the wasting of the land. The infertility called for a renewal of both king and kingdom. The model for the procedure is to be found in the ancient Irish "echtra," journeys of heroes to the otherworld where occur both the necessary asking of the question and the naming of kings on the cup.

The quest of the grail that scattered Arthur's round table and sent the knights wandering through the wilderness on separate ways was what today we recognize as a form of "vision quest." It had a long history in Irish tradition, in the *echtra*[31] of youthful heroes who were candidates for the kingship, journeys which served as their ritual initiation and trial of their fitness for the bestowing of this destiny. Chretien's account of Perceval's visit to the grail castle has distinct affinities with the *echtra* of Conn in a tale called the "Phantom's Frenzy," an expression more properly translated as "a supernatural being's prophetic ecstasy."[32] It tells of the hero's losing his way, receiving an invitation to a dwelling that turns out to be the magnificent mansion of Lug — the god of both sun and thunder, and Ireland's first king. A beautiful maiden with golden crown serves them rich fare and filling a golden cup asks of Lug, "To whom shall the cup be given?" to which the reply is, "Pour it for Conn." She is the Sovereignty, and her cup designates the kingship. Upon repetition of the question, Lug names the future descendants of Conn who will inherit the throne. All vanishes at the last, palace, host, and maiden, leaving Conn with the golden cup.

Another version of an *Echtra* (in the "Adventure of Art")[33] contains the wasteland motif. The same Conn here is married to an evil woman who brings upon the land a disastrous spell, spoiling grain and milk. In order to revive the land, Conn sets out upon a journey over the sea in a coracle and comes upon an island palace with wondrous features in bronze and crystal, with hazel trees in blossom, with entertainment appearing magically of itself, and a drinking horn. All is presided over by the fair niece of the sea god, Manannan Mac Lir. Upon Conn's return, the evil wife is banished and fertility presumably restored to the land. The tale affords a clear picture of the magical role of the royal couple in maintaining the fertility of the land, and when evil strikes, the disastrous wasteland that results; the cure is a vision quest for renewal of the royal life-giving potency. Yet another legend tells of Conn's grandson Cormac visiting the Land of Promise. [34] His wife was carried off by a stranger, and in pursuit he finds himself in the magnificent otherworld mansion of Manannan, full of similar wonders. After being lavishly entertained by the god and a beautiful maiden and by their magical fare, the hero wakes in the morning on the lawn of Tara with his wife beside him and a truth-telling cup. This theme of the abduction of the queen by an otherworld lord occurs frequently in the Arthurian romances, providing the occasion for the heroic journey to the otherworld, for the renewal and the gift it provides.

With the gradual elaboration of the old Celtic motifs in Christian hands, we discover a development of the messianic element in the concept of the kingship. Arthur himself was thought of as deathless, and there was a strong conviction among the Celtic peoples that he would return from the realm of the otherworld to establish a new golden age, as he had done in the sixth century. The line of thought followed the classical stages of the concept of sacral kingship. It began with the desire for the reestablishment of the ideal of the kingship as an actual form of governance. However, the grail quest pushes beyond that to the vision of a purely spiritual kingdom to be attained through the cultivation of knightly virtue. In this sense, the kingship of the grail is an internal one, of the soul. Its expression culminates in the thoroughly christianized tale of Galahad's quest.[35] This hero, a creation of the Cistercian Order, is the epitome of the monastic ideal, of stainless chastity and self-mastery, seeking the mystical union with God. He is introduced to Arthur as a messiah, the long-awaited one "who is descended from the lineage of King David." The grail becomes at this point a pure vision bringing upon the assembled knights the light of grace of the Holy Spirit.

Individuality and the Love Experience

In looking into the meaning of these romances, one must guard against our secular propensities to regard such stories as a species of novel and love story. They are, on the contrary, real myth in which the parts are not played by ordinary people but by archetypal personages. This is hinted at by the fact that these are derived from erstwhile deities. More than that, however, their doings address the profound cultural and spiritual or emotional issues of the times in dramatic form, spelling out the meaning-in-depth of new movements under way in the unfolding of current history.

In the twelfth century a new individuality was in the making, emerging from under the heavy constraints of feudal collectivity and finding its epitome in the vicissitudes of the love experience. In Jung's psychology, this would be framed as the activation of the anima and animus components of the collective unconscious,[36] and their collision with the values and mores expressed in the collective persona as fashioned by the feudal culture. The convinced outward adaptation to established ways was creaking and groaning under the heavy impact of a newly aroused spiritual necessity for individual self-determination and fulfillment. Fresh passions were being stirred, and persons were finding their relations with each other in a different framework.

The trial of true myth seems to me to be the question whether the spoken narrative is also accompanied by some ritual expression in action. The answer is made abundantly clear by the role of these mythic epics as explicative of the ways of courtly love and behavior. There was a distinct ceremonial in which a knight pledged his *triuwe* to his lady, sealed it with the formal kiss, and rendered his unswerving service to her. These loves were passionate but far from chaotic, and they were conducted along the lines of established and agreed rules. Spring festivals were held to bring young knights and ladies together.[37] There were apparently even courts of love. in which women deliberated the complaints of violation of the code by individuals. There was a discipline by which the passions of knights were tempered and refined by their ladies, and gentility was an aim of education of young men and women. The experience of such courtly love was in its essence a spiritual quest in which both parties sought a rebirth, transformation, and fulfillment of their noblest nature.

In this perspective, the legends of the grail take on a special significance. In contrast to the tragedy of the Tristan and Iscult myth, in which the opposing pulls of the spiritual quest and of the constraints of the mundane structure led to failure, the quest of the grail signified a reconciliation of these opposites. The quester was promised, if he perfected his knightly qualities, the reward of a kingship in another realm than the mundane. The cup of the sovereignty was to be won at the hands of a grail damsel as a mythic expression of the fulfillment of selfhood through the trials of the courtly love experience. Such a kingship was then to be realized in a mythic and mystic dimension of inner being, safely in hiding from the mundane world and yet at the same time necessary to it spiritually. Throughout there is implied a characteristically Celtic reconciliation of the contraries: this world and otherworld, mundane and spiritual, temporal and eternal, and outer law and inner law. Also the symbols of grail and lance are eloquently expressive of the spiritual union of female and male, animus and anima, out of which a fresh and passionate vitality would emerge on the stage of history to renew the society.

The crucial turning point in the narrative for good or for ill, success or failure, is the asking of the question. In Gawain's visit to the grail castle,[38] he is accompanied by two companions, Perceval and Calogreant, who slumber as the Fisher King tells his story; even Gawain himself falls asleep before the tale is done. He is in consequence only half successful in his mission as healer. This tells us that the fault is in unconsciousness, and that success would hang upon the quester's insistence on knowing, on consciousness. Health and wholeness, then, arise from an advance in heroic consciousness, and this is expressed in the symbol of the union of female and male in the grail and lance and the accompanying kingship.

The Outer and Inner Kingdoms

In the romances of the round table and of the grail, we easily find ourselves perplexed as to the interrelation of this world and otherworld so typical of Celtic lore. I find it clarifying to regard the story of the Arthurian Kingdom of Logres as the mythic model for the Celtic way of governance, addressed to the aspirations of the actual Celtic kingdom in twelfth-century Europe; and to regard the Grail Kingdom as in turn the mythic model of the Celtic way of personal redemption, addressed to the needs of Arthur's Logres for the fulfillment of the heroic individual. The two kingdoms thus constitute a mythic level behind a myth, one this worldly and one otherworldly, one a kingdom of society, one a kingdom of the soul. When the mythic Logres is on the verge of sterility by becoming too set in its institutional ways, the needs of structure and of persons, of society and of individuals, are constellated as opposites. A crisis is thus engendered which becomes the occasion for a healing process to restore balance and vitality; this is the challenge to the quest, to the visionary journeys of heroes that might bring renewal. All is addressed, in turn, to the corresponding need of twelfth-century Europe for revitalization when the feudal system congeals and crumbles.

In fact, a new breath of energy did sweep through Europe at this time. A generation of "new men" did rise into prominence,[39] gaining positions of authority and power that left the older aristocracy of the feudal titles off to one side, while they took the posts of "*ministeriales*," administrators of domains who did the actual work of conducting the practical affairs of the culture. In Europe's case, unlike China's and India's, this democratization and freedom of individuality arose concurrently with the establishment of their urban civilization.

Tragedy was mixed with triumph, however, in the outcome of the courtly culture. With the encouragement of Bernard of Clairvaux, several crusades were carried out in southern France against the Cathari, Waldenses, and Albigenses, because of their heretical teachings and practices. Tens of thousands of souls were slaughtered, a holocaust that at the same time wiped out the adherents of the courtly culture, cutting the life span of that venture to a mere three or four decades. Spiritually, though, it went on blossoming as its literary genre throve in Germany, Italy and England.

Great testimonies to the radical novelty of the tradition were created. The cult of woman found its more orthodox expression in the elevation of the Virgin to the status of Queen of Heaven and to her enthronement at Chartres,[40] and indeed in the profusion of such edifices through the "cathedral age." Mary became the divine personage that was more accessible to the people, while Christ was viewed as Judge at the Last Judgment, somewhat too austere for the common man, and God himself too remote. When one was in need of a compassionate hearing, one went to Our Lady, Queen of Heaven. Meanwhile on the mundane plane, great women ruled on the thrones of various parts of Europe.

Wolfram captured the spirit of the New Kingdom of the Heart in his description of Parsival as the awaited one, more familiar to us in Wagner's operatic retelling[41] in which the hero is "Durch Mitleid Wissend" (enlightened through compassion).

Summary

The twelfth-century romances, then, give us a rich demonstration of the role of myth-making in a time of critical culture change appearing to us less remote than the myth and ritual of antiquity. As in many of those of earlier times, poetry served as the main vehicle of mythic expression and had as its main theme the emergence of a new individuality in the making, in the framework of the mutual spiritual development of young men and women. A perplexing question arising for us in many of these tales is the relation between the personal love experience and that more universal love that takes the form of compassion and ardent feeling for the entire human world. For the people of those centuries, they surely were bound together, as the work of Dante showed shortly after.

In the next essay, we will find poetry extolled as the medium for prophetic utterance. The ardor that had been expressed in the romances led in the nineteenth century to the enthusiasm of the romantic movement in poetic myth-making.

Revolution and World Regeneration 9

"Poets are the hierophants of an unapprehended inspiration; the mirrors of the gigantic shadows which futurity casts upon the present"[1]; in these words Shelley claims for poetry the prophetic function of giving direct utterance to the seminal images of the future that are germinating in the depths of the psyche. He says further, "In ancient times, what we call prophets were the poets," inasmuch as poetry is the "Faculty which contains within itself the seeds at once of its own and of social renovation . . . poetry could redeem the time: it is ever still the Light of life; the source of whatever of good or generous or true can have place in an evil time."[2] Shelley thus saw that the poetic, mythic images of an improved state of society were "the children of airy hope, the prophets and parents of mysterious futurity."[3]

Shelley: Prophet and Revolutionary

It has been a delight to me in recent years to rediscover Shelley in a new light. From my early schoolday impressions of him I was inclined to visualize him as a typical young romantic, dreamily writing of nightingales and asphodels, or of fantasmagoric landscapes of craggy pinnacles, dim caves, and vine-tangled primordial forests; his familiar portrait seems to render him as effeminate and scarcely able to concern himself with the world of human strivings.

From his life and writings, on the other hand, we find him to be a man of stature, filled with immense vitality and vigor, and to be an ardent revolutionary and philosopher of social reform and liberation from tyranny. The visionary perceptions that fill his *Prometheus Unbound* appear before us as prophetic utterances that "speak to our condition," to our own cultural transition that is so stressful at this particular juncture today. With an uncanny aptness he addresses the problems that many of us are wrestling with: revolution for cultural renovation, nonviolent methods of conflict, the reexamination of Christian assumptions, the role of the visionary mind, the image of world regeneration, and in this the function of love in the transformation of society.

Striking evidence for the special significance of Shelley for today's concerns is to be found in the flurry of commentaries that have appeared in only the last two decades. This particular reception of him parallels that of William Blake: both men were genuine mythmakers. Only recently, in a generation that has learned much through various experiences of altered states of consciousness, has the power of the visionary mind been granted special recognition.

The commentaries over the last decades have emphasized the dimensions of depth in Shelley's work. Bloom wrote of his "mythmaking" in a new vein,[4] Woodman of his mystical quest and "apocalyptic vision,"[5] Webb of him as a "voice not understood"[6] (i.e., classed among romantics seen as avoiding the concerns of the real world in favor of the subjective realms of fantasy and feeling). Young has explicated in full the poet's explorations of the potentials for non-violent conflict.[7] Bhalla speaks lucidly for the oriental point of view in recognizing Shelley's familiarity with and zealous interest in Indian mystical philosophy.[8]

Shelley as Mythmaker

Formerly, the *Prometheus Unbound* had been regarded as allegory, to be decoded and also criticized in terms of success in respect to clarity and consistency. True myth is concerned with neither of these, and lately Shelley's capacities as a mystic and mythmaker have come into recognition. Allegory translates conscious rational thought into symbolic expressions which when grasped are to be translated back into the rational thought out of which they sprang. Much writing went into conjectures about what the poet meant to say; each differed from the other.

Real myth is comprised of the manifestation of archetypal symbols arising on their own initiative out of the imaginal mind, and the writer can only weave them into an art form in the spell of the inspiration that causes them to glow with a light of their own. He may secondarily attempt to interpret them into rational modes of thought, but their original character is nonrational. The symbol, as Charles Williams put it, is a "shape . . . understood to be an image of things beyond itself";[9] or, as C. S. Lewis has reminded us, in the Platonic sense the symbol is "the really real of which the material world is a mere copy"; therefore, for the symbolist "it is we who are the allegory."[10] Bhalla points out that Shelley specifically warns his reader against the mistake of allegorical interpretations of his work, and urges us to abide by the poet's own intentions."[11]

Shelley has remained his own best commentator, particularly in respect to his intentions in making poetry the vehicle for visionary reform of the human being and hence of the world. In his "Defense of Poetry" he declares that poetry "creates for us a being within our being. It makes us the inhabitants of a world to which the familiar world is a chaos."[12] That is. as Woodman points out, the imaginal mind is for him "a creative power at work upon the chaos of man's familiar world, forcing it to assume a form which is the image of the 'divinity in Man.' "[13]

Shelley was clearly concerned with world regeneration, and understood it in its psychological as well as political sense. As he perceived it, our fixed assumptions and habits of thought have a deadening and stultifying effect when they become unreflecting, and hence automatic; only the revivifying light of the divine in man can break through this darkness and renew one's experience of the world. Thus, he says, "The interpenetration of a diviner nature through our own quickens the imagination to create anew the universe, after it has been annihilated in our minds by the recurrence of impressions blunted by reiteration."[14] One is reminded of Deikman's formulation of the mystical experience as an introduction of a new consciousness which "deautonomatizes" our overly habitual and limited modes of experience.[15]

"Prometheus Unbound" in Summary

Prometheus Unbound, considered by Shelley his greatest work, was his most explicit statement of social revolution, reform, and world renewal. To outline briefly the dramatic poem, it is a myth that depicts a turn in cosmic history. It takes up the story where Aeschylus had left off in his *Prometheus Bound*, in which the Titan railed against Zeus who was punishing him for giving to man the stolen gifts of fire, wisdom, and the arts and crafts; the Titan brought down a curse upon the god. As Shelley's drama opens. Prometheus is bound to the rock in the Caucasus (where an eagle periodically devours his liver to increase his sufferings). In spite of the admonitions of the Titan when he had given to Zeus the kingship over gods and men, this high god had let himself be carried away by zeal to dominate, oppress, and enslave his subjects, and suffering consequently prevailed over the world on a vast scale; the worldly powers of church and state in like manner oppressed their subjects. Prometheus now wrestles with his own recognition that in his curse upon Jupiter (Zeus) he had become like his oppressor, and that to free himself and mankind from such self-enslavement the only means are pity, compassion, and forgiveness. His consort, Asia (Aphrodite-Venus), depicted as Love and Nature in one, undergoes a parallel transformation by descending into the deepest darkness of the cave of Demogorgon to stir him into his mission to overthrow the tyrant Jupiter, since his hour had arrived. When he is freed from his icy rock, the Titan and Asia, with her two sisters, retire to a cave paradise in which are experienced the archetypal forms that generate the arts. The world is regenerated, transformed by Asia's love and Prometheus's wisdom; evil is eliminated, and power in the world is superceded by love among mankind. An ecstatically visionary and symbolic celebration of the renewed cosmos in song closes the drama.

Shelley's Authentic Visionary Experience

The entire thrust of the poem is classically messianic. It conforms to that pattern of visionary reform in which the oppressive "establishment" is overthrown and a new reign of love and brotherhood prevails in a world regenerated. It must be constantly reiterated that true myth-making is not a rational process of conceptualizing by discursive thought and conscious intent but is the product of altered states of consciousness in dreams, visions, or other transports. Shelley was no exception, and his *Prometheus* has all the hallmarks of true mythic experience, as did Blake's and Milton's works. His style is more serene in its feeling tone than Blake's, whose cosmos resounds with anguished howlings, tears, and rage emanating from passionate beings encircled by flaming fire and blood coursing through immense eternities of time and space. This contrasts with Milton's cosmos, enveloped in the official Judeo-Christian mold of divine personages and angels. In their several ways, these poets were equally genuine fashioners of true myth.

The authenticity of Shelley's mythmaking is born out by considerable evidence. Some five years previous to his writing of *Prometheus*, he had made attempts to present himself to the Irish people as a leader of their revolutionary moves against the oppressions of English rule and had laid forth to them a program of nonviolent rebellion almost as explicit as Gandhi's a hundred years later.[16] In his disappointment at not being accepted by them in this role, he resolved to make his appeal to mankind for these modes of achieving true spiritual revolution and reform through his poetry, even if it meant addressing himself to the cultivated and aware revolutionaries of the society of some distant future.

Along with others of the romantic movement, Shelley had watched with dismay the failure of the French Revolution to achieve its desired ends. What had promised to become a regeneration of society through the ideals of liberty and fraternity had turned out instead to become a mere change of hands holding the power of tyranny and oppression. He found himself increasingly convinced that there is no transformation of society without first the accomplishment of the transformation of the individuals composing it, or at least leading it.[17] He therefore plumbed deeply into the philosophical and spiritual issues involved in such a mystic quest, and composed translations of Plato's *Symposium* and *Republic* along the way of his search.

In the winter of 1817–1818,[18] matters came to a critical turning point for Shelley. Some months previously there had taken place a massacre of an assembly of republican reformers in Manchester at the hands of a tyrannical government. More recently the poet had learned that this same government was about to enforce his separation from his infant child because of his irregular marital complications. His only choice was to flee his native country, never to see it again. In his self-exile to Italy he suffered erosions of his physical strength from consumption (TB), and his child was also about to die. We are not left to conjecture about the effects of these hardships on the poet's state of mind, for he described them in explicit terms to a friend in a letter written three months before quitting England's shores — at the time that he was first conceiving the shape of his new *Prometheus*. Any of us who are familiar with the experience of altered states of consciousness, through whatever means, are able instantly to recognize the signs of it that the poet describes in this account of his subjective state:

> My feelings at intervals are of a deadly and torpid kind, or awakened
> to such a state of unnatural and keen excitement, that only to instance
> the organ of sight, I find the very blades of grass and the boughs of
> trees present themselves to me with microscopic distinctness. . . . [17]

What could be a more clear expression of that peculiar state of
the psyche named "psychedelic," associated so much with
psychotropic substances like peyote and mushrooms that it is easy to
forget that nature has its own ways of throwing us into these
transports without our bidding? Also, he did use laudanum.

These states were not particularly welcome to the poet, who
found himself often to

> remain for hours on the sofa between sleep and waking, a prey to the
> most painful irritability of thought. . . . [19]

This clearly is the mental ground out of which his myth of Prometheus germinated and came to flower. I point to it particularly as
essential to the understanding of the mythic character of the *Prometheus* because his wife, Mary, in her illuminating notes on the three
volumes of his poetry, did the same. She began her comments on the
Prometheus with the quotation of this letter, obviously to convey to
the reader that the poet was in an unnatural state of mind at the time
of his first writing it.[20]

I would add further that the poet was at a significant age during
the unfolding of his new myth (1819, his twenty-eighth year). Those
of us who do analytic work in depth with the psyche find that there
is a cluster of individuals who present themselves with an activated
psyche at the age of twenty-eight or so (better put as twenty-seven to
twenty-nine). It appears to be as significant a turning point in psychic
development as fourteen or so, the time of the activation accompanying puberty and the adolescent upheavals, and perhaps also as
thirty-five, which Bucke has pointed to as the classical time for the
experience of what he called "cosmic consciousness," or enlightenment.[21] These multiples of seven have been brought into discussions
of development by such authors as Levinson and, before him, Rudolph
Steiner.[22]

A Prophet of Nonviolent Revolution

I would therefore stress the significance of Shelley's twenty-eighth year as a time of intense revolutionary fervor which gave birth to his excited appeal to resistance against oppression in his "Song to the Men of England," and his anguished longing for strength of prophetic voice in his "Ode to the West Wind."[23] Aware of being already too soon in his declining years, in the latter verse he still knows himself as a man possessed of a restless vitality akin to that of the stormy wind: "A heavy weight of hours has chained and bowed/One too like thee: tameless, and swift, and proud." He begs the wind to grant him the gift of the charisma that would make his voice heard through the world: "Make me thy lyre, even as the forest is . . . /Be thou, spirit fierce,/My spirit! Be thou me, impetuous one!/Drive my dead thoughts over the universe/Like withered leaves to quicken a new birth . . . /Be through my lips to unawakened earth/The trumpet of a prophecy! O wind. . . . "

As already noted, Shelley was all too aware that he was not being heard in his own time, and so was content to address his prophetic verses to a future generation. It is not generally recognized that he was indeed harkened some eighty years later by Gandhi who, when he was living as a barrister in London, attended meetings of the Shelley Society and heard the poet's proposals to resist oppressive authority by nonviolent means. He never acknowledged his debt because of the poet's advocacy of free-love, which offended him as being out of keeping with the requirements for a campaign of Satyagraha (Truth-Force), which necessitated a blameless purity of spirit. Nevertheless, what Shelley foresaw in his prophetic vision in his "Masque of Anarchy."[24] is readily recognized in the methods of Indian Swaraj, its nonviolent war of independence, a hundred years later, won by confronting the opposition fearlessly with folded arms.

'Stand ye calm and resolute,
Like a forest close and mute,
With folded arms, and looks which are
Weapons of an unvanquished war.
. . . .
'And if then the tyrants dare,
Let them ride among you there;
Slash, and stab, and maim, and hew;
What they like, that let them do.

With folded arms and steady eyes,
And little fear, and less surprise,
Look upon them as they slay,
Till their rage has died away:

'Then they will return with shame,
To the place from which they came
· ·

'And that slaughter to the nation
Shall steam up like inspiration,
Eloquent, oracular,
A volcano heard afar:
· ·

(')Shake your chains to earth, like dew
Which in sleep had fallen on you:
Ye are many — they are few!'

I find it altogether uncanny that Shelly had given his heroine personifying transformative love the name, Asia, apparently being familiar with some of India's philosophy. and that it should turn out to be Asia in which his recommendations for nonviolent war would be heard!

This part of Shelley's life was also a time of deep research into his gradually maturing mystical philosophy in his labors over Plato's *Symposium*, and over the role of the Orphic Eros in both the greater cosmos and man's microcosm. His "state of unnatural and keen excitement" may have made him suffer, but in these transports the Muse conveyed to him the gift of high lyricism and vivid imaginal powers.

The "Prometheus Unbound," a Mythic Drama

In his dramatic poem, the condition of creation emerges in the first two acts as the poet depicts the earth groaning under the oppression of tyranny that the king of the gods had allowed himself to create by a betrayal of trust. For, as Asia tells of it, Prometheus in the start of his reign

Gave wisdom, which is strength, to Jupiter,
And with this law alone, "Let man be free,"
Clothed him with the dominion of wide Heaven.
To know nor faith, nor love, nor law; to be
Omnipotent but friendless is to reign;
And Jove now reigned; for on the race of man
First famine, and then toil, and then disease,
Strife, wounds, and ghastly death unseen before,
Fell . . .

She speaks of terror, madness, crime, remorse, and

Abandoned hope, and love that turns to hate;
And self-contempt, bitterer to drink than blood . . .

The drama opens with a soliloquy of Prometheus hanging in
agony upon the icy rock in the Caucasus, prepared at this point for
the enantiodromia; he declares that he survives through

The wingless, crawling hours, one among whom —
As some dark Priest hales the reluctant victim —
Shall drag three, cruel King, to kiss the blood
From these pale feet, which then might trample thee
If they disdained not such a prostrate slave.
Disdain! Ah no! I pity thee . . .

Here occurs the turning point in the cosmic history. It represents the
essence of the nonviolent resistence to oppressive powers:

. . . I speak in grief,
Not exultation, for I hate no more,
As then ere misery made me wise. The curse
Once breathed on thee I would recall.

No one he summons could dare to repeat the dread words, but his
mother Earth comes to his aid, reminding him there are "two worlds
of life and death."

One that which thou beholdest; but the other
Is underneath the grave, where do inhabit
The shadows of all forms that think and live
Till death unite them and they part no more;

The phantasm of Jupiter is conjured forth and reiterates the words of
the curse as they had occurred three thousand years before. Prometheus replies forgivingly:

It doth repent me: words are quick and vain;
Grief for a while is blind, and so was mine.
I wish no living thing to suffer pain.

He is tempted by the envoy of the high king to make a deal that would
offer a compromise and relieve the sufferer; Mercury tries, like the
"company man," to persuade him. Then follow Furies to torment him

to yield. Prometheus continues to defy the King by means of the suffering inflicted by him, which works to undo its perpetrator:

> . . . though dread revenge,
> This is defeat, fierce king? not victory.

After choruses tell of the woes of the world under the enslavement of the cruel tyrant, and the longing for "Wisdom, Justice, Love, and Peace," the Titan resolves to defy.

> . . . I would fain
> Be what it is my destiny to be,
> The saviour and the strength of suffering man,
> Or sink into the original gulf of things:

What the Titan has realized during these encounters is that his erstwhile raging against Jupiter in hate had only debased him into the same enslavement to evil as the king-god's.[25] He had then to settle his accounts with the opponent within himself. The only release from the evil clearly lay through the hard path of suffering and forgiveness; only then could love prevail.

Hence, in the second act, Asia's sister Panthea recounts to her a dream vision of an encounter with the renewed Prometheus, transformed into his light-body from which the pains and wounds of his suffering have sloughed off:

> . . . his pale wound-worn limbs
> Fell from Prometheus, and the azure night
> Grew radiant with the glory of that form
> Which lives unchanged within, and his voice fell
> Like music which makes giddy the dim brain,
> Faint with intoxication of keen joy . . .
> . . . The overpowering light
> Of that immortal shape was shadowed o'er
> By love; which . . .
> Streamed forth like vaporous fire; an atmosphere
> Which wrapped me in its all-dissolving power . . .

In this transport she neither saw, nor heard, nor moved but

> . . . only felt
> His presence flow and mingle through my blood
> Till it became his life, and his grew mine
> And I was thus absorbed, until it passed.

The transport seems to me to be also Shelley's, who was at the time himself infatuated with the recognition of "the divinity in man," of which this visionary image represented the archetype. It marks the completion of the Titan's transformation.

A second dream of Panthea then comes to her mind in which the spirit voices call to her, "Follow, follow!" and upon this recollection the spirits call upon the sisters to follow. Thus is begun the initiation process by which Asia undergoes her own transformation. In this, as La Cassagnere has pointed out,[26] there are three stages: her entering into the mysteries of the forest, her descent into the deepest depths of the cave of Demogorgon, and her ascent to her luminous transfiguration on the mountain. This commentator also suggests, as do others, that the poet meant this cave of the depths to represent the center of the world. It is enveloped in a "brilliant darkness," in which the person of Demogorgon is scarcely perceivable since he "hath neither form nor limb." He represents that edge of chaos at which cosmos is on the verge of taking shape — "where nothing becomes something";[27] he also has something of the quality of Plato's Necessity under whose persuasion the creative process moves.[28] When Asia encounters him, she demands answers to the questions of from where the world's evils have come. He gives enigmatic responses, saying only, "He reigns," until she asks whom he calls God, and he replies that "Jove is the supreme of living things." Since Jupiter is himself enslaved by his own evil, she asks who is the master of the slave. He replies:

> . . . If the Abysm
> Could vomit forth its secrets. But a voice
> Is wanting, the deep truth is imageless.

As Demogorgon rises in his chariot to do his work of dethroning Jupiter, the Spirit of the Hour arrives to take Asia and Panthea to the mountain. Panthea is struck with the brilliance of a glow in the clouds around them, thinking it must be from the sun. Their charioteer corrects her surmise; it is Asia transfigured. Panthea exclaims to her in wonderment:

> How thou art changed! I dare not look on thee;
> I feel but see thee not. I scarce endure
> The radiance of thy beauty. Some good change
> Is working in the elements, which suffer
> Thy presence thus unveiled . . .
> . . . love like the atmosphere

Of the sun's fire filling the living world,
Burst from thee, and illumined earth and heaven
And the deep ocean and the sunless caves . . .

Given the whole context of Shelley's quest after the meaning of the Orphic and Platonic Eros, I tend to read this visionary experience of Asia's luminosity as an expression of the poet's own ardent apprehension of her.

There follows an unusually lovely ovation, a veritable litany, to Asia as a luminous goddess of love, sung by a spirit.

Life of Life! thy lips enkindle
    With their love the breath between them; . . .
Child of Light! thy limbs are burning
    Through the vest which seems to hide them; . . .
Fair are others; none beholds thee,
    But thy voice sounds low and tender . . .

Lamp of Earth! where'er thou movest
    Its dim shapes are clad with brightness, . . .

She is not to be beheld, only sensed. All of nature resonnates to the warm breath of her atmosphere, for she is after all an *anima mundi*, the soul of the world which will inform it with her quality.

Hearest thou not sounds i' the air which speaks
the love
Of all articulate beings? Feelest thou not
The inanimate winds enamored of thee? . . .

Asia on her part reflects this perception of the new atmosphere suffusing the world.

Realms where the air we breathe is love,
Which in the winds on the waves doth move,
Harmonizing this earth with what we feel above.

Asia now responds to the singing of the spirit by a truly remarkable rendition of the groundplan of a rite of passage, in which a regression stage by stage to infancy and thence into death is followed by rebirth and paradise. She tells of her feeling in her experience of the spirit's song, that her soul is an enchanted boat floating upon the silver waves of the sweet singing.

We have passed Age's icy caves,
And Manhood's dark and tossing waves,
And Youth's smooth ocean smiling to betray:
Beyond the glassy gulfs we flee
Of Shadow-peopled Infancy,
Through Death and Birth, to a diviner day;
A paradise of vaulted bowers . . .

The narrative in Act III opens with the arrival of Demogorgon to take Jupiter off his throne and into the depths. Jupiter demands who this awful shape might be, and the answer comes:

Eternity. Demand no direr name.
Descend, and follow me down the abyss . . .
. . . and we must dwell together
Henceforth in darkness. Lift thy lightnings not.

Tyrannous reign, he declares, is never to exist again.

The tyranny of heaven none may retain,
Or reassume, or hold, succeeding thee.

The poet is emphatic that the evil kingship in heaven is brought to its final demise, to fall back into chaos out of which creation had arisen.

. . . Sink with me, then
We two will sink on the wide waves of ruin,
Even as a vulture and a snake outspent
Drop, twisted in inextricable fight,
Into a shoreless sea . . .

When Hercules has unchained the Titan from his icy rock, Prometheus and Asia are joined together again in their love, ending their three thousand-year separation. He invites her and her two sisters to live with him in the cave paradise that awaits them, "All overgrown with trailing odorous plants, and a fountain/leaps in the midst with awakening sound." This cave has affinities with that of Plato's metaphor in the *Republic*, illustrating the contrast of being beguiled by the mere shadows of reality and of turning in contemplation to behold the pure light of heaven and the forms. The poet's grammar here becomes inscrutable, and Prometheus's speech to the sisters needs paraphrasing: The mind, "arising bright from the embrace of Beauty," (whence come "the forms of which the appearances are the

phantoms"), casts upon lovely apparitions "the gathered rays which
are reality"; these lovely apparitions which shall visit us are the
"progeny immortal" of the various arts, and of "arts, though unim-
agined, yet to be." In other words, the three sisters and the Titan
together preside over the newly regenerated world by a truly Platonic
contemplation; today we might compare it to the Taoist concept of
rule, according to which, if the ruler is dwelling in the Tao, the world
takes care of itself in perfect harmony.

Now by the winding tones of a horn which Prometheus long ago
had given Asia, as it traverses over the world in the hands of the Spirit
of the Hour, the world is transformed. He reports to the four personages what he has seen; not only is evil transcended, but love now
prevails over all.

> . . . the impalpable thin air
> And the all-circling sunlight were transformed,
> As if the sense of love, dissolved in them,
> Had folded itself round the sphered world.

All of humanity now lives in the harmony of true equality:

> And behold, thrones were kingless, and men walked
> One with the other even as spirits do,
> None fawned, none trampled; hate, disdain, or fear,
> Self-love or self-contempt, on human brows
> No more inscribed . . .

On the model of Prometheus's own earlier recognition of the true
place of kingship, man is now king over himself in a united world.

> The loathsome mask has fallen, the man remains
> Sceptreless, free, uncircumscribed, but man
> Equal, unclassed, tribeless, and nationless,
> Exempt from awe, worship, degree, the king
> Over himself; just, gentle, wise . . .

Nor does the poet overlook the particular equality that is so much
under urgent consideration today, that of the liberation of women
from their various restrictions. We can perhaps sense here the influence of Mary Shelley, daughter of Mary Wollstonecraft, one of the
early heroines of the movement.

> And women, too, frank, beautiful, and kind . . .
> From custom's evil taint exempt and pure;

> Speaking the wisdom once they could not think,
> Looking emotions once they feared to feel,
> And changed to all which once they dared not be,
> Yet being now, made earth like heaven; . . .

Men and women are to hold the same mutual respect and love as their newly presiding archetypal models, Prometheus and Asia.

For the purposes of the present discussion, it is particularly noteworthy that, while the drama as such ends at this juncture, Shelley was not content to close the poem. Some months later, while living in Florence, he felt moved to add a fourth act consisting essentially of a visionary and hymnic cosmic dance of images. The attainment of paradise by the world regeneration was not quite enough, and we find Panthea continuing to have visions. It appears to be her role, throughout the poem, to be the visionary one, as we have seen in her image of the transfiguration of Prometheus and again Asia. One might say that the poet's own visionary experiences were assigned to her in the drama. Now in the final act she beholds a series of cosmic mandalas.

> And from an opening in the wood
> Rushes, with loud and whirlwind harmony,
> A sphere, which is as many thousand spheres,
> Solid as crystal, yet through all its mass
> Flow, as through an empty space, music and light:
> Ten thousand orbs involving and involved,
> Purple and azure, white, green and golden,
> Sphere within sphere; . . .

Unimaginable shapes people the spaces as lights, colors, scents, and music tumble over each other, whirling and spinning on myriad axles and also kneaded into an aerial mass drowning the senses. Then:

> . . . Within the orb itself,
> Pillowed upon its alabaster arms
> Like to a child o'erwearied with sweet toil,
> On its own folded wings, and wavy hair,
> The Spirit of the Earth is laid asleep, . . .
> And from a star upon its forehead, shoot, . . .
> Enbleming heaven and earth united now,
> Vast beams like spokes of some invisible wheel
> Which whirl as the orb whirls, swifter than thought,
> Filling the abyss with sun-like lightnings,
> And perpendicular now, and now transverse,
> Pierce the dark soil, and as they pierce and pass,
> Make bare the secrets of the earth's deep heart.

This appearance of ecstatic imagery of mandalas, and other visions of the birth of the newly regenerated world, leads us now to remind ourselves of what a world image means. It becomes perhaps the central point of the entire archetypal drama. The transformation of the image of the world is one and the same as that of the self. Selfhood involves not only a way of experiencing one's own nature, the inner world, but equally of experiencing the outer world and its nature — in other words, an outlook, a Weltanschauung. Hence, it is at the heart of Shelley's point, that there is no redeeming society without also transforming the individuals composing it.

The Spirit of the Earth and that of the Moon now sing to each other a love duet of many stanzas. Finally, Demogorgon rises up out of the earth in his darkness, and the poem closes with his final statement of the ethical intent of the poem.

Mythic Foundations of Democracy

A characteristic of messianic visionary myths such as this is that they lay forth images from the archetypal psyche that are preparing the new cultural moves of the near future[29] — are "parents of mysterious futurity," as Shelley phrases it. In our review of the historical material concerning the Bronze Age, we have seen that the outstanding feature of its new religious forms was that they gave expression to emotional drives that were channeled into an altogether new scale of organization, of dominance, masterful rulership, aggression, military might, and empire building. Those were times of extreme cruelty and violence, but these qualities were sacralized as manifestations of the new potentials for mastery and power. With the Revolution of Democratization, on the other hand, new virtues were proclaimed: Violence and tyranny were looked down upon as evil and the good was found rather in compassion, peace, nonviolence, and benevolence. One might have thought that love among the people would have been sacralized from the beginning as the bonding principle in society and the dynamic of its integration. Yet, it came only later and as an outcome of the differentiation of the image of the center.

This history suggests a deeper meaning of the concept of democracy than we usually recognize. In our practice of this form of government, we have come to take it for granted that it involves fair and equal representation and the universal franchise to vote; order in society then is effected by those persons who are elected to preside and assume power. Yet, we are finding that order tends to crumble when the will of the people becomes focused on vested interests and self-seeking. Not only Plato viewed this form of rule as unstable and prone to lead to tyranny, but our own founding fathers preferred a republic and looked askance at democracy as altogether unpromising. The history of democratization, on the other hand, reveals a different and more significant process in its evolution. Whereas the sacral kingship had projected out into manifest ceremonial expression all the features of psychic centering and integration, its democratization effected an internalization of these so that they might become realized within the individual. Personal piety and moral responsibility of the citizenry was entirely the product of the Revolution of Democratization. Then the motivations towards orderly social organization were to come from within the individual; ethics came into being as a religious concern.

The freedom that Shelley was so passionately enamored of and that he labored and wrote in behalf of, meant exactly what Prometheus said of it when he declared his liberation from the tyranny of Jupiter and from his own inner enslavement; speaking to the Furies he declared, "Yet am I king over myself, and rule/The torturing and conflicting throngs within,/As Jove rules you when Hell grows mutinous." In this freedom, what holds society in order is no longer a strong power from above enforcing a dominance over the people, but rather now a self-mastery and a strong, ardent sense of relatedness and brotherhoood that arises spontaneously from within each person.

However, this shift from power and dominance, asserted from its pinnacle outside and above, to love and brotherhood, springing from the depths inside, is not merely wished into being by idealistic good intentions. It comes as a revolutionary upheaval, involving the overthrow of those high powers to clear the stage for the infusion of the new motivations from the psychic wellsprings. Thus, a revolution of this kind must take place first within the archetypal foundations of those new motivations. The mythic king god must first be toppled before there is any meaningful unseating of the powers of political rule. The new order of freedom makes itself known first in visionary states and the myth forms that emanate from them, representing the burgeoning of new and unfamiliar potentials of the psyche for self-rule. Shelley was quite clear that there can be no integration of society apart from the integration of the individuals composing it.[30]

Wisdom and Love

What is beautiful in Shelley's perceptions is that he discerned very clearly the movements of the archetypal psyche in preparing these new motivations to meet the demands of new times. He knew very well that he was no longer speaking in terms of the rational ideals of intelligent reforms and improvement; if he were, his writing would have been allegory. His mythic images were presented, pure, as they came from the depths, and he was addressing himself to people of the future who could bring them into effect in the world when the time would be ripe. The rational reforms which Godwin had put forward,[31] and urged Shelley to accept as sufficient, were not enough for the poet. If there is to be true caring and a sense of belonging to each other, love is the necessary redeeming factor in society. Hence, "Wisdom without love is impotent," he declared, and in the myth, Asia's part is clear.[32] Yet such mutual caring is to apply not only to living in society but also to our relation to nature — an issue that has become far more urgent in our day than in Shelley's. On this account, Asia not only represents Venus-Aphrodite as Love, but, as Mary Shelley points out, she is Nature.[33] We might venture a paraphrase and suggest that "social order without ecological order becomes impotent."

When Prometheus redeems both himself and suffering mankind from servitude and pain, his efforts thus hinge entirely upon Asia and his reunion with her, as Wisdom with Love. She undergoes her own transformation paralleling that of the Titan; the entire regenerative process involves the transfiguration of each of them.

The connotations of the figure of Prometheus are rich. Shelley in his own introduction to his myth[34] says of him:

> The only imaginary being resembling in any degree Prometheus is the Satan of Milton. Prometheus is a more poetical character, because in addition to courage, majesty, and firm and patient opposition to omnipotent forces, he is exempt from the taint of ambition, envy, revenge, and the desire for personal aggrandizement. Prometheus is the type of the highest perfection . . . .

In addition, various virtues are attributed to him. This analogy to Satan might surprise us at first if we are inclined to think of that figure as embodying pure evil; but beyond such moralistic bias we are led into a rich set of connotations of his nature and role in the psychology of archetypal process.

The term "Satan" signifies the "Adversary," acting in opposition to the high god.[35] There have been various heresies springing from Gnosticism that have perceived the biblical creator as a dark and jealous demiurge who tried to prevent mankind from becoming conscious.[36] The true high god was "the great first alien life from the worlds of light, the sublime that stands above all works," thus the wholly transcendant, the "beyond." The world was created, on the other hand, by the demiurge, the first great archon, whose existence derived from the passion of the feminine and her will to create. Of him it was said, that in his ignorance and *hybris*, "He boasted of what was taking place at his feet and said, 'I am Father and God, and there is none above me'" to which his mother retorts, "Do not lie, Ialdabaoth: there is above thee the Father of all, . . . " In Eden he thus forbade the first man to taste of the tree of knowledge of the opposites which would give him wisdom and make him like the gods. We know today that the Israelites combined into one figure two prototypes: Yahweh, who was a storm god having affinities with the Canaanite Baal, and El Elyon, who was a god of the high and bright sky having affinities with the Canaanite god of the same name.[37] El was the greater, and it seems that certain heresies later restored his supremacy over the lesser and jealous demiurge. Lucifer in this context is indeed the "light-bringer" who tempts the first man to defy the oppression of the creator and win for himself the wisdom that was his due. Yet this consciousness did throw man into the riven state of being torn by the conflict of the opposites; paradise then belonged to his future, to be regained through his redemption, that is, his rediscovery of his own inner divinity.

Shelley intended his Prometheus to play such a role as the "Adversary," opposing the oppressive reign of the governing powers of the *status quo*, personified in Jupiter; in no sense was he the opponent of the good. When the time is ripe, then, for cultural renewal and world regeneration, this Adversary appears in the eyes of the Establishment as threatening disorder and disruptive evil. To the proponents of change, on the other hand, he is recognized as the redeemer and savior who brings to mankind the boon of the new order.

Hence, in Shelley's myth Jupiter as king god of the sky had punished Prometheus for his insubordination and rebellion in giving the gift of fire and wisdom to man, condemning him to three thousand years of intense suffering as a wrongdoer. Only when the course of time and history reached the point where the archetypal enantio-dromia must take place, did Jupiter himself become seen as the tyrant promoting evil and suffering in the world, and Prometheus as the suffering savior introducing a new order into that world. Hence, he represented the supreme good.

In the world regeneration that ensues, then, the New Heaven and New Earth are presided over by a divine couple, Prometheus as Wisdom suffused by love, Asia as Love suffused by wisdom. Logos and Eros are to live in harmony and balance together. Eros in this case represents the Platonic and ultimately Orphic principle: In the mystic quest for the One, love is both the means and the end, as La Cassagnère has pointed out.[38] Yet the same principle applies in this issue as in that of social reform: Well intended conscious efforts do not suffice to release the wellsprings of this dynamism. The capacity for this loving must first be transformed from its latent state of mere potentiality. Thus, as we have observed, Asia herself undergoes an initiation process in descending into the deepest darkness to the cave of Demogorgon, and reascending into her transfiguration in brilliant light and warmth, which suffuse through the world and transfigure it. The world of humanity then lives together in this glow of the One, which becomes experienced in the feeling of love.

This installation of the goddess of love as a divine partner in the new order of the regenerated world makes Shelley's myth particularly relevant today. For it is becoming evident to those who watch the moves of the archetypal psyche that the image of the goddess is becoming activated and receiving attention widely. I am speaking of something more than the intellectual recognition being given her in the flurry of recent literature on the history of this figure; more striking and perhaps at the root of all this interest, is the present dynamism in the collective psyche that takes on her image.

The End of the Era of Kingships

The past two centuries have accomplished the end of a long era of five millenia in which monarchy has prevailed throughout the world. Shelley and Blake and other romantics, as already mentioned, watched the French Revolution with great hopes, only to be disappointed by the demise of the freedom it fought for and the ideal of the society that it had envisioned. Blake turned his face away from political concerns thereafter. Shelley, on the other hand, wrote arduously on behalf of the revolutionary ideal. He concluded that man is made of two components, the "Imaginative Being" and the "Social Being," and that one of these may not be transformed without the other.[39] After their time, World War I became the second great historic event that sounded the final death knell of monarchy; since then, the few remaining kingships have been rendered purely ceremonial, out of a respect for tradition.

I see in Shelley's *Prometheus*, then, a true and profound expression of mythic changes in the archetypal psyche. It is a typical visionary experience of world regeneration, well-informed of the philosophical issues yet free in its spontaneous imagery, in which love replaces power as the dominant modality of living in society and in the world of nature. The overthrow of Jupiter is a mythic perception that the sacral kingship, established by the Urban Revolution so long ago, molding the world as we know it, is now coming to an end as the mythic expression of the means to order the world of mankind and nature.

Summary

In our present times the problem of alienation gives men and women of our sprawling cities the dismal sense of not belonging either to a well-knit social setting or to the integrity of their natural environment. To remedy this plight, it is not enough to seek programs of change by rationalistic recommendations emerging out of idealistic thinking. Deep concern is required, and the psyche can only be moved by the highly charged and rich images of myth, as Shelley well knew. His mythic drama gives full expression to the psychic dynamics of the end of an era, at the turning point where patriarchy yields place to the feminine and to the equality of men and women under the aegis of the divine couple.

The drama ends with stirring words from Demogorgon.

To suffer woes which Hope thinks infinite;
To forgive wrongs darker than death or night;
   To defy Power, which sccms omnipotent;
To love, and bear; to hope till Hope creates
From its own wreck the thing it contemplates:
   Neither to change, nor faulter, nor repent;
This, like thy glory, Titan! is to be
Good, great and joyous, beautiful and free;
   This is alone Life, Joy, Empire, and Victory!

Conclusions for Our Times

Individuality in Evolution 10

hrough these explorations of myth and ritual in governmental
ceremonial, prophetic movements and visionary poetry, the
gist of history stands out clearly. As individuality emerges
from the social matrix of the collectivity, hand in hand with it arises
the cultivation of caring and compassion from the duty of obedience
to higher authority. In these two fruits of cultural development we
may discern a complementary interplay and a historical necessity
which now invite exploration.

Individuality and Social Concern

When the maintenance of social order is no longer the sole
prerogative of those in the position of power and control, and instead
becomes a concern for the common individuals to look after, what is
there to prevent an outbreak of unruly anarchy and self-seeking? In
those Times of Troubles that occurred in the several cultures in the
foregoing histories, this was no mere speculative question; it was a
horrendous problem born of catastrophe and suffering. Ambitious
individuals were competing for power and territory with unbridled
violence, making use of new technologies of warring and policing to
overrun their worlds with callous predations.

In the midst of these extreme conditions emerged again and again
the answer to the urgent problem fully equal to it in clarity and prac-
ticality: Only the sense of spontaneous personal responsibility toward
one another for the general well-being of the people could create a
new mode of social cohesion strong enough to replace the previously
imposed rule. This suggests that in the evolutionary process of history,
the freedom of individuality is purchased by the price of a strict

obligation to be mindful of the needs of other individuals. One is reminded again of the Confucian phrasing of this principle: Only in seeking the fulfillment of others can one find fulfillment.

We find, then, that individuality and social caring form a complementarity, appearing on the historical scene bound together hand in hand. The fact that visionary and revolutionary effort has been required to introduce these onto the stage of the evolutionary drama is striking; for with our rationalistic modern mentality we might have expected that just clear-headed good thinking would have sufficed to come to these conclusions. Therefore, these complementary principles invite now a penetrating scrutiny.

Individuation

Individuality is achieved by its differentiation out of the collectivity, whether of the family system, the subculture, or the general culture. One may well raise the question: Is not everyone an individual, and do we not all have qualities distinguishing us from one another? Fortunately, of course, this is so. Here, however, we are concerned not with appearances or traits but with a measure of uniqueness in terms of self-determination in respect of one's own system of values, structure of meanings, and world outlook. These result in one's knowing consciously one's criteria of moral choice and one's understanding of the world one lives in, of nature and of human nature. One's design of life becomes an expression of all these.

Individuation as Jung has defined it[1] is the process of becoming what one is, as distinct from all the other possibilities in human endowment. It means self-fulfillment by being obedient to the law of one's own being. This accomplishment of wholeness is a task requiring decades of experience and reflection, an adventure of fearless exploration of emotional involvements with persons and with concerns and undertakings, with constant questioning of meanings and testing of values.

This modern psychology of individuation has an altogether different ring from the character of a collectively determined existence. In the ancient Egyptian culture, for example, we have observed that obedience to the king in all matters, and a constant mindfulness of the customs and traditions established by the ancestors, were the means by which one achieved a good and fruitful life. For emphasis, I will repeat what was written by a king to his son, capturing the essence of this way of conducting oneself and finding one's place in the world: For the wise man "Truth comes to him well-brewed, after the manner of the ancestors. Imitate thy fathers, thy ancestors, . . . for lo, their words abide in writing. Open, that thou mayest read and imitate knowledge."[2]

This typifies the spirit of a collectively oriented society that then provides myth forms that satisfy all thirst for understanding, and ritual practices in which its emotional processes are handled. To be integrated psychologically is then to be living in a spirit of conformity with the entire system. Such is the atmosphere of a culture that puts into the ceremonial forms of the state all the myth and ritual imagery of the psyche, externalizing these contents in such fashion that the various symbolic processes that the psyche requires are experienced in the form provided by the established tradition for the entire membership. This is the sense in which Jane Harrison and her school saw in myth and ritual the "expression of collective emotion." [3]

The Image of the Center

We have noted in the review of various cultures that among the images so externalized, the representation of the center predominated, along with a four-fold structuring of space around it. Whole kingdoms, cities, temples, reliquaries, thrones, and so on were given this geometric shape. At this center the sacral king functioned as its personification, undergoing all the symbolic processes that are the work of this component of the psyche.

Called in many cultures the Great Man, the sacral king was the Unique Individual, the only person endowed with an immortal soul, in the case of early Egypt, or with the privilege of becoming one of the *Ti*, the royal ancestors composing Heaven, in the case of early China. From attributes such as these we observe how the potential of individuality itself was projected out into the ceremonial forms, to be experienced by the populace only in its externalized expression. At the same time, bound up in his person were the qualities of benevolence, mercy loving-kindness and caring for people. All this tells us that the complementarity under discussion, that of individuality and of compassionate societal concern, was originally a unity embracing them both in the royal image of the center.

The democratization of the kingly forms, and their internalization representing a dawning realization that these expressed the processes that belong to the inner life and spiritual cultivation of individuals, were the work of the affect-image of the center. Upheavals, transitions, transformations, renewals, all are operations that take place in the image of the center; they are apparently instigated and guided by it, suggesting that this image represents the governing component of the psyche.

To return to Jung's formulation of the integrative processes of the psyche, individuation is the task of developing a relation to the archetypal center, the image of the Self in its wholeness.[4] This is a function in the psyche that makes itself known to consciousness through affect-images portraying its nature and that gradually takes over the leadership in the developmental process. It is a center of the entire psyche, organizing it in the same manner that the ego as a center of the conscious field orders its contents. It therefore is experienced as an inner authority superordinate to the ego.[5] This is only an abstract way of expressing the experience of not being quite the controllers of our lives, and of being led from point to point in our growth and development from somewhere inside, being enticed into concerns, endeavors, entanglements, and relationships that we little expected and hardly chose. The influence of the Self is felt in the form of inner promptings from a source that turns out to know more than we do consciously about what is in store for us, for our more complete development.

The psychic center, the Self, like any other archetypal entity, is observable only in the way it portrays itself in its image. On this account, we learn most about its nature and its functioning by its myth and ritual expressions in various cultures. Especially important to our understanding of it is the observation that to a certain extent ontogeny repeats phylogeny; that is, the individual psyche is like other organs of the body in repeating the phases of its evolution. Thus, what has shown itself as a prevailing and typical trend in the maturing of cultures over the past five millenia is found also in the development of the psychic life of the individual.[6]

The Capacity to Love

The historical trend that our present investigation is concerned with is, of course, the transition from the phase in which power and dominance were sacralized in various cultures to that in which human-hearted caring and compassion were honored, each as the means toward social cohesion. My observations of visionary turmoil in psychosis testify to the occurrence of this same transition from one to the other in the individual.[7] Presumably, the motivation for such a development of the capacity to love is not only expressive of the need of the individual psychic organism for its own wholeness but equally the requirement of the social organism for its integrity and well-being.

Learning how to be deeply caring toward one's fellow beings is showing itself to be more difficult than might be expected, judging by all the signs of our contemporary cultures. In watching individuals growing into this capacity, it appears that one does not love by just getting used to it bit by bit. It seems rather to require a more profound transformation in the psychic system, amounting to a rite of passage. The most familiar form of this is the outbreak of ardor in the love experience that is sensed as a transformation of one's nature, leaving the former limited self behind and entering a new dimension of one's own selfhood and a new awareness of, and honoring of the selfhood of the partner. One is not the same person after this upheaval. On this account I have made a special point of including the twelfth-century culture of courtly love in this study, to glean from it some of the makings of this transformative love experience through its mythic representation. The more universal lovingness characterized in the Christian *agape* was reached also by transformative process, that is, by means of the baptismal rite of passage and visionary "resurrection" into the new consciousness. In the Buddha's teaching, compassion was likewise an accompaniment to the overhauling of the very foundations of one's being through enlightenment.

In these doctrines and practices, we are informed again and again that achieving the capacity to live in deeply caring relatedness to one's fellow beings is accomplished only with the utter renewal of one's being. No amount of humanistic right thinking and good intentions can equal the power of this archetypal experience that delivers one into this new state of being, like a birth into a revivified world.

In the material of myth and ritual recounted in the foregoing chapters, it becomes evident that the great religions and prophetic or philosophic movements all were primarily concerned with governance and social order. More specifically, they paid most attention to the questions of how best to integrate a society and to integrate oneself in a manner to live in it most fruitfully and harmoniously. This is consonant with Jung's early realization that the psychic energies conveyed in the archetypal images divide at the very foundations of the psyche into those that go into behavior and those that motivate the formation of culture.[8]

In this framework of the evolution of cultures, individuation can be understood as the heritage, for the common man and woman, of properties that had once belonged solely to the role of the personage personifying the archetypal center, the sacral king. The outer aspect of this legacy is found in the various prerogatives yielded over to the people. The corresponding inner aspect lies in the assimilation by the conscious personality of those potentials that in the early phases of development were comprised within the psychic center. Both psychology and the disciplines of spiritual cultivation endeavor to grasp the meanings and methods of this inner developmental process. Jung often mentioned the observation that his formulation of the individuation process, while stressing the inner enrichment and fulfillment of the personality's individual uniqueness, was never intending to overlook the bearing it has on the accompanying experience of kinship with one's fellow beings.[9] Yet in the handling of individuation processes since, there has been an inclination to focus on this inner unfolding of individual wholeness and to leave relatively blurred the issues of the societal concerns that are involved in the process itself.

These considerations of individuation bring us back now to further probing into the nature of the complementarity of the requirements of individuality and those of selfless social sensitivity.

The Emergence of Individuality and Its Hazards

Looking first at the psychology of the Urban Revolution, we may observe that the age of the early great sacral kingships produced a kind of consciousness that characterized the needs of ego development. The principal mythic figure expressing the psychology of the royal personage was the king-god, the divine counterpart, in the society of the gods, of the monarch on the earthly plane. In the ancient Near East, from which our western traditions arose,this kingly deity was the storm-god and warrior-god.[10] He possessed all the properties that play a part in the concerns of the ego: the urge to mastery, the power motivations that win prestige, the assertive-aggressive emotions that give strength to fighting, the ambitions that drive toward expansion of rule and empire-building, the acquisitive tastes that gain the accumulation of wealth, and the technological acuity that could produce a Bronze Age. The awareness of ever-changing historical progress began with these.

With the democratization of the kingly prerogatives, as we saw, the unrestrained exercise of these talents gave rise to a ruthless predatory aggression and an immense destructiveness that brought not only devastation to the populace at the hands of lesser great individuals but even came close to disintegrating the social structures within which they did their predatory work. This unrestrained self-aggrandizement occasioned the Time of Troubles in Egypt's and China's Feudal Age. The Mesopotamian kingdoms subdued and dismantled one another in sequence until in the end Assyria spent itself in warring into its demise. These were the conditions that gave rise to the crises of rapid culture change and the consequent revitalization movements that have been examined in the foregoing studies.

The peril, therefore, from the effects of the storm-god and his earthly representative is great indeed when there is yet no counterbalance. The saving factor each time has been that the archetypal psyche has its own homeostatic capacities and ways of providing the means to restore viability to societies in these dire straits, through its own mysterious processes. The visionary work of the great reformers amounted essentially to their giving voice to this psyche as it was proferring remedies to their ailing cultures. The genius of their contributions lay primarily in the wisdom of this psyche as it made its designs known to them, and then also in their superbly gifted articulation of those revelations.

Two Modes of Order: Imposed and Evoked

The much needed counterbalancing principle that was introduced by these visionaries arose from an activation of the archetypal motivations belonging to the "Receptive" and to "human-heartedness," to use the Chinese terms. In Jung's language these allude to the "Eros" mode of relating to the world, a "category of experience" in mutual counterpoise with the "Logos" mode[11] Where the Logos moves us to understand meaning by a process of abstracting from experience, the Eros urges us toward entanglement in it, thus to find meaningfulness in the interrelatedness.

Organization can come by either mode. The sacral kingship ideology was preoccupied with cosmic and social order, personified in the god of the high heaven. The image of the sun figured prominently in this role, as instanced in Egypt's Re. This order was imposed in turn by the monarch upon his people by his power, and they in return rendered their obedience to his authority. The sky-god of Mesopotamia, for instance, was Anu, whose name meant absolute authority that compels obedience.[12] The appetite for this power became so gripping that the zeal to impose the particular order of a realm did not stop within its bounds but gave rise to a hunger for conquest, with the intention of imposing it upon other societies and creating empires. It was the duty, for example, of China's kings to bring the neighboring barbarian tribes into the order of the realm by conquest, as part of their cosmocratic function, as we have already noted. This expansive subduing of increasing numbers of peoples was a new phenomenon in the world as a corollary of the mentality of the Urban Revolution. The history of nations shows that whenever a new species of cultural order makes its appearance it urges men to impose it upon others, as with Sargon of Akkad's revelation to antiquity of what empire can be, Alexander's conquest of the entire known world, Islam's holy wars and Christendom's response in kind in the crusades, of the contemporary ideologies of our century vying to bend the world to their system.

The ideologies of the great reformers and prophets that envisioned the democratization of the kingly forms were equally concerned with cosmic and social order, but they perceived it as attainable through an altogether different avenue. Here, societal harmony was not to be imposed upon the system but evoked from within it. In the very nature of things, in this view, people have been endowed by the divine powers with inclinations to feel empathy and regard for the well-being of one another. This Eros mode implies far more than a benevolent kindliness of demeanor. It is a dynamic that by its interweaving quality binds families, communities, and whole societies together in mutual belonging and cooperative enterprise. The welfare and well-being of the members become then a mutual concern arising spontaneously from within themselves through the feelings of caring concern.

Separateness and Oneness

In the contrast of these two modes of arriving at the ordering of society, the complementarity of individuality and societal sensitivity takes on further clarity. The power motivations emphasize separatenss, one person or group pitted against another in a competition of strength. The Eros mode, set in counterbalance to that, arrives at a perception, the other way, of the oneness of all beings in a system of interrelatedness binding them together into a whole. In the former way, the organism to be fostered is the individual fending for himself; in the latter, it is the social organism that is to prosper by the mutuality of individuals.

The Differentiation of the Logos and Eros Modes

The rise of the patriarchy in the Urban Revolution is in our times, of course, the object of vehement expressions of negative feeling and criticism for its subordination of woman, leaving her in a position of degradation and pushing out the role of the goddesses into an equally falsified and diminished place in the pantheon. When we look over this five thousand-year span of cultural development, we cannot help wondering how it can be that woman came to be so devalued and humiliated for so long. It appears to us that a gigantic error had been committed throughout the world in its forward moving histories. We could wish that it had been done differently, with more humane regard for the equality of the sexes, thus maintaining the reverence for woman that had been the traditional habit before that time.

Yet can it be that history creates gargantuan mistakes lasting five millenia? Can these developments instead be viewed less judgmentally as the very costly growth pains of the human psyche producing, as it usually does, much suffering along the way?

Although there was much injustice and persistent blindness to the significance of loving-caring as a bonding principle, it nevertheless seems to have been a compelling need in human beings to develop this mastery in the masculine mode before feeling ready to develop its opposite. This pattern follows the psychological law that any orientation that is employed to handle the issues of life is clung to up to the point at which it fails to take care of important new circumstances. At such junctures, it appears to defeat itself. Only then can it give over to its opposite by a process that Jung has called an *enantiodromia*, that is, a turning over into the opposite.

If we view the course of historical development in this light, then we can recognize patterns of progress that can give it some meaning. These can be discerned as processes of differentiation of opposite modes of experiencing the world and functioning in it, each swelling to such predominance that they by turn occupy center stage and push the other off into the wings until their particular act in the drama of history is concluded.

The patriarchy of the Urban Revolution ushered in an exercise of the functions that would sharpen the acuity of consciousness for the application of technical mastery of ever-increasing complexity: The art of metallurgy led to the forging of weapons and agricultural implements and other tools; the skills of the arts and crafts grew in refinement; the sciences of measuring space and time prospered; and above all, the new use of writing allowed records to be kept that transformed the capacities of commerce and law and written tradition. This species of focused consciousness we now are inclined to link with left-brain functioning.

The reformers in the Revolution of Democratization explored with comparable vigor that other kind of consciousness that takes into itself the configurations of the whole, of the entire world system and social system. Integration was the keynote; the integration of the spiritual potentials in persons, that of the requirements for the welfare of the populace, and that of the relations between the natural and the human environment. This species of consciousness that is more holistic than focused, more receptive than directive, and more inclined to operate through image and feeling than through the fine-pointed rational processes, we now are coming to associate with right-brain functioning.[13]

I have suggested elsewhere[14] that the history of cultures, as seen through their myth and ritual developments, renders an account of the successive differentiations of these left- and right-brain functions over the past five thousand years of human evolution. That is only one framework, however; one appealing to those who are inclined to find more sense of reality in the physical or physiological than in the purely psychological. It is a way of thought that paradoxically is more theoretical than experiential, however, and hence has the ring of the abstract however much it purports to speak of the materially "real"!

The data of observation found in the histories of cultures provide the more experiential form of pairs of opposites as recounted in these chapters: individuality and social sensitivity; power and love; imposed and evoked order; externalized and internalized governance, and so on. It hardly needs emphasizing that the need of human evolution is to find ways of coordinating these contraries so that they may function together in balance and harmony. This reconciling and uniting of opposites is one of the classical features of the archetypal center.

We find ourselves today at a point of transition in our cultural outlook in which we are feeling the need to think in terms of considering mankind as fitting into relation to the whole of his setting rather than as a collection of individuals striving to fend for themselves and get what they can for their prosperity. In this lies a striking parallel to the Times of Troubles of ancient cultures, in which the overassertion of individuality was spelling doom for entire peoples unless compensated by a new development of societal sensitivity.

The New Paradigm in Evolutionary Thinking

We are coming into a world view quite different from that of a few decades ago. We now look out upon our cosmos and our planet as evolving constantly from the lower and simpler into ever higher levels of complexity and order. We see life forms no longer as separate phenomena struggling for survival in their own linear developments but rather as elements in patterns of interrelationships all evolving together in an ever-evolving environment. The mode of thought is the language of interrelations, patterns, integration of parts in wholes, and self-organizing systems. The words that recur constantly are *co*evolution, *co*existence, *co*operation of life forms, indicating their working together in relation to each other. All these are eloquent indicators of the kind of orientation that is fastened upon the interweaving of things, the hallmark of the Eros mode.

The resulting image appearing in the thinking of today's science is of an organic world in a self-organizing universe. Erich Jantsch has made an all-encompassing synthesis of these findings and conclusions with great vision in his *The Self-organizing Universe*,[15] and Fritjof Capra has interrelated them with other cultural issues in his *The Turning Point*,[16] a painstaking work of broad scope. I will summarize sketchily this current concept of evolution to indicate the composition of the background to my present study of the history of cultures. In doing so, I must first apologize to the reader for expressing these concepts in a language far more abstract than might be wished; it serves the purposes of condensation of material that otherwise might require an entire essay to expound.

Evolution in Terms of Self-organizing Systems

Living systems are seen as ones whose higher levels of order and complexity include those of lower levels, and as wholes, whose properties and laws are not reducible to those of the component parts they comprise. On the contrary, while these smaller units have their own order, it is in some respects determined by the order of the organisms of which they are parts. For example, cells have their own very complex organization yet serve the interests of the body.

In previous decades, scientists were puzzled by a seemingly still unresolvable contradiction between the concept of the Second Law of Thermodynamics,[17] by which the universe is seen as "running down" by entropy, losing energy amid increasing disorder (toward equilibrium), and the evolutionary concept of the building up of increasing levels of order in biological systems. The formulation of dissipative structures by Prigonine[18] not only provided a link between chemical systems and living ones but also provided a resolution to the quandary of decreasing and increasing orders: These structures have the character of self-organizing systems and of being able to "import energy and export entropy."[19]

At the various ascending levels, the organisms are not quite uniformly ordered but preserve a free play of flexibility in each and of variability among them. They maintain a stabiliy, but one that is "far from equilibrium." It is a dynamic stability undergoing perpetual fluctuations, the constancy of the state of the organism then being held in balance by homeostasis, its self-regulation among the opposing influences toward change, as for example, those of body temperature.

Self-organizing systems hold in this way a balance preserving their self-maintenance. On the other hand, their fluctuations which play an essential role in their self-maintenance, lead on beyond preservation toward change. The systems then have also the character of self-transcendence, of making creative thrusts beyond their former physical and mental parameters. This flux becomes one of the prime features of organisms contributing to the progress of evolution. This presents an essentially new view contrasting with the previously generally accepted assumption that evolutionary change came about by mutations of the genes; one of the more mechanistic theories has been that chance hits of cosmic rays might have given the impetus to change, providing the opportunity for variants of a species to compete more successfully in the struggle for survival if they thereby happened to become better equipped for adaptations than their cousins. In the self-organizing systems framework, flux is an element in the very nature of biological organisms that opens the possibility for successful creative experiment leading to new modifications of species.

The role of these fluctuations amid stability is to create stress of varying degrees of intensity, which may be handled within the self-maintaining system up to a point; beyond a critical degree of stress there occurs the creative thrust of self-transcendence to adapt to the changed conditions with new structures and behavior. Again, process gives rise to form.

This new picture of the ascending order of organisms rests no longer only upon the assumption of the battle for survival in competition, no longer only of a series of victories of adaptation to a set environment, all in the framework of linear developments of separate species in stable settings. This current view sees patterns of ascending orders of interrelationships of both organisms and their environments, in which both coevolve in mutual cooperation. The environments are ecosystems which in themselves behave as organisms with the usual properties of self-maintenance and of self-transcendence with change, belonging to the character of self-organizing and self-regulating systems. The relationships within the ecosystems are essentially cooperative, and any competition remains contained within this overall cooperative mode.

In the new framwork of biological evolution, then, the essential dynamic lies in the interplay of adaptation and creativity, of competition and cooperation, and of self-maintenance and self-transscendence. Survival becomes not so much that of the particular species as that of the whole pattern of organization in the process of coevolution. In this pattern of interrelations, any tendency toward aggressive self-assertion of a species requires the balance that comes out of the necessity for integration into the containing system, by fitting into it cooperatively.

Two Super-systems: Biosphere and Noosphere

The grand picture of the superecosystem comprising all lesser ecosystems has been portrayed by Lovelock and Margulis.[20] Beginning with the problem of how to determine whether or not there is life on Mars, as part of the NASA project, they decided that an answer would be found in making an analysis of the composition of the atmosphere, which would betray the presence of substances that could only be produced by living forms. The proving ground would be that of our own planet. In making a study of our entire planetary biosphere with great exactness, they concluded that it revealed indications of its operating as a gigantic self-regulating system with homeostatic processes to preserve the constancies necessary for life over hundreds of millions of years in the composition, for instance, of the atmosphere and of the seas. The biosphere therefore is found to be a mammoth self-organizing system, a superorganism comprising all lesser systems of organisms. To it they gave the mythic name of Gaia, the earth goddess of the Greeks, thus abiding by the human custom of rendering in myth form that which cannot yet be readily grasped by the rational intellect. She operates at such a high level of order and complexity that one is tempted to endow her with some kind of mentation, but only at the biological level.

Standing at the summit of the evolutionary process, all the while, is mankind with his highly developed consciousness. The totality of mankind also represents, I suggest, a superorganism with the individual humans as parts in the overall psychic system of the social organism, the "noosphere" in Teilhard de Chardin's rendition.[21] His mind gives man the choice to fit into the ecosystem cooperatively or through his technological capacities to dominate or destroy it.

The Task of Consciousness

In regarding this choice, I am reminded of Jung's comments in 1925,[22] when in a seminar he was speaking of the Age of Aquarius about to make itself known in the late decades of our century. He commented that this would be the age of psychological man, and what that means is that it would be the time at which man would have the awareness necessary to realize fully his capacity for evil! In the 1920s that was a shocker; today it is almost a self-evident fact of our relation to our world.

Mankind's consciousness is the great problem of our time, not only for our own welfare but for that of the superorganism to which we belong, Gaia. Our species has a mind making us capable of unleashed aggressive self-assertion against the interests of integration of the containing ecosystem. We are a species with a capacity for immense destructiveness resulting from our freedom of will and choice, due to the circumstance that the higher the level of order and complexity, the more a species is independent in respect to its environmental conditions.

We have observed already that a society's world image and outlook determines its behavior. Thus far in history, the psyche has shown itself to be possessed of the resources to rescue societies from their folly. One hopes that it will again be capable of rendering a comprehension of our predicament, before our predatory interests in the service of self-aggrandizement — in our search for convenience, comfort, gain, and property — wreak havoc beyond remedy. We are already on the verge of realizing our part in our ecosystem and our need to live cooperatively within it. One might express the quandary as a tussle between the interests of the ecosystem and the ego-system!

Our left-brain technological mastery has led us into a spending spree for five centuries, taking all that we can grasp or force from our environment and its resources. A right-brain compensation to this thrust could lead us to sufficient maturation of outlook to reach an attitude of caring such that a tender regard for the entire ecosystem would be realized as vital for its survival. The supreme mastery could then be found in our acting as guardians rather than plunderers of our setting, as parts behaving in the interests of the whole.

In this we find history coming around full-circle to the image of the first Great Individuals' role in their relation to nature. The sacral kings of Sumer, called "Lugal," "Great Man," had as their function to act as "Gardener of God," ritually enacting the care of the cyclical processes of the vegetation through the sequence of seasons.[23] Now we are at the other end of this five thousand-year development, at a point where we know once more than we can become "Gardeners of God," now with our newly developed consciousness and its capacities to take care of the rounds of nature with accurate comprehension. In Israel, Adam, "The Man," another gardener in his Eden, was believed to have been granted the privilege of being master of all living beings, and that in eating of the tree of knowledge he became conscious of good and evil, "like unto the gods," and of being able to make the choice.

The Holistic View

The long history since Western Europe's archaic era has moved characteristically through the phase of aggressive self-assertion and dominance far enough to reach a crisis of stress in which we find ourselves on the brink of our own Time of Troubles. The critical level of stress converts self-maintenance into self-transcendence. Those are the confitions in which the love and caring in the Eros mode — along with its world view that perceives the interrelatedness and oneness of all living beings — make themselves manifest. Again, we know ourselves as parts in the system of the whole, and our behavior as accountable to the operation of the whole, growing by cooperation, coexistence, and coevolution.

The nature of the whole is reflected in all the parts. That is the holographic model of orgnization,[24] a present-day variant of the correspondence of macrocosm and microcosm. It is a view with roots in ancient philosophies, such as Plato's, for whom mind replicated the form of the cosmos, or that of Mencius, who could state that "The ten thousand things (of all creation) are complete within us." It is found in ancient religions, such as Gnosticism's advocating the exploration of inner mental experience there to encounter the whole world and finally God.[25] Also, it occurs in the pioneers of science at its threshold, such as Paracelsus, who found the seven planets represented in the seven metals of the organism along with their astrological influences on the life of the psyche.[26]

It has often been remarked in recent years that man stands at the summit of evolution at which the universe can become conscious of itself: The whole becomes aware of itself in the parts. There is a beautifully clear demonstration of this principle in the operations of the archetypal world image, discussed in chapter 3. This is the component in psychic depth that represents the experience of the whole. When an archaic city kingdom fashioned itself in the image of the world or the cosmos, it was symbolizing the intuition of man's relation to the social organism and the world organism. This affect-image of the quadrated world, as the archetype of the center, is the dynamic source of the self-organizing operations of the human organism. It provides the fluctuating stability of self-maintenance and the creative thrust of self-transcendence. That is, it integrates the individual psyche, looking after the self-assertive interests of the unitary organism, and it motivates individuals toward relating to the higher levels of order, looking after the integrative interests of the social superorganism. It is the focus through which we trace the evolution of the human individual psychic organism and of the collective social organism. Also, it is the image through which we read the meaning of the world, and thus it motivates our conduct in it.

Constantly in the forefront among the visionary concepts of social cohesion was the nature and functioning of this center. The midpoint of the realm was the locus ceremonially occupied by the figure of the sacral king personifying not only the center but also the totality of the realm; all its life was symbolically compacted in his image. The character of this central configuration in the phase of its development in the Urban Revolution, composed as it was of motivations of power, prestige, and aggression, could be summarized as urging the separateness arising out of competing in strength. With the internalization of the royal image in the Revolution of Democratization, it again represented not only a center of inner governance but also the totality of the whole; that is, it became the focus of the individual's inner rule, but also and most significantly, it was found to represent "the One." The sense of commonality and of community with the fellow members of society arose here not only out of feelings of caring and compassion, but, more deeply, out of this archetypal experience of the essential unity of all beings.

Summary

My conclusion from these excursions into cultural histories is that the psyche and society are both organisms that are self-healing in conditions of turmoil and self-organizing in the course of evolution. The differentiations occurring during this long development are visibly traceable through the myth and ritual imagery portraying the organizing work of the archetypal center. Out of this arises the caring love that acts as the bonding principle in the social organism, and that is doubtless the human modality of experiencing the same cohesive property that has been constantly working at all phases in the evolving process of ascending levels of organization in the cosmos. It has increasingly been known to mankind as God.

Modern Myth
and Nuclear Nemesis

11

In the excursions we have been making into the histories of culture change and transformation through Times of Troubles in various parts of the world, it will not have escaped the reader's notice that in them we recognize features of our own critical predicament of today's world. The power-motivated drive to extend spheres of influence and dominate whole populations outside of the bounds of the nation itself goes on as it did in the time of the Bronze Age, but this time with a competitiveness of a thousand-fold greater intensity in the Nuclear Age. The fallacy of separateness, that trait so characteristic of the power mode, is by now reaching its acme in the adversarial confrontation of the two halves of the world, locked into their antagonisms and escalations toward supremacy in destructive capacity. We look on and stand appalled, feeling all but helpless.

Mythic Images Activated by the Nuclear Crisis

We are only almost beyond help, however. For we are learning from the great crises of the past that the archetypal psyche has customarily and almost magically revealed its wisdom and its guidelines to resolve them in time to avert final destruction. From all my searches into the experience of many cultures in many eras, I have come to a convinced belief that once again, under the pressure of today's urgency, the psyche will be found ready to come up with new leading myth forms and spiritual practices that can give rise to creative problem-solving efforts. If a major step in evolution is required for this solution, it would bring into play processes beyond self-maintenance and on the level of self-transcendence. How, then, are we to read the presently gathering storm of crisis in terms of its mythic foundations?

Thunderweapon and Nuclear Blast

While nuclear weapons are new enough in their unimaginable power of destruction, the mythic imagery underlying the motivation to use them is not. Indeed, in all these investigations I have found a surprisingly exact myth and ritual representation of such weapons all through early history following the Urban Revolution, namely in the thunderbolt in the hands of the warrior storm-god,[1] enabling him to assert a destructiveness equally unthinkable in those times.

If we trace back the earliest genesis of this thunder-image, we find it in the bull-roarer used in many archaic cultures ritually for its potency in effecting transformation. A vivid example still to be observed in our century exists among the Arunta of Australia who use this implement in their initiation rites.[2] A plaque of wood, oblong in shape and carved to indicate streaks of lightening, is suspended on a thong to twirl it. The elders grouped around the initiant all hold and twirl one of these until it produces its moaning and whirring, an eerie sound named "The Voice of Thunder," once given to man by the Old Grandfather in the Sky, Daramulun. It alone has energy from the thunder immense enough to drive the process of the boy's passage through death and into his birth as an adult man.

In the more advanced agrarian economy and lifestyle of the Neolithic Age, in which myth and ritual were concentrated particularly upon the task of fostering increase, the awesome thunderbolt became a visible sign of the vigor of the weather-god as he united with the earth mother in a sacred marriage to render her fertile by his rains.[3] The potency of the bolt was in this case serving a phallic function of generativity, a benign function of the god looked back upon in later times as one of the elements of the Golden Age with its peace and prosperity provided abundantly by the earth.

Then, with the advent of the new concerns of societies in the Urban Revolution,[4] as we have noted already, the personages of myth underwent radical alterations, all as reflections of the need to represent the significance of the changes and to lead the motivations into new channels of cultural activity. The patriarchal bias put the male deities into an unprecedented predominance that emphasized especially the aggressive dynamism energizing the new commerce, war-making, and empire-building. The old weather-gods, formerly so beneficent, now underwent a corresponding metamorphosis into their new demeanor and functions as king-gods and warrior-gods bearing aloft their deadly thunderweapon, ready to strike.

All through the ancient Near East of that period, this awesome divine personage, under many names yet usually serving similar functions, was venerated as the celestial model of the sacral kingship of the world of mortals. He was depicted in verbal form in many hymns and mythic anecdotes, and in plastic form in numerous stelae and figurines. Whether in Sumer, Akkad, Assyria, Anatolia, Canaan or Israel in that zone, or the Indo-European area with Greece, Rome or India, his fearsome appearance was always much the same, stridently brandishing his explosive weapon. He portrayed in his guise the very essence of the aggressive motivations to wipe out enemies, raze their cities, and build empires. We know him to be the same weather-god as of old, for, paradoxically, he continued to be the spouse of the earth mother represented by the sacral kings in the annual renewal festivals. There was in this no contradiction, however, at least on the symbolic level of ritual, since his role in these ceremonials was to conduct his cosmic combat to preserve life against death and order against chaos by defeating his mythic enemies.

Yet the deadly thunderweapon did not serve merely to punish or blast an enemy into submission. Not stopping with that scale of destructiveness, it sometimes would threaten the total annihilation of the world; in this larger role it became closely similar to its modern form, the explosion that can bring an end to life in the cold darkness of nuclear winter.

If the reader is still left with any mental reservations about the thunderweapon being the mythic image behind the nuclear blast, let me resolve it by telling a truly remarkable mythology found in ancient Etruria,[5] that beautifully refined culture that preceded the grosser one of Rome. The shape of the Etruscan cosmos had the usual four-fold arrangement, dividing the dome of heaven into quadrants and then again into eight sections. Each of these contained a particular potency of nature and a certain quality playing its part in divination. Each was personified by a deity bearing a thunderbolt and standing upon one of the eight points of the compass portrayed in his own color. The high god Tinia took his place, as we are by now ready to expect, at the central cosmic axis as the ninth presiding over the other eight. This was no static kind of cosmos, for the quadrants represented the four world ages characterized by their customary metals, each coming to a close by a metamorphosis into a new era. Now Tinia's power was so supreme as to be capable of terminating in cataclysm the present Etrurian age. The means by which he could bring this about sound altogether familiar to our ears. He possessed a stockpile of three thunderbolts, each for special use; the third he held in reserve by cautious restraint since that one had the capacity to annihilate the entire world order, the whole generation of men and gods! Safeguards to limit this frightening possibility ruled that before he could release the final explosive device, a governing body of twelve gods, the *Di Consentes*, must be called upon to consult together and come to mutual agreement to give or withhold their approval, the jurisdiction over the use of it being in their hands. I sometimes wonder if we would trust even twelve gods to tell us when we must not use the bomb!

These various glimpses of the mythology of the thunderbolt therefore leave little room for doubt that the nuclear blast that we hold in so much dread today is apprehended in the same archetypal affect-image. The scale of our present nuclear plight may be of much greater magnitude, but its ingredients are the same, even including the fearful vision of the end of the known world. This fear we must now consider as well, to see what we learn in the light of our investigations of myth.

World Destruction and Regeneration

It is imperative for us constantly to remind ourselves that the horrific vision of world destruction is part and parcel of the mythic imagery of rapid culture change and of world views in transition, as we have observed already. Beholding the world coming to its end amid storm, earthquake, flood, and fire we have found to be a typical experience of a prophet whose psyche is registering the emotional impact of the end of an era. The ensuing world regeneration is then the picture of the ushering in of a new age, meaning by this an innovative cultural effort whose configuration is outlined in a fresh myth and ritual form. This pattern of transformation is basic to the revitalization movements and crisis cults throughout history. It is fearful and promising, filled with dread and equally with hope, seeming to be a literal ending and yet a transformation.

This literal interpretation, the tendency to take such visions as material fact, is the stumbling block which was seen in our discussion to be the occasion of much grief and hardship in many cultures. There is a term in Jungian psychology for this turn of events: "concretistic misunderstanding," implying that an image and its accompanying emotional component are taken not as symbol but as fact. Many are the suicides, for instance, that result from taking literally the symbolic death that the psyche has introduced in the manner of its own expression of the process of change and transition. Many are the holy wars that are what scholars have recognized as "historifications" of the ritual cosmic combat belonging to the ceremonial rites of renewal of the king and kingdom.[6] In all such cases tragedy results from the misinterpretations of symbolic expressions, even though they are easily accountable by the fact that imagery of this kind is accompanied by such a strong emotional charge that it is experienced as an altogether compelling impulse to be "acted out."

The Archetype of the Enemy

Added to these forbidding mythic images in the process of culture change is that of the enemy; from its history also we have much to learn. For such radical upheavals necessarily must arise out of conflict between the old and the new, and also between the possibility of disintegrative forces overwhelming those of the new organizational effort. We have found the image of the enemy also to be a regular element in the rites of renewal; customarily the imagery is not only of order pitted against chaos, but more dangerously, the order of the realm against its neighbors. In other words, this imagery as well is concretized by the familiar habit of projection. The enemy can otherwise be quite recognizable as one's own inner contradiction and opponent. For instance, we can easily discern this in the history of revolutions against autocratic rule in which the leaders become ludicrously tyrannous themselves when they assume power.By the intensification of this projection of the antagonist on the international scale, our present world has been divided in two, each half claiming to live in the light, while the other wallows in darkness.

The Role of the Mythic Images

From all these observations, we must conclude that mythic images are already at work in our emotional involvement in the pressing issues that confront us. Man's ultimate power to destroy was heretofore represented as the thunderblast, and now it is as the nuclear derivative of it. Its effect promises the familiar picture of world destruction. The opposites are constellated as a pair of supposedly irreconcilable enemy forces dividing the world image in two.

How can this be regarded merely as myth, one might ask, when these are very matter-of-fact truths of our situation in very material reality? This is exactly the point, however. For, so at the start of the Urban Revolution were the bronze battle axe and spear very real facts playing their part in the wholly new and horrible scale of warfare of that era. So drastic were the implications of these and other innovations that new myth forms were required to render the meaning of these creations that were changing the culture. Hence, they became attributes of the warrior storm-god personifying the new psychology of conquest, never before experienced in such magnitude.

Fear and Faith

In the emotional turmoil of a culture dealing with new challenges, issues arise that are at first beyond comprehension and thus beyond the capacity of the consciousness of the time to handle. At such turbulent junctures, all the signs and symptoms of fear make their appearance as part of the syndrome of rapid culture change. These then activate the archetypal psyche, whose myth forms are made manifest to give some orientation to the new circumstances and to set the process of transformation under way.

Today we can see that the experience of terror is kept only at the outer margin of awareness, perhaps because of the unthinkability of the possible consequences. Now, unthinkability spells unconsciousness. There seems at present to be no known way to cope with the issues and prevent what is transpiring. We sense that a relentless progress of escalation is blindly moving ahead and that no one really is in any position to control it. When there is no such conscious management, it is by the same token being left to the autonomy of the unconscious psyche to carry the leadership. However, it is only our consciousness that is blind in this situation, for the psyche does have the wherewithal to throw light on the whole process by its myth-forming capacity to give leads. The evidence of history assures us that in the most dire predicaments the psyche manifests its wisdom again and again through the visionary perception of its images on the part of gifted individuals. Is is any wonder that salvation is such a common theme in the mythic imagery of revitalization movements?

Mitigating Images

Among the many instances of this work of the visionary psyche that have been reviewed throughout this study, few mythic forms have had specific reference to the means for mitigating or countering the overwhelming force of the thunderweapon and its emotional accompaniments: Etruria's Di Consentes served this function before Rome's empire put a stop to that culture; Shelley's mythic drama portrayed the nonviolent spirit necessary to the overthrow of the tyrannical thundergod but was not accepted into the culture of the British Empire as a guideline.

One of the most poignant expressions of this issue is to be found, however, in the evolution of the thunderbolt in India and Tibet. The ancient king-god Indra wielded the same kind of lightning shaft as his other Indo-European counterparts, such as Zeus or Jupiter, one that was grasped at the center and that extended into four prongs at each end. This *vajra* was taken over into Mahayana Buddhism as the *dorje*, with some modifications. This small brass symbol, three or four inches in length, serves as one of a pair of ritual implements: the "vajra-sceptre" coupled with the "vajra-bell," held in the right and left hands, respectively, of the lama in certain ceremonials. They symbolize the supreme goal of spiritual cultivation in the paired opposites known as wisdom and compassion, the qualities of mind which lead the adept to the recognition that in the universe all is the One. The vajra connoting this wisdom is called the Adamantine Body or Diamond Body, incorruptible and invulnerable as this jewel.

The myth explaining the origins of these forms[7] tells that Avalokita, the Bodhisattva who personifies the grace of compassion (a male figure who in crossing the mountains into China became the female Kuan-Yin),[8] gave a great gift to the world. This was the well known mantra, *Om Mani Padme Hum*, "Behold the Jewel in the Lotus!" chanted throughout the Buddhist world in meditation. An image representing this is the *vajra* contained in the lotus, *padma*, as the supreme masculine and feminine, respectively. This image we have encountered in the chapter on Buddhism in the form of the legendary Diamond Throne or Vajra Throne, marking the spot where the Buddha attained his enlightenment. On this round stone, it was said, was carved the lotus, *padma*, surrounding at the center the *vajra*, the Diamond Body. The implication is startingly forceful and beautiful: That which had been the deadly weapon of the king-god, wielded to blast his enemies, is refined to a spiritual force that is here contained within the opposite principle enfolding it; the gigantic masculine assertion of power now held in the embrace of the feminine lotus, tempered and restrained by it in an eternal embrace and union of opposites.

Compacted in this magnificent image lies the secret of a potential mitigation and containment of the otherwise wild and undomesticated force embodied in nuclear fission that drives relentlessly towards destroying. The symbol does not spring out of our own cultural soil, but it does portray in a condensed visual form a cluster of associations around the issue of the complementarity of power and love — of the drive that tends to break free of restraint and that which tends to provide restraint — both being the fruits of the emergence of individuality in evolution.

The Fear of Change

The consideration of these various mythic associations now leads to a further point about the experience of fear of the threat of nuclear nemesis and the blast that would bring the known world to an end. From all that we have reviewed of the imagery of such cataclysmic world destruction it has become clear that this horrific image is constellated at times of acute cultural crisis and culture change. In these, what has been the familiar world of a society's *ethos* and *eidos*, its values and meanings by which its life and ways have been governed, is no longer viable; the familiar emotional investments that have served to motivate the people must be foregone. Only by letting go into an uncertain future are the new possibilities free to come into effect. What could be a greater occasion for fear!

When we look at what is transpiring in this time in our own crisis, do we perceive hints as to what is on the move in the archetypal psyche for our cultural reorientation?

The new rise of the feminine is a phenomenon that can be said to promise the most far-reaching implications. One might object that our most visible and dramatically impressive developments come from the extremely fast-growing achievements in our technology, opening up the computer age and the conquest of space made possible by it. While these are stunning leaps into new dimensions of our capacities, they do not represent changes in our basic orientation but rather the continuous advance in scientific mastery. All this has sprung from the tradition of science since its inception, one that is avowedly founded upon a masculine bias. Its great founders in the seventeenth century made the point in no uncertain terms, as for instance Bacon's declaring the intent of the new discipline to "torture" from nature her secrets and thereby to master her and bind her to the "service" of man as a "slave," "hounded in her wanderings" and "put in constraint," all in the imagery of subduing witchcraft.[9]

After almost five centuries of this demand that nature serve our purposes at any cost to her, it begins to dawn upon us that by this approach to her we are contriving a predicament of our own making. It is becoming all too obvious that by our predatory attitudes of wresting from our environment what we happen to desire, and forcing it to produce for us without taking heed of its own requirements, we can well exhaust the resources that the planet has so generously provided, and even foul beyond redemption the soil, the seas, and the atmosphere. Our environment of nature and of nations, too, has needs of us, and for us to learn an attitude of serving these needs the "receptive" mode is drawn upon. This is an orientation that pays heed to the nature of "the other," whether a person, a nation, or an environment, and prepares the response that can foster mutual well-being. The ecological frame of thought, and the "new paradigm" that studies the interconnectedness of all the parts of a system, lead to a recognition that all phenomena are members of a whole and thus can only be adequately understood in the perspective of the unity of the whole. This is a view that requires changes in our consciousnesss.

The overturning of familiar ways of a culture is always fraught with dismay and reluctance. This dread of change is what is at the heart of the vision of the end of the known world, as I see it, the real fear that is being objectified in the specter of the nuclear blast. Could it even be that it is easier to see ourselves blowing up a world than changing it? In our discomfort, though, we lose sight of that which lies beyond this threshold of change. The mythic imagery tells us that the vision of the world's end is midway to its regeneration, and that the blast of the thunder has traditionally been the expression of intense transformative power. If we ride out these perils and not act them out, essentially gentle things await us.

The Psyche's Response

The history of myth leads us to the conclusion that the new kind of awareness is the work of the archetypal psyche, constellating the feminine principle and the receptive mode as it has so often done in the past with powerful impact upon the ensuing developments of great cultures. The frame of mind that keeps its focus on the needs of the whole and on the interrelationships of the members of the whole, has close affinities with the spirit of the visionary movements that we have been reviewing. What visions of the *polis* of a new order might be awaiting us now?

Ahead   # 12

From this journey through the long spans of space and time in cultural history, exploring the visions of forward moving change, what do we glean for our current circumstances? How do we read the mythic guidelines that are appearing for our orientation to the changes ahead?

Myths and Utopias

It must be understood that in real myth and vision there is no proposing of Utopias. Those have been attempted at various points in history and have usually led to disappointment. Utopias are born of idealistic abstractions conceived by cognitive process; they come from the top of the head. Archetypal myths on the other hand, while they might appear at first glance to have the ring of ideals, come from a different level of experience; they are gifts from the very foundations of the psyche and give expression to emotional motivations. The thinking mind might be persuaded by an ideal picture of a good society, but myth seizes the whole person with its fervor.

Old Myths and New

We have observed that myths make their appearance only at certain critical junctures that have the character of urgency, and as long as they are current and alive, they are indicating the ways ahead which a people are already prepared to recognize. In this way they behave somewhat like dreams: We dream something only when we are about ready to assimilate its meaning and bring that into our lives. In like fashion, a myth is "received" by a people when it is found convincing, which happens when it corresponds to what is already at work in the collective psyche of the populace; otherwise, it fades like a seedling on unfertile soil.

In our present cultural climate, we are experiencing a renewed fascination with mythology, delving into various ancient myth and ritual forms in order to bring to light what they have meant for their societies and therefore might hold for us today. Particularly, there has been a burst of enthusiastic exploration of myth in the past couple of decades on the part of feminist spokespersons to find fitting expression of the qualities of womanhood. In this reaching into the past to find myth forms for today, there arises the danger of a confusion as to what is specific to a culture and a time. This question concerns me as I write this, for it could look as if I were doing the same thing, searching into past myth and ritual forms of antiquity to learn from them what might be relevant today. But the intent of this study is in fact not the same. It is an inquiry into the myth-making process: its origin in the condition of mind of a society in stressful times; the function of the image of the archetypal center governing it; its tendencies to sacralize one or another mode of experience at certain junctures as creative experiments for adaptation to new conditions. In this way, my hope has been to find guidelines from the past about what to expect of myth-making, but not to find there the substance for actual myth.

I will illustrate my point by a few examples. We have noted how the Arthurian Cycle functioned in its own twelfth-century context as an expression of the problems of the individuality emerging out of the constraints of the feudal structure, and as a probing into the potentials of love relations as transformative agencies in that process. These myths belonged to the Celtic people, and these problems to the culture of the time: The lusty Lancelot would be a problematic model for the male of today, or the fairy queen Guinevere for the female, or Arthur for ruling in today's world. Inanna (Ishtar), Mesopotamia's beloved Queen of Heaven and Earth, spouse of Dumuzi, is warmly appealing to all who read of her, and her cultic poetry is deeply moving; yet these verses were created for rituals of fertility and for festivals of the Sacred Marriage, the sexual union of god and goddess for the magical promotion of increase, matters no longer belonging to our industrial or agricultural ways.

We can love these mythic personages, feel enriched by these tales and verses, truly resonate to them and encounter them in our dreams, yet they do not belong to us in the sense of being created out of our cultural conditions of today but only out of other contexts. Through them we catch glimpses of what is eternal in the nature of woman and man and of the cycles of life and death, but not what is temporal in the issues the psyche is working on in our times. By way of analogy, when any of us might feel a strong urge to create a work of art, we do not merely visit the museum to see what Renoir did with his. So our culture, profoundly in need of new vision, cannot merely borrow those of other times and places.

It is my impression, from studying myths in relation to their cultural functions, that a particular form of a myth is truly alive for a few generations at best in those cultures that are progressing and developing; modifications and alterations follow upon one another from century to century. It has a far longer life when enshrined in traditional cultures that revere and conserve the ways of the ancestors undisturbed. As soon as culture change is in question, new myths for new times are in order.

The psychology of this issue of the eternal and the temporal has been well formulated in Jung's model. In this the archetypes in themselves are dynamic propensities that are universal, but as soon as activated they become known through their representation in images that are specific to their context in time and place. In these dimensions, they differentiate as the psyche goes through its evolution. The function of historical symbolic forms is in this case to serve as metaphors or as parallels in the process of amplification for our better assimilation of contents from the unconscious. The explorations that have been set forth in this book have had this intention, to alert our awareness to the role of myth and increase our understanding of it so that we may recognize the psyche's work when it happens.

New Consciousness and Prescribed Behaviors

Equally problematic are the cultic prescriptions of ways of behavior to be followed as if learned by rote. That way of following instructions starts from the outside in the vain hope that it permeates to the inner person. The Christian *agape* has had an unpromising history and has become a threadbare sentimentality perhaps chiefly due to its having had its inception as a commandment, as instruction as to how to be and what to do to be a good follower of the way. Whatever the Buddha might have said originally, it was soon codified into precepts of right thinking and right acting. Confucius was content to train a few disciples to cultivate a certain awareness of issues in the midst of the work of governing and politics, but his concepts were soon turned so much into formulas that the Taoists were quick to comment that Confucians were talking too much and paying too little attention to the way of nature, to what came from their inner being. If you have to talk so much about how to get to some behavior, then you show you are not there yet. Obviously, if one carries the heavy burden of knowing that one should be doing something, one does not yet feel like doing it spontaneously.

Therefore, in seeking out the appearance and development of the Eros mode, the Yin, as a cohesive force in society, we have not been looking for a set of ideals or prescriptions of behavior. The effort has been rather to see how visionaries portray a state of the psyche in which the Yin prevails, one that moves into the field of conscious experience by a spontaneous developmental process when the circumstances of a culture demand it for its survival. This move on the part of the myth-forming, archetypal psyche produces an outlook, a way of experiencing and living and relating, that is accompanied by felt motivations. For these archetypal, emotional components of the psyche's development, the mythic images are the natural and effective expressions. From them we learn how one tends to behave when the Yin is given its due place, and we do not need then to be told how to behave in order to bring the Yin into its due place. As we have seen, the visionaries gave it various names, all implying a way of being in the world and of experiencing it: human-heartedness (*Jen*), universal love (*Chien-ai*), brotherhood, compassion and kindliness, brotherly love (*Agape*), and such terms for a mode of relationships in society that might redeem it from its destructive capacities.

Power and the Receptive

This principle of relating, this Eros, stands in counterbalance to the Logos principle. We have been observing the lesson of history that tells us that the masculine principle personified in the god of the bright sky or sun has consistently tended to motivate societies toward dominance and power. This mode imposes designs of how things ought to be or must be according to a certain concept of order, and is prone to enforce conformity to them; thus, a strongly active-assertive relation to the surroundings is encouraged.

In the personal sphere, these modes operate in the same ways as in the collective. The relations between "self and other" apply not only to those between individuals but also between the individual and the society, or between a society and other nations, or between mankind and the world of nature. What the visionaries have consistently pointed to as the difficulty with the active-assertive masculine principle is that it creates the illusion of the separateness in any of these respects, separateness of self and other or self and world. It might be most concisely expressed in the blindness of the statement, "The concerns of nature are no concern of mine." This outlook could be said to typify the attitude toward our world that prevailed among urban industrial societies until quite recently, naively fending off any awareness of the intricate system of interrelatedness of all beings in nature as if we were no part of them. This is an example of what is meant by the "illusion of separateness."

The receptive mode, on the other hand, takes in a multiplicity of perceptions of what the full nature of "the other" comprises, and by the same token motivates us to relate fully to it. It is colored by a caring respect that then minimizes the distinctions between oneself and persons or things of the world, that is, between "self and other." In all facets of life, the relations to nature and to nations, or between persons in child-rearing, love experiences, friendships, institutions, or corporations, all, the same polarity appears: Power urges us to impose order by domination, the receptive to evoke order by arriving at a sense of mutual affinity. Between partners in relationships, one may be demanding of the other to be a certain way rather than enjoying the pleasure of discovery of the other's unique way. In child-rearing, a willful parent may hold an entire life plan to impose on a son or daughter and even cut him or her off at the pockets if the expectation is not agreed with, over against experiencing the delight in encountering what is unexpected in the child's spontaneous development. In education, the concept of teaching as an authoritarian pumping in of information may impede the cultivation and nurturing of the child's natural wisdom. On the societal level, the issues are often more obvious, such as the imposing of ideologies on other nations rather than fostering their own nascent cultural preferences. In many such areas of experience, there is the tendency to find one's own concept most convincing and the unexpected one coming from the other party more unpromising.

In its conformity with right-brain functioning, the receptive mode openly takes in what is out there in "the other," and hence is possessed of a certain realism. Left-brain activity, on the other hand, is characterized by a more focused attention and filters out information that might seem irrelevant and thus hinder clarity; this selectiveness may in consequence limit its tolerance to the actualities of what is out there in "the other." This contrast between the two modes in turn involves the issue of tolerance and acceptance.

Separateness and Relatedness

When we ponder the proposals of visionaries like Chuang-tse or the Buddha — that separateness is an illusion to be broken through and transcended — we find ourselves at the heart of the knotty problem of what that means in respect to the fulfillment of individuality. Is this expressive of a contradiction or merely a paradox?

Naturally, we of this psychological age tend to assume as self-evident that knowing oneself makes for better relationships. Indeed, it is almost axiomatic that what we resist and close ourselves to in our inner psychic life, we also resist accepting in others. That is, we can be open to an "other" only to the extent that we are willing to be open toward our own interior "other," the conflicting elements in our makeup that present inconsistencies or flat contradictions to what we prefer to be. In this interrelation of inner and outer in our psychic life, there is a kind of mirroring: If we are regardful and accepting of what is in our own nature, then we can be so to the same extent toward what is in the nature of the other person. In this openness, there can be more than tolerance; there may be even a delight in the otherness, in all our differences and idiosyncrasies. Hence, the more we differentiate our individuality, the more we become aware of the meaning of these differences from others. Far from being separative or isolating, this individuality can provide the means for developing our fullest capacities for real relatedness. I am belaboring the point because there is a certain brand of New Age thinking that encourages minimizing differences in order to foster the sense of oneness between fellow beings; I would suggest such melting into oneness produces the opposite effect than that hoped for.

All this provides another framework in which we can recognize the meaningfulness of the fact that at the turning points in various cultures individuality and the Eros principle of relatedness emerge together into expression. The visionaries all the way from Confucius to Shelley have perceived that a fulfilled society must necessarily be founded upon the fulfillment of the individuals composing it. A culture must therefore attend to personal self-cultivation as it strives to mend itself.

In discussing relationships in these terms, the line of thought concerns the ego-conscious level with its separateness of individuals in their differences. Individuality involves "making distinctions," the point the Taoists objected to in their preference to rise to the level at which such "cutting up" was irrelevant. Emphasizing individual differences stands in contrast to the deeper psyche's perception that we are all fundamentally one — where the differentiations and separations are perceived as all illusory. Yet, we have necessarily to hold on to our ego-conscious world view and mundane reality-sense if we are to continue to navigate the world of the ordinary realities and manage our lives, relationships, and responsibilities. What is difficult is that we equally have to hold on to our connection with the experience and realization of oneness if we are going to remain psychically whole. It helps to bear in mind that apart from merely knowing about oneness and appreciating it, we can only actually apprehend it directly, only experience it in its immediacy, when we are in an altered state of consciousness. The two modes of experience, the customary normative conscious state and the altered state, exist together, equally accessible to us, the one at the level of the ego, the other at that of the Self. The task is to harmonize them and give each its due.

In relationships, the Eros mode reaches across the differences, individual to individual; by it, we are also in touch with the awareness that we are one. The ego-consciousness tends to experience loving in a scale of preferences; some persons are more and some less cherished and important to us. The Self, on the other hand, tends to feel compassion for all existence supra-personally. These two ways complement each other, both being necessary to the fullness of relating. Otherwise, we may find ourselves loving certain persons to the exclusion of compassion for and kinship with other beings; or we may feel at one with all existence and have only the most rudimentary capacity to relate sensitively to those persons close to us.

Our Predicament

Are we then just to sit back and wait for this mysterious move of the collective psyche to occur? What gets it under way? History has shown us that when a culture is in dire straits, the collective psyche is activated, just as it is in the case of individuals. The psyche is an organism that responds creatively to new challenges, to necessity. Dire straits of this kind are now upon us, awaiting us just ahead.

Specifically, we are discovering our immense potential for destruction and our proclivity toward it. We can wipe out, poison, or eat up as many of our fellow creatures as we allow ourselves to, even to the point of bringing all other species to termination if we so choose. We are on the way to killing the arable soil's humus beyond reviving. We are fast cutting down our jungles and forests, and the life forms they support. Our fresh water is being polluted beyond repair in many areas, as are even the rains. In short, we are preparing our own crisis, our Time of Troubles. We are doing this just as it has always been done in history, by aggressive self-assertion that disregards the needs of the whole.

Scenario of a Renewal Process

If we do indeed deplete our resources to the critical point, then, in a world living by the competitive motivations, we would turn upon each other. That is the point at which we would know we are in trouble, and that is the set of conditions that would jog the psyche into its customary renewal process. One might well put it that at that point, we would show that we had gone over the edge into craziness, and the psyche's typical reconstitutive process would take over. In it, the themes of world destruction and world regeneration would become the crucial issues. In our blindness, we might let ourselves act them out and release the nuclear blasts themselves. The other way, one hopes, we might make a leap of consciousness and realize what it is that gives rise to world-destruction impulses: a process of radically dismantling our familiar emotional investments in the established cultural habits, by then gone sour, and of releasing a flood of new possibilities in a creative world-regeneration. The critical factor here — in this choice between concrete world-destruction and its psychic equivalent, between annihilation and transformation — is the sharp awareness of the issue, of the fact that there is a choice; and then, with this awareness, to let go of our accustomed ways of thought and action. This revolution would be entirely psychic long before it would find political articulation. It would be a time of hope and a time of fear, of the appalling dismay of not knowing what waits ahead in the near future. Those most afraid and least trusting of the creative innovations under way would dig in to hold onto an ultraconservative stand against change, opposing the more adventurous part of the population that would recognize that things simply cannot remain as they are, without renewal.

The accomplishment of this change would be most readily recognized at the time when we could look back upon the former ways of the late twentieth century with an appalled astonishment at their absurdity; governed by a competitiveness that goes for the jugular; conducting corporate practices without ethics; locked into adversarial relations between the strata of those in power and those working for them; prone to isolate groups, families, and children; impoverished to the bone amidst abundance by the draining of resources into dangerous armaments for supposed positions of strength; carelessly filling the land, water, and air with new chemicals little understood for their destructive capacities; stuffing the body with substances that violate and distort its natural functions of self-regulation; creating devastating frustrations by whipping up the desire for things that are never enough and can never satisfy in any event; and in all this, going on a spree of consuming and using up all the resources the earth has provided, as fast as possible before the final endpoint of depletion. It would look in that retrospect like the folly that it is.

What, then, would be the distinguishing signs of the basic transformation of outlook, of the fundamental shift to include a Yin mode of living in the world? The poetic and prophetic souls possessing the great vision of the new way would become the mouthpieces of the psyche in its dynamic upheaval of renewal. Their effect upon the culture would be to stir a momentous rush of enthusiasm into new concerns.

The Greek *enthousiasmos*, we should remember, means the divine (*thous*, from *theos*) moving in (*en*); hence, an "engodding." Sacredness is endowed upon what is experienced as most valued and at the same time as most mysterious because of its newness, its unfamiliarity. It is the mark of that which is just hovering on the threshhold of consciousness as it emerges from its dormancy in depth, still colored by the numinous aura of the archetypal world of myth. We have observed how the qualities of dominance and power, when they first were activated in the Urban Revolution, were sacralized and personified in king-gods and war-gods, and how later, those of love and compassion were sacralized in the Revolution of Democratization. Sacrality, I suggest, is about to make a move again into a new focus, marking a new experience of what is held dear and desirable, that is, of values and of meanings that are rearranged into a transformed configuration. Powerful energies would be released when this upheaval occurs, accompanied by enthusiasm for great undertakings.

With sacrality appears reverence, the deep esteem for what is held in awe for its majesty. In parallel with the world view that our visionaries have been developing in recent years, even our science itself, the very epitome of the mode of mastery and power, is presenting us its new vision: the awesome picture of creative coevolution constantly giving birth to the superorganism of the biosphere, which is our heritage, and to the superorganism of the society of mankind, which is our responsibility. Both evoke our wonderment and reverence, and motivate us to care for them.

Caring is the leitmotif of this whole study. The word itself sends off a rich shower of associations. Derived from the Latin *caritas*, holding dear, it has the same connotations as the Greek *agape*; both imply cherishing, loving, "affection" as the rousing of affects. These are the qualities of the Eros mode as it rises to take its place in our new world image and world view. The *claritas*, the clear knowing represented in our science, and the *caritas*, the warm caring accompanying our new world vision, would stand side by side: the Yang and the Yin, in balance; Vajra and Padma; Wisdom and Compassion; Prometheus and Asia in their partnership presiding over a transformed world image. This is the picture of wholeness, of healing, of achieving oneness.

Notes

1. The Psyche and the Evolution of Cultures

1. Perry, J.W., "Reconstitutive Process in the Psychopathology of the Self," *Annals of the New York Academy of Sciences*, XCVI, art., 3, 27 January 1962, pp. 853–76.

2. Eliade, M., *The Myth of the Eternal Return*, Bollingen Series XLVI, New York,Pantheon, 1954.

3. Perry, J.W., *Lord of the Four Quarters*, New York, Braziller, 1966.

4. Childe, V.G., *New Light on the Most Ancient East*, New York, Evergreen Books, Grove Press, 1947.

5. Toynbee, A.J., *A Study of History*, New York, Oxford University Press, 1947.

6. Jung, C.G., "Concerning Mandala Symbolism," *Archetypes of the Collective Unconscious*, trans. R.F.C. Hull, *Coll. Works*, Vol. 9, 1, Bollingen Series XX, New York, Pantheon, 1959.

7. Maslow, A., *Religion, Values and Peak Experiences*, New York, Viking, 1970.

8. Teilhard de Chardin, P., *The Phenomenon of Man*, New York, Harper and Row, Torchbooks, 1961.

9. Frazer, J.G., *The Golden Bough*, London, Macmillan, 1890–1915.

10. Reinach, S., *Orpheus*, New York, Liveright, 1935.

11. Raglan, F.R.S. Lord, *The Hero*, London, Methuen, 1936.

12. Perry, W.J., *The Children of the Sun: A Study in the Early History of Civilization*, London, Methuen, 1923.

13. Raglan, F.R.S. Lord, *Jocasta's Crime*, London, Thinker's Library, 1940.

14. Freud, S., *Moses and Monotheism*, New York, Knopf, 1947.

15. Jung, C. G., "On Psychological Understanding," *The Psychogenesis of Mental Disease*, trans. R. F. C. Hull, Coll. Works, Vol. 3, Bollingen Series XX, New York, Pantheon, 1960.

16. Darwin, C., *The Descent of Man*, London, Murray, 1871. Also See *The Origin of Species*, New York, Appleton, 1880.

17. Drummond, H., *The Ascent of Man*, New York, J. Pott, 1894.

18. Drummond, H., *Natural Law in the Spiritual World*, New York, J. Pott, 1887.

19. Whitehead, A.N., *Process and Reality*, New York, Macmillan, 1936.

20. Henderson, L.J., *The Order of Nature*, Cambridge, Harvard University Press, 1925.

21. Needham, J., *Time, The Refreshing River*, London, Allen and Unwin, 1953.

22. Needham, J., *Science and Civilization in China*, 5 volumes, Cambridge University Press, 1954 et. seq.

23. Jung, C.G., "On Psychological Understanding."

2. *Lo! They Beheld*

1. Perry, J.W., *The Far Side Of Madness*, Englewood Cliffs, Prentice-Hall, 1974, pp. 30–31.

2. Sundkler, B.G.M., *Bantu Prophets in South Africa*, London, Lutterworth, 1948 Also, Lanternari, *The Religions of the Oppressed*, Mentor Book, New York, New American Library, 1965, pp. 46–47.

3. Lanternari, *The Religions of the Oppressed*, p. 47.

4. Mooney, J., "The Ghost Dance," *Report of the Bureau of American Ethnology*, XIV, 1972, Pt. II.

5. Lame Deer, J., *Lame Deer, Seeker of Visions*, R. Erdoes, ed., New York, Washington Square Press, 1976.

6. Lanternari, *The Religions of the Oppressed*, pp. 239–49.

7. Fuchs, Stephen, *Rebellious Prophets: A Study of Messianic Movements in Indian Religion,* New York, Asia Publishing House, 1965.

8. LaBarre, W., "Materials for History of Studies of Crisis Cults, A Bibliographical Essay," *Current Anthropology*, XII, No. 1, 1971, pp. 3–44.

9. Worsley, P., *The Trumpet Shall Sound: A Study of Cargo Cults in Melanesia*, London, 1957. Also, Lanternari, *The Religions of the Oppressed*, pp. 166 ff.

10. Lanternari, *The Religions of the Oppressed*, pp. 191–96, 209–10.

11. Wallace, A.F.C., *The Death and Rebirth of the Seneca*, New York, Knopf, 1970.

12. LaBarre, W., "John Wilson, The Revealer of Peyote," Appendix 7 of *The Peyote Cult*, New York, Schocken Books, 1971, pp. 151–61.

13. Lanternari, *The Religions of the Oppressed*, pp. 118–20.

14. Ibid., pp. 143–50.

15. Ibid., pp. 168–69.

16. Ibid., p. 134.

17. Wallace, A.F.C., *Culture and Personality*, New York, Random House, 1961, pp. 188–99.

18. Sullivan, H.S., *Schizophrenia as a Human Process*, New York, Norton, 1962, p. 20.

19. Jung, C.G., "On Psychic Energy," trans. R.F.C. Hull, *Coll. Works*, Vol. 8, Bollingen Series XX. New York, Pantheon, 1960.

20. Jung, C.G., "Symbols of Transformation," trans. R.F.C. Hull, *Coll. Works*, Vol. 5, Bollingen Series XX. New York, Pantheon. Also, Jung, "On Psychic Energy."

21. Lanternari, *The Religions of the Oppressed*, p. 241.

22. Ibid. pp. 248–49.

23. Wallace, A.F.C., "Stress and Rapid Personality Change," *International Record of Medicine and General Practice Clinics*, 169, No. 12, 1956; Latourette, K.S., *The Chinese: Their History and Culture*, New York, Macmillan, 1946; Fitzgerald, C.P., *China*, New York, Praeger, 1961.

24. II Esdras, Ch. XIV, *The Apocrypha*, ed. M. Komroff, New York, Tudor, 1936. p. 67.

3. World Images in Turmoil and Transition

1. Perry, J.W., "Reconstitutive Process in the Psychopathology of the Self," *Annals of the New York Academy of Sciences*, XCVI, art. 3, 27 January 1962, pp. 853–76.

2. Perry, J.W., *Roots of Renewal in Myth and Madness*, San Francisco, Jossey-Bass, 1976.

3. Perry, *The Far Side of Madness*.

4. Perry, J.W., "Emotions and Object Relations," *Journal of Analytical Psychology*, II, No. 2, 1937, pp. 137–52.

5. Perry, J.W., *The Self in Psychotic Process*, Berkeley, University of California Press, 1953, provides a full study of this case.

6. Perry, *Lord of the Four Quarters*.

7. Campbell, J., *Oriental Mythology, The Masks of God*, Vol. 2, New York, Viking, 1962, uses this term.

8. L'Orange, H.P., "Studies in the Iconography of Cosmic Kingship in the Ancient World," Cambridge, *Institutett for Sammenlignende Kulturforskning*, Harvard University Press, 1953.

9. Cammann, S.V.R., "Suggested Origin of the Tibetan Mandala Paintings," *Art Quarterly*, Spring, 1950.

10. Vaillant, G.C., *The Aztecs of Mexico*, Garden City, Doubleday, Doran, 1941; republished, Penguin, 1953.

11. Von Vacano, O.W., *The Etruscans in the Ancient World*, trans. S.A. Ogilvie, London, Edward Arnold, 1960.

12. Von Hagen, V.W., *Realm of the Incas*, Mentor Book, Ancient Civilizations, New American Library, 1957.

13. Mercer, S.A.B., *An Egyptian Grammar for Beginners*, Oriental Research Series, No. I, London, Luzac, 1929.

14. MacCana, P., *Celtic Mythology*, London, Hamlyn, 1970, p. 1178.

15. Jung, C.G., *The Secret of the Golden Flower*, London, Kegan Paul, Trench & Trubner, 1935.

16. Maslow, A.H., *Religion, Values, & Peak Experiences*, New York, Viking, 1970.

4. A Legacy of Pharaohs

1. Sources drawn upon for this account of the sacral kingship of Egypt: Blackman, A.M., "Myth and Ritual in Ancient Egypt," *Myth and Ritual*, ed. S.H. Hooke, London, Oxford University Press, 1953; Breasted, J.H., *The Dawn of Conscience*, New York, Charles Scribner & Sons, 1933; Childe, *New Light on the Most Ancient Near East*; Fairman, H.W., "The Kingship Rituals of Egypt," *Myth, Ritual, and Kingship*, ed. S.H. Hooke, Oxford, Clarendon, 1958; Frankfort, H., *Kingship and the Gods*, Bk. I, Chicago, Chicago University Press, 1948; Gaster, T.H., *Thespis: Myth, Ritual, and Drama in the Ancient Near East*, Garden City, Anchor Books, Doubleday, 1961; and Wilson, J.A., *The Culture of Ancient Egypt*, Chicago Phoenix Books, University of Chicago Press, 1960.

Further detailed references are found in Perry, *Lord of the Four Quarters*.

2. Frankfort, *Kingship and the Gods*, Ch. 2.

3. Ibid., Ch. 1.

4. Ibid., pp. 32, 133–35.

5. Ibid., Ch. 5.

6. Wilson, J.A., "Egyptian Observations," *Ancient Near Eastern Texts Relating to the Old Testament*, ed. J.B. Pritchard, University of Princeton Press, 1955, p. 431.

7. Ibid., p. 431.

8. Breasted, *The Dawn of Conscience.*

9. Wilson, J.A., "Egyptian Oracles and Prophecies," *Ancient Near Eastern Texts*, pp. 446–47.

10. Breasted, *The Dawn of Conscience*, p. 39.

11. Ibid., p. 144.

12. Ibid., p. 154. Text found in *Ancient Near Eastern Texts*, pp. 414–18.

13. Wilson, "Proverbs and Precepts," *Ancient Near Eastern Texts*, pp. 412–13.

15. Wilson, "Egyptian Oracles and Prophecies," *Ancient Near Eastern Texts*, pp. 441–44.

16. Breasted, *The Dawn of Conscience*, p. 201 ff. Text in Wilson, "Egyptian Oracles and Prophecies," pp. 444–46.

17. Breasted, *The Dawn of Conscience*, p. 203.

18. Toynbee, A.J., *A Study of History*, Oxford, Oxford University Press, 1947, pp. 30–33.

19. Frankfort, H., *The Birth of Civilization in the Near East*, Garden City, Anchor Books, Doubleday, 1961. pp. 28 ff.

20. Breasted, *The Dawn of Conscience*, Ch. XIV.

21. Ibid., p. 249.

22. Ibid., p. 249.

23. Ibid., pp. 235–37.

24. Ibid., pp. 296–97.

25. Ibid., pp. 292–93.

26. Ibid., p. 293.

27. Ibid., pp. 291–92.

28. Wilson, *The Culture of Ancient Egypt*, pp. 309–18.

29. Ibid., p. 314.

5. *Sages and Sons of Heaven*

1. Sources drawn upon for this account of the sacral kingship of China: Bodde, D., "Harmony and Conflict in Chinese Philosophy," *Studies in Chinese Thought*, ed. A.F. Wright, Chicago, Chicago University Press, 1953; Chavannes, E., *Les Memoires Historiques de Se-ma-ts'ien*, Paris, E. Leriaux, 1895–1905; Creel, H.G., *The Birth of China*, New York, Frederick Ungar, 1937; Creel, H.G., *Chinese Thought*, Chicago, University of Chicago Press, 1953; Fitzgerald, C.F., *China: A Short Cultural History*, New York, Praeger, 1961; Granet, M., *Chinese Civilization*, New York, MacMillan, 1958; and Soothill, W.E., *The Hall of Light: A Study of Early Chinese Kingship*, New York, Philosophical Library, 1952.

Further detailed references are found in Perry, *Lord of the Four Quarters*.

2. Needham, J., *Science and Civilization in China*, 5 volumes, Cambridge, Cambridge University Press, 1954 et. seq.

3. Needham, J., "Human Laws and Laws of Nature in China and the West," *Journal of the History of Ideas*, XII, 1951, p. 250.

4. Bodde, *Harmony and Conflict in Chinese Philosophy*, p. 23.

5. Creel, *The Birth of China*, pp. 182–84; Waley, A., *The Analects of Confucius*, New York, Vintage Books, Random House, undated, pp. 41–43.

6. Creel, *The Birth of China*, pp. 342–43.

7. Ibid.

8. Creel, *The Birth of China*, p. 137; Tung Chung-shu, "Ch'ien ch'u fan-lu," sec. 43, trans. B. Watson, in "The Imperial Age: Ch'in and Han," in *Sources of Chinese Tradition*, Part II, ed. W.T. de Bary, New York, Columbia University Press, 1960.

9. Soothill, *The Hall of Light*, pp. 1–2.

10. Fung Yu-lan, *A Short History of Chinese Philosophy*, trans. D. Bodde, New York, Macmillan, 1960, p. 57.

11. Granet, *Chinese Civilization*, Bk. IV, Ch. 1; Creel, *The Birth of China*, p. 337.

12. Soothill, *The Hall of Light*; Granet, *Chinese Civilization*.

13. Granet, *Chinese Civilization*, p. 12.

14. Creel, H.G., *Confucius and the Chinese Way*, New York, Harper and Row, Torchbooks, 1960, p. 36.

15. Fung, *A Short History of Chineses Philosophy*, pp. 201–02.

16. Ibid., pp. 206–07.

17. Waley, *The Analects of Confucius*, p. 49.

18. Ibid., pp. 27–29.

19. Ibid., p. 28.

20. Fung, *A Short History of Chinese Philosophy*, p. 42; Confucius, *Analects* XII:22:1, *The Four Books*, trans. J. Legge, Shanghai, The Commercial Press, undated.

21. Confucius, *Analects*, XII:2; see also XIV:35:1–3.

22. Confucius, *Analects*, VI:22:1.

23. Confucius, *Analects*, VI:28 and XXVIII:2; Fung, *A Short History of Chinese Philosophy*, p. 43.

24. Dai, B., "Being Fully Human: A Chinese Ideal of Mental Health," *Highland Highlights*, Asheville, Office of Information Services, Sept. 1981., pp. 9–13.

25. Confucius, *Analects*, IV:15; Fung, *A Short History of Chinese Philosophy*, pp. 43–44.

26. Confucius, *Analects*, XII:2; Creel, *The Birth of China*, p. 131.

27. Creel, *The Birth of China*, pp. 123–31.

28. Confucius, *Analects*, XII:22.

29. Confucius, *Analects*, X; Waley, A., *The Way and Its Power*, New York, Grove Press, 1958, pp. 160–61.

30. Waley, *The Way and its Power*, p. 34.

31. Fung, *A Short History of Chinese Philosophy*, pp. 69 ff; Creel, H.G., *Chinese Thought: From Confucius to Mao T'se-tung*, Chicago, Chicago University Press, 1953, pp. 91 ff.

32. Mencius VII (I) 4:1, *The Four Books*.

33. Mencius II (I) 2:11–15. "The Great Morale" is Fung's term, *A Short History of Chinese Philosophy*, pp. 78–79, "vast, flowing passion nature" is Legge's, *The Four Books*.

34. Mencius VI (2) 2:1.

35. Fung, *A Short History of Chinese Philosophy*, p. 76; Creel, *Chinese Thought*, p. 81.

36. Waley, *The Analects of Confucius*, pp. 34–37.

37. Legge, *The Four Books*, p. 347; Fung, *A Short History of Chinese Philosophy*, pp. 170 ff.

38. "The Golden Mean" XXII, Legge, *The Four Books*; Fung, *A Short History of Chinese Philosophy*, p. 176.

39. "The Golden Mean" XXII, Legge, *The Four Books.*

40. Fung, *A Short History of Chinese Philosophy*, pp. 191–203; see Perry, *Lord of the Four Quarters*, pp. 208–09, for further quotes.

41. Perry, J.W., *Lord of the Four Quarters*, p. 209.

42. Ibid.

43. Tung Chung-shu, *Ch'un-ch'iu Fan-lu*, Ch. 36, Fung, *A Short History of Chinese Philosophy*, p. 195.

44. Fung, *A Short History of Chinese Philosophy*, Ch. 5; Mo-tse, in Lin Yu-tang, *The Wisdom of the East*, New York, Random House, 1942, pp. 785 ff.

45. Lin Yu-tang, *The Wisdom of the East*, p. 625.

46. Fung, *A Short History of Chinese Philosophy*, pp. 112–16; Lin Yu-tang, *The Wisdom of the East*, p. 625.

47. Fung, *A Short History of Chinese Philosophy* pp. 112 and 114.

48. *Chuang-tse*, II:3, in Lin Yu-tang, *The Wisdom of the East*, p. 636; Fung, *A Short History of Chinese Philosophy* p. 112.

49. *Chuang-tse*, II:3, 5, 7, in Lin Yu-tang, *The Wisdom of the East*, pp. 636 and 639.

50. *Chuang-tse*, II:10, in Lin Yu-tang, *The Wisdom of the East,* p. 642; Fung, *A Short History of Chinese Philosophy*, p. 114.

51. Lao-tse, *Tao Teh Ching*, XVIII.

52. Lao-tse, *Tao Teh Ching*, XIX, in Lin Yu-tang, *The Wisdom of the East*, p. 592.

53. Lao-tse, *Tao Teh Ching*, III, in Waley, *The Way and its Power*, p. 145.

54. *Chuang-tse*, IX:2, in Lin Yu-tang, *The Wisdom of the East*, p. 670.

55. *Chuang-tse*, VI:3, in Lin Yu-tang, *The Wisdom of the East*, p. 658.

56. *Chuang-tse*, IV:1, in Lin Yu-tang, *The Wisdom of the East*, pp. 645–46.

57. Lao-tse, *Tao Teh Ching*, VI, in Waley, *The Way and its Power*, p. 149.

58. Lao-tse, *Tao Teh Ching*, II.

59. Lao-tse, in Waley, *The Way and its Power*, pp. 34–35.

60. Wilhelm, R., *The I Ching or Book of Changes*, Bollingen Series XIX, New York, Pantheon, 1950, Book I.

61. *Shuo Kua*, III:10, in Wilhelm, *The I Ching*, p. 294.

62. *I Ching*, Oracle I, "Ch'ien, The Creative," in Wilhelm, *The I Ching*, pp. 1–9.

63. *I Ching,* Oracle II, "K'un, The Receptive," in Wilhelm, *The I Ching,* pp. 9–15.

64. Lao-tse, *Tao Teh Ching,* X, in Waley, *The Way and its Power,* p. 153.

65. Saso, M.R., *Taoism and the Rite of Cosmic Renewal,* Washington State University Press, 1972.

6. Kingship and Compassion

1. Sources drawn upon for this account of the sacral kingship of India: Barnett, L.D., *Antiquities of India,* New York, Putnam, 1914; Basham, A.L., *The Wonder That Was India,* London, Sidgwick and Jackson, 1956; Campbell, J., *Oriental Mythology, The Masks of God,* Vol. 2, New York, Viking, 1962; Griffith, R.T.H., *Hymns of the Rigveda,* Benares, Lasaruz, 1896; Hocart, A.M., *Kings and Councillors,* Cairo, Egyptian University, Barbey, 1936; Hocart, A.M., *Kingship,* London, Oxford University Press, 1927; Masson-Oursel, P., *Ancient India and Indian Civilization,* trans. M.R. Dobie, London, Kegan Paul, Trench, & Trubner, 1934; and Raghavan, V., and R.N. Dundekar, "Hinduism," *Sources of Indian Tradition,* ed. W.T. de Bary, New York, Columbia University Press, 1958.

Further detailed references found in Perry, *Lord of the Four Quarters.*

2. Masson-Oursel, *Ancient India and Indian Civilization;* Jacobsen, T., "Mesopotamia," *Before Philosophy: The Intellectual Adventure of Ancient Man,* London, Penguin, 1954.

3. Manu VII, 3–8, quoted in Basham, *The Wonder That Was India,* p. 845.

4. Basham, *The Wonder That Was India,* p. 81; Eggeling, J. "The Satapatha Brahmana," *Sacred Books of the East,* ed. F.M.Muller, Vol. 41, Oxford, Clarendon, 1900.

5. Eggeling, "The Satapatha Brahmana."

6. Ibid.

7. Ibid.; Basham, *The Wonder That Was India,* p. 81; Barnett, *Antiquities of India,* #21, pp. 169–70.

8. Barnett, *Antiquities of India,* #18, pp. 166; Basham, *The Wonder That Was India;* Eggeling, "The Satapatha Brahmana."

9. "Suvarnaprabhasottana Sutra," in DeBary, W.T., *Sources of Indian Tradition,* New York, Columbia University Press, 1960, pp. 185–86.

10. Basham, *The Wonder That Was India,* pp. 83–85.

11. "Maha Parinibbana Suttanta," XVI:11–22, in Rhys Davids, T.W. and C.A.F, "Dialogues of the Buddha," in *Sacred Books of the Buddhists*, London, Oxford University Press, 1899, Vol. III, Pt. 2, Ch. 5, pp. 154–56.

12. Basham, A.L., "Buddhism in India," *The Buddhist Tradition in India, China, and Japan*, ed. T. de Bary, New York, The Modern Library, 1969, Ch. 1; Rahula, W.S., *What the Buddha Taught*, New York, Grove Press, 1959, p. 84.

13. . "Mahavastu," Perry, *The Children of the Sun*.

14. "Digha Nikaya," Thomas, E.J., *The Life of the Buddha as Legend and History*, New York, Barnes and Nobe, 1960, Ch. 1.

15. "Nidana-katha, Jaraka, Kuttaka-nikaya." Birth stories are found in "Lalita-vistara, and Mahavastu," Thomas, *The Life of the Buddha*, Ch. III.

16. "Lalita-vistara," Thomas, *The Life of the Buddha*, p. 40.

17. "Mahavastu" 2., Thomas, *The Life of the Buddha*, p. 53.

18. "Mahavastu" 2., Thomas, *The Life of the Buddha*, Ch. VI.

19. "Maha Parinibbana Suttanta" 5, Thomas, *The Life of the Buddha*, pp. 39–40, 220 ff.

20. "Ambattha-Sutta," III, I, 5, in Rhys Davids, T.W., *Sacred Books of the Buddhists*, Vol. II, "Dialogues of the Buddha," London, Oxford University Press, 1899, pp. 110–11.

21. "Lakkhana Sutta," Thomas, pp. 217 ff.

22. Rahula, *What the Buddha Taught*, Ch. VI.

23. "Majjhima Nikaya," I, Basham, "Buddhism in India," p. 27; "Metta-Sutta, Suttanipata" I, 8, Rahula, *What the Buddha Taught*, p. 97; Conze, E., *Buddhism in Essence and Development*, New York, Harper Torch Books, 1975, pp. 102–02.

24. "Digha Nikaya," I, 4 ff. Basham, "Buddhism in India," pp. 32–34.

25. Basham, *The Wonder That Was India*, p. 81; Dundekar, R.N., "Hinduism," *Sources of Indian Tradition*, ed. W.T. deBary, New York, Columbia University Press, 1958, pp. 236–57.

26. "Sutta Nipata," Basham, "Buddhism in India," p. 38.

27. Ibid., pp. 36–37.

28. "Digha Nikaya," I, 4 Basham, "Buddhism in India," p. 33.

29. "Dhammapada," 223, Rahula, *What the Buddha Taught*, p. 132.

30. "Dhammapada," 3–5, Basham, "Buddhism in India," pp. 38–39.

31. Rahula, *What the Buddha Taught*, p. 84.

32. "Jataka" I, Rahula, *What the Buddha Taught*, pp. 84–85.

33. Nikam, N.A. and R. McKeon, *The Edicts of Asoka*, Chicago, University of Chicago Press, Phoenix, 1959, p. 41.

7. Agape and Anointed Ones

1. Sources drawn upon for this account of th sacral kingship of Israel: Bentzen, A., *King and Messiah*, London, Lutterworth, 1955; Guthrie, H.H. *Israel's Sacred Songs: A Study of Dominent Themes*, New York, Seabury, 1966; Hooke, S.H. et al., *Myth and Ritual*, London, Oxford University Press, 1953; Hooke, S.H. et al., *Myth, Ritual, and Kingship*, Oxford, Clarendon, 1958; James, E.O., *Myth, and Ritual in the Ancient Near East*, New York, Praeger, 1958; Johnson, A.R., *Sacral Kingship in Ancient Israel*, Cardiff, University of Wales, 1955; and Mowinckel, S., *He That Cometh*, trans. G.W. Anderson, New York, Abdingdon, 1954.

   Further detailed references are found in Perry, *Lord of the Four Quarters*.

2. Guthrie, *Israel's Sacred Songs*, Ch. I.

3. Allbright, W.F., *Archeology of Palestine*, Baltimore, Penguin, 1960, p. 183; Johnson, *Sacral Kingship in Ancient Israel*, p. 29.

4. James, *Myth and Ritual in the Ancient Near East*.

5. Johnson, *Sacral Kingship in Ancient Israel*, p. 56.

6. Ibid; Mowinckel, S., *He That Cometh*.

7. Perry, *Roots of Renewal in Myth and Madness*.

8. Johnson, *Sacral Kingship in Ancient Israel*, p. 81; Birkeland, H., *The Evildoer in the Book of Psalms*, Oslo, Avhandlinger utgitt av det Norske Videnskaps — II, Akademi I, Oslo II, 1955.

9. Mowinckel, *He That Cometh*, pp. 102–02.

10. James, *Myth and Ritual in the Ancient Near East*, p. 99.

11. Johnson, *Sacral Kingship in Ancient Israel*, p. 119.

12. Guthrie, *Israel's Sacred Songs*, Ch. 2.

13. As in note 8.

14. Klausner, J., *The Messianic Idea in Israel*, trans. W.F. Stinespring, New York, Macmillan, 1955, Ch. IV.

15. Ibid.

16. Ibid., Ch. V; Mowinckel, *He That Cometh*, Chs. IV, V, VI.

17. Mowinckel, *He That Cometh*, Ch. VI; Johnson, *Sacral Kingship in Ancient Israel.*

18. Perry, *Lord of the Four Quarters*, reviews the developments, pp. 175–82. Also see Mowinckel, *He That Cometh*, Ch. VI.

19. Jeremiah, 31:33. See Klausner, *The Messianic Idea in Israel*, Ch. VIII.

20. Isaiah 56 to 66. See Mowinckel, *He That Cometh*, Ch. VII, and Klausner, *The Messianic Idea in Israel*, Ch. XII.

21. Levy-Bruhl, L., *Primitive Mentality*, London, Allen & Unwin, 1923.

22. First Servant Song: Isaiah 42:1–7; Second Servant Song: Isaiah 49:1–9; Third Servant Song: Isaiah 50:4–11; Fourth Servant Song: Isaiah 52:13 to 53:12.

23. Mowinckel, *He That Cometh*, Ch. VII.

24. Ibid., pp. 189–205.

25. Klausner, *The Messianic Idea in Israel*, pp. 176–77, 218–19, 259–63; Dimont, M., *Jews, God and History*, New York, New American Library, 1972.

26. I Enoch, *The Apocrypha and Pseudepigrapha of the Old Testament*, ed. R.H. Charles, Los Angeles, Work of the Chariot, 1970.

27. Ibid. Section I, Ch. 1:5–7; II Esdras 13:12, 39 ff; Mowinckel, *He That Cometh*, p. 381.

28. I Enoch, Ch 14:8, 71:1, Charles, *The Apocrypha*.

29. Ibid., Ch. 34:3–5.

30. Ibid., Ch. 46:1–3.

31. Barnabas VI:13.

32. Mowinckel, *He That Cometh*, pp. 346–48.

33. II Esdras 113:1 ff., trans. Mowinckel, *He That Cometh*, p. 390. Also in Komroff, M., *The Apocrypha*, New York, Tudor, 1936, p. 62.

34. Daniel 7:13 ff.

35. II Esdras 13:5 ff., trans. S. Mowinckel, *He That Cometh*, p. 397; II Esdras 62:12, Klausner, *The Messianic Idea in Israel*, p. 360 .

36. I Enoch 25:3–6, 69:29, 48:5; Mowinckel, *He That Cometh*, Ch.X:12.

37. I Enoch 51:12–20, 61:12, 70:4, 32:3; Mowinckel, *He That Cometh*, Ch. X:9; Klausner, *The Messianic Idea in Israel*, pp. 295–6. The earliest mention of resurrection: Isaiah 26:19.

38. I Enoch 54:3–6, 55:4, 56:1–4; II Baruch 29:1, 73:1. Mowinckel, *He That Cometh*, Ch. X:13; Klausner, *The Messianic Idea in Israel*, p. 246.

39. I Enoch, 10:17–19, II Esdras 7:28 ff; Baruch 29:4. Mowinckel, *He That Cometh*, Ch. X:16; Klausner, *The Messianic Idea in Israel*, pp. 343.

40. I Enoch 71:14–17. Mowinckel, *He That Cometh*, Ch.X:16; Klausner, *The Messianic Idea in Israel*, pp. 356 ff.

41. II Esdras 7:28 ff. Klausner, *The Messianic Idea in Israel*, p. 354.

42. I Enoch 93:17–17; cf. Isaiah 65:17, and 66:22; Mowinckel, *He That Cometh*, X:16; Klausner, *The Messianic Idea in Israel*, pp. 354 ff.

43. I Enoch 48:1 ff., 39:6–7. Klausner, *The Messianic Idea in Israel*, p. 290.

44. Dimont, *Jews, God, and History.*

45. Mowinckel, *He That Cometh*, p. 445 ff.

46. Ibid., p. 510, quoting Klausner.

47. Ibid., pp. 448–49.

48. II Enoch, *The Book of the Secrets of Enoch, The Apocrypha and Pseudepigrapha*, ed. R.H. Charles.

49. Mark 12:29–31.

50. John 15:1–12.

51. Bentzen, *King and Messiah*, pp. 44–46, quoting the thesis proposed by Nyberg; Johnson, *Sacral Kingship in Ancient Israel*, p. 2.

52. Paul, I Corinthians 12:12–27.

53. Paul, Romans 6:1–11.

54. Smith, M., *The Secret Gospel*, New York, Harper & Row, 1973, Ch. 12; Pagels, E., *The Gnostic Gospels*, New York, Vintage Books, Random House, 1981, Ch. I.

55. Nygren, A., *Agape and Eros: A Study in the Christian Idea of Love*, trans. A.G. Hebert, London, Society for Promoting Christian Knowledge, 1952.

56. Paul, Galatians 4:5–7.

8. Quests and the Kingdom of the Heart

1. Sources drawn upon for this account of the sacral kingship of the Celts:

Heer, F., *The Medieval World*, trans. J. Sondheimer, New York, Mentor Books, New American Library, 1963; Loomis, R.S., *Celtic Myth and Arthurian Romance*, New York, Columbia University Press, 1927; Loomis, R.S., *The Grail from Celtic Myth to Christian*

Symbol, New York, Columbia University Press, 1963; MacCana, P., *Celtic Mythology*, London, Hamlyn, 1970; Markale, J., *King Arthur: King of Kings*, London, Gordon and Cremonesi, 1977; and Markale, J., *Women of the Celts*, London, Gordon and Cremonesi, 1975.

2. Heer, *The Medieval World*, Ch. II.

3. Sayers, D.L., *The Song of Roland*, Baltimore, Penguin, 1957.

4. Heer, *The Medieval World*, Ch. VII; DeRougemont, D., *Love in the Western World*, trans. R. Belgian, New York, Fawcett, World Library, 1956.

5. Terry, P., *Lays of Courtly Love*, Garden City, Anchor Books, Doubleday, 1963; Fowles, J., *The Lais of Marie de France*, trans. R. Hamming and J. Ferrante, New York, Dutton, 1978.

6. Terry, *Lays of Courtly Love*.

7. Zimmer, H., *The King and the Corpse*, ed. J. Campbell, Bollingen Series XI, Princeton, Princeton University Press, 1971, pp. 162–76.

8. Markale, *Women of the Celts*.

9. Ibid., pp. 128–42.

10. Capellanus, A., *The Art of Courtly Love*, trans. J.J. Parry, New York, Frederick Ungar, 1959.

11. Heer, *The Medieval World*.

12. Bedier, J., *The Romance of Tristan and Iseult*, trans. H. Belloc and P. Rosenfeld, Garden City, Doubleday, 1955.

13. Markale, *Women of the Celts*, pp. 217 ff.

14. Campbell, J., *Creative Mythology, the Masks of God*, Vol. VI. New York, Viking, 1968, pp. 44 ff.

15. Markale, *Women of the Celts*, p. 240.

16. Ibid., pp. 217 ff.

17. Ibid., p. 213.

18. Ibid., p. 226.

19. Ibid., pp. 226–27.

20. Heer, *The Medieval World*.

21. MacCana, *Celtic Mythology*, pp. 117–21.

22. Ibid., p. 117.

23. Ashe, G. et al., *The Quest for Arthur's Britian*, ed. G. Ashe, St. Albans, Herts, Paladin, 1968; Markale, *King Arthur: King of Kings*.

24. Markale, J., *King Arthur: King of Kings*, pp. 54 ff.

25. Ibid., quoting the E. Kohler, *L'Aventure Chivaleresque*, Paris, 1974.

26. Loomis, *The Grail from Celtic Myth to Christian Symbol; Celtic Myth to Arthurian Romance*, Ch. XXIII.

27. Loomis, R.S., *Celtic Myth to Arthurian Romance*, New York, Columbia University Press, 1939; Brown, A.C.L., *The Origin of the Grail Legend*, Cambridge, Harvard University Press, 1943.

28. Brown, *The Origin of the Grail Legend*.

29. Loomis, *The Grail from Celtic Myth to Christian Symbol*.

30. Ibid.

31. Ibid., pp. 47–49.

32. Ibid., pp. 48–49.

33. Ibid., p. 75.

34. Ibid., p. 76–77.

35. Ibid., Ch. XII.

36. Jung, C.G., *Two Essays on Analytical Psychology*.

37. Heer, *The Medieval World*, pp.170–72.

38. Weston, J., *Sir Gawain at the Grail Castle*, London, Nutt, 1903.

39. Heer, *The Medieval World*.

40. Adams, H., *Mont-St-Michele and Chartres*, Cambridge, Houghton Mifflin, 1936.

41. Wagner, R., *Parsifal*, trans. H.L. & F. Corder, New York, Rullman, pp. 6–7.

9. Revolution and World Regeneration

1. Woodman, R.G., *The Apocalyptic Vision in the Poetry of Shelley*, Toronto, Toronto University Press, 1964, p. 71, quoting Shelley's "Defence of Poetry."

2. Webb, T., *Shelley, A Voice Not Understood*, Manchester, Manchester University Press, 1977, p. 124, quoting Shelley's "Defence of Poetry."

3. Webb, *Shelley, A Voice Not Understood*, p. 147.

4. Bloom, H., *Shelley's Mythmaking*, New York, Cornell University Press, 1969.

5. Woodman, *The Apocalyptic Vision*.

6. Webb, *Shelley, A Voice Not Understood*.

7. Young, A., *Shelley and Nonviolence*, The Hague, Paris, Mouton, 1975.

8. Bhalla, M.M., *Studies in Shelley*, ed. F.E. Krishna, New Dehli, Associated Publishing House, 1973.

9. Williams, C., *The Figure of Beatrice*, New York, Noonday Press, 1961, pp. 7 ff.

10. Bhalla, M.M., *Studies in Shelley*, p. 67.

11. Ibid.

12. Woodman, *The Apocalyptic Vision*, p. 19.

13. Ibid., p. 16.

14. Woodman, *The Aporalyptic Vision*, p. 3, quoting Shelley's "Defence of Poetry."

15. Deikman, A., "Bimodal Consciousness," *Archives of General Psychiatry*, 45, pp. 181–89, 1971.

16. Young, *Shelley and Nonviolence*.

17. Webb, *Shelley, A Voice Not Understood*.

18. Shelley, P.B., *The Poetical Works of Percy Bysshe Shelley*, ed. Mary Shelley, London, Edward Moxon, 1857, Vol. I, p. 367 ff.

19. Ibid.

20. Ibid.

21. Bucke, R.M., *Cosmic Consciousness*, New York, Dutton, 1969.

22. Levinson, D., *The Seasons of a Man's Life*, New York, Ballantine, 1979.

23. Shelley, *Poetical Works*, Vol. II, pp. 417 ff.

24. Ibid., Vol.III, pp. 359 ff.

25. Wilson, M., *Shelley's Later Poetry*, New York, Columbia University Press, 1959.

26. La Cassagniere, C., *La Mystique du Prometheus Unbound de Shelley*, Paris, Lettres Modernes, Minard, 1970.

27. Wilson, *Shelley's Later Poetry*, p. 135.

28. Webb, *Shelley, A Voice Not Understood*, p. 175.

29. Perry, J.W., "The Messianic Hero," *Journal of Analytical Psychology*, Vol. 17, pp. 184–98, 1972; "Psychosis and the Visionary Mind," *Journal of Altered States of Consciousness*, Vol. 3, (1), pp. 5–41, 1977–78.

30. Webb, *Shelley, A Voice Not Understood*, p. 68.

31. Young, *Shelley and Nonviolence*.

32. Webb, *Shelley, A Voice Not Understood*.

33. Shelley, *Poetical Works*, Vol. I, pp. 371–372.

34. Ibid., pp. 263 ff.

35. Scharf, R., "Die Gestalt des Satans im Alten Testament," in C.G. Jung *Gestalt des Geistes*, Zurich, Rascher, 1953.

36. Robinson, J.M., *The Nag Hammadi Library*, New York, Harper and Row, 1977, especially pp. 161 ff; Pagels, E., *The Gnostic Gospels*, Vintage Books, New York, Random House, 1981, Ch. 2.

37. Perry, *Lord of the Four Quarters*, pp. 97–111.

38. La Cassagniere, *La Mystique du Prometheus Unbound de Shelley*, p. 126 ff.

39. Young, *Shelley and Nonviolence*.

10. Individuality in Evolution

1. Jung, C.G., "Conscious, Unconscious, and Individuation," and "Concerning Mandala Symbolism," *The Archetypes of the Collective Unconscious*, trans. R.F.C. Hull, *Coll. Works*, Vol. 9, Part I, Bollingen Series XX, New York, Pantheon, 1959; *Two Essays on Analytical Psychology*, trans. R.F.C. Hull, *Coll. Works*, Vol. 7, Bollingen Series XX, New York, Pantheon, 1953, pp. 108, 171 ff, 238.

2. Breasted, *The Dawn of Conscience*, p.154.

3. Harrison, J.E., *Themis*, Cambridge, Cambridge University Press, 1927, pp. 45–46, 122–23.

4. Jung, C.G., *The Development of Personality*, trans. R.F.C. Hull, *Coll. Works*, Vol. 17, Bollingen Series XX, New York, Pantheon, 1954.

5. Jung, C.G., *Psychology and Religion*, Terry Lectures, New Haven, Yale University Press, 1938.

6. Neumann, E., *The Origins and History of Consciousness*, Bollingen Series XLII, New York, Pantheon, 1954.

7. Perry, *The Far Side of Madness*; *Roots of Renewal in Myth and Madness*.

8. Jung, "On Psychic Energy."

9. Jung, "Zarathustra," seminars privately mimeographed.

10. Perry, *Lord of the Four Quarters*.

11. Jung, *The Secret of the Golden Flower*.

12. For sources, see Perry, *Lord of the Four Quarters*, p. 63, and notes.

13. Ornstein, R.E., *The Psychology of Consciousness*, San Francisco, Freeman, 1972.

14. Perry, J.W., "Psychosis and the Visionary Mind," *Journal of Altered States of Consciousness*, Vol. 3, No. I, 1977–78, pp. 5–14.

15. Jantsch, E., *The Self-organizing Universe*, Oxford and New York, Pergamon Press, 1980.

16. Capra, F., *The Turning Point*, New York, Simon and Schuster, 1982.

17. Needham, J., "Evolution and Thermodynamics", *Time, The Refreshing River*, London, Allen and Unwin, 1943.

18. Prigonine, I., *From Being to Becoming*, San Francisco, Freeman, 1980.

19. Jantsch, E., *The Self-organizing Universe*, Ch. 2, quote on p. 32.

20. Lovelock, J.E., *Gaia*, Oxford, Oxford University Press, 1979.

21. Teilhard de Chardin, P., *The Phenomenon of Man*, New York, Harper and Row, Torchbooks, 1961.

22. Jung, 1925 Seminars, privately mimeographed.

23. Widengren, G., "The King and the Tree of Life in Ancient Near Eastern Religion," *Uppsala Universitets Arsskrift*, Vol. 4, Uppsala, Sweden, Lundequisttika Bokhandeln, 1951.

24. Wilber, K., et al., *The Holographic Paradigm*, ed. K. Wilber, Boulder, Shambala, 1982.

25. Jonas, H., *The Gnostic Religion*, Boston, Beacon Press, 1963; Pagels, E., *The Gnostic Gospels*, New York, Vintage Books, Random House, 1981.

26. Jacobi, J., *Paracelsus, Selected Writings*, Bollingen Series XXVIII, New York, Pantheon, 1951.

11. Modern Myth and Nuclear Nemisis

1. Perry, *Lord of the Four Quarters*; Blinkenberg, C.S., *The Thunder-weapon in Religion and Folklore*, Cambridge, Cambridge University Press, 1911.

2. Frazer, J.G., *Balder the Beautiful*, Part II, *The Golden Bough*, Vol. XI, London, Macmillan, 1919, pp. 226–31.

3. Harrison, *Themis*, pp. 95–117, 116–83.

4. Childe, *New Light on the Most Ancient Near East*.

5. Von Vacano, *The Etruscans in the Ancient World*, pp. 38–40.

7. Conze, *Buddhism in Essence and Development*, pp. 183 ff.

8. Blofeld, *The Bodhisattva of Compassion*, *The Mystic Tradition*.

9. Merchant, C., *The Death of Nature*, San Francisco, Harper and Row, 1983, pp. 168–72.

Bibliography

Adams, H. *Mont-St-Michele and Chartres*, Cambridge, Houghton Mifflin, 1936.

Allbright, W. *The Archeology of Palestine*, Baltimore, Penguin, 1960.

Ashe, G. *The Quest for Arthur's Britain*, ed. G. Ashe, St. Albans, Herts, Paladin, 1968.

Barnett, L.D. *Antiquities of India*, New York, Putnam, 1914.

Basham, A.L. *The Wonder That Was India*, London, Sidgwick and Jackson, 1956.

_____. "Buddhism in India," *The Buddhist Tradition in India, China, and Japan*, ed. T. deBary, New York, The Modern Library, 1969.

Beal, S. *Buddhist Records of the Western World*, trans. S. Beal, Boston, Osgood, 1885.

Bedier, J. *The Romance of Tristan and Iseult*, trans. H. Belloc and P. Rosenfeld, Garden City, Doubleday, 1955.

Bentzen, A. *King and Messiah*, London, Oxford University Press, 1953.

Bhalla, M.M. *Studies in Shelley*, ed. F.E. Krishna, New Delhi, Associated Publishing House, 1973.

Birkeland, H. *The Evildoer in the Book of Psalms*, Oslo, Avhandlinger utgitt av det Norske Videnskaps -ii, Akademi i, Oslo II, 1955.

Blackman, A.M. *Myth and Ritual*, ed. S.H. Hooke, London, Oxford University Press, 1953.

Blinkenberg, C.S. *The Thunderweapon in Religion and Folklore*, Cambridge, Cambridge University Press, 1911.

Blofeld, J. *The Bodhisattva of Compassion, The Mystic Tradition*, Boulder, Shambala, 1978.

Bloom, H. *Shelley's Mythmaking*, New York, Cornell University Press, 1969.

Bodde, D. "Harmony and Conflict in Chinese Philosophy," *Studies in Chinese Thought*, ed. A.F. Wright, Chicago, Chicago University Press, 1953.

Breasted, J.H. *The Dawn of Conscience*, New York, Charles Scribner & Sons, 1933.

Brown, A.C.L. *The Origin of the Grail Legend*, Cambridge, Harvard University Press, 1943.

Bucke, R.M. *Cosmic Consciousness*, New York, Dutton, 1969.

Cammann, S.v.R. "Suggested Origin of the Tibetan Mandala Paintings," *Art Quarterly*, Spring, 1950.

Campbell, J. *Oriental Mythology, The Masks of God*, Vol. 2, New York, Viking, 1962.

Capellanus, A. *The Art of Courtly Love*, trans. J.J. Parry, New York, Frederick Ungar, 1959.

Capra, F. *The Turning Point*, New York, Simon and Schuster, 1982.

Charles, R.H. *The Apocrypha and Pseudepigrapha of the Old Testament*, ed. R.H. Charles, Los Angeles, Work of the Chariot, 1970.

Chavannes, E. *Les Memoires Historiques de Se-ma-ts'ien*, Paris, E. Leriaux, 1895–1905.

Childe, V.G. *New Light on the Most Ancient East*, New York, Evergreen Books, Grove Press, 1947.

Creel, H.G. *The Birth of China*, New York, Frederick Ungar, 1937.

_____. *Chinese Thought*, Chicago, University of Chicago Press, 1953.

_____. *Confucius and the Chinese Way*, New York, Harper and Row, Torchbooks, 1960.

Dai, B. "Being Fully Human: A Chinese Ideal of Mental Health," *Highland Highlights*, Asheville, Office of Information Services, 1981.

Darwin, C. *The Descent of Man*, London, Murray, 1871.

_____. *The Origin of Species*, New York, Appleton, 1880.

DeBary, W.T. *Sources of Chinese Tradition*, Part II, ed. W.T. deBary, New York, Columbia University Press, 1960.

Deikman, A. "Bimodal Consciousness," *Archives of General Psychiatry*, 45, 1971.

DeRougement, D. *Love in the Western World*, trans. R. Belgian, New York, Fawcett, World Library, 1956.

Drummond, H. *The Ascent of Man*, New York, J. Pott, 1894.

_____. *Natural Law in the Spiritual World*, New York, J. Pott, 1887.

Dundekar, R.N. "Hinduism," *Sources of Indian Tradition*, ed. W.T. deBary, New York, Columbia University Press, 1958.

Eggeling, J. "The Satapatha Brahmana," *Sacred Books of the East*, ed. F.M. Muller, Vol. 41, Oxford, Clarendon, 1900.

Fairman, H.W. "The Kingship Rituals of Egypt," *Myth, Ritual, and Kingship*, ed. S.H. Hooke, Oxford, Clarendon, 1958.

Fitzgerald, C.F. *China: A Short Cultural History*, New York, Praeger, 1961.

Fowles, J. *The Lais of Marie de France*, trans. R. Hamming and J. Ferrante, New York, Dutton, 1978.

Frankfort, H. *The Birth of Civilization in the Near East*, Garden City, Anchor Books, Doubleday, 1961.

_____. *Kingship and The Gods*, Bk. I, Chicago, Chicago University Press, 1948.

Frazer, J.G. *The Golden Bough*, London, Macmillan, 1890–1915.

Freud, S. *Moses and Monotheism*, New York, Knopf, 1947.

Fuchs, S. *Rebellious Prophets: A Study of Messianic Movements in Indian Religion*, New York, Asia Publishing House, 1965.

Fung, Y.L. *A Short History of Chinese Philosophy*, trans. D. Bodde, New York, Macmillan, 1960.

Gaster, T.H. *Thespis: Myth, Ritual, and Drama in the Ancient Near East*, Garden City, Anchor Books, Doubleday, 1961.

Granet, M. *Chinese Civilization*, New York, Macmillan, 1958.

Griffith, R.T.H. *Hymns of the Rigveda*, Benarcs, Lasaruz, 1896.

Guthrie, H.H. *Israel's Sacred Songs: A Study of Dominant Themes*, New York, Seabury, 1966.

Harrison, J.E. *Themis*, Cambridge, University of Cambridge Press, 1927.

Heer, F. *The Medieval World*, trans. J. Sondheimer, New York, Mentor Books, New American Library, 1963.

Henderson, L.J. *The Order of Nature*, Cambridge, Harvard University Press, 1925.

Hocart, A.M. *Kingship*, London, Oxford University Press, 1927.

———. *Kings and Councillors*, Cairo, Egyptian University, Barbey, 1936.

Hooke, S.H. *Myth and Ritual*, London, Oxford University Press, 1953.

———. *Myth, Ritual, and Kingship*, Oxford, Clarendon, 1958.

Jacobi, J. *Paracelsus*, Selected Writings, Bollingen Series XXVIII, New York, Pantheon, 1951.

Jacobsen, T. "Mesopotamia," *Before Philosophy: The Intellectual Adventure of Ancient Man*, London, Penguin, 1954.

James, E.O. *Myth and Ritual in the Ancient Near East*, New York, Praeger, 1958.

Jantsch, E. *The Self-Organizing Universe*, Oxford & New York, Pergamon Press, 1980.

Johnson, A.R. *Sacral Kingship in Ancient Israel*, Cardiff, University of Wales, 1955.

Jonas, H. *The Gnostic Religion*, Boston, Beacon Press, 1963.

Jung, C.G. *The Archetypes of the Collective Unconscious*, trans. R.F.C. Hull, Coll Works, Vol. 9, Part I, Bollingen Series XX, New York, Pantheon, 1959.

———. "Concerning Mandala Symbolism," *Archetypes of the Collective Unconscious*, Coll. Works, Vol. 9, 1, Bollingen Series XX, New York, Pantheon, 1959.

_____. "Conscious, Unconscious, and Individuation," *Archetypes of the Collective Unconscious*, Coll. Works, Vol. 9, Bollingen Series XX, New York, Pantheon, 1959.

_____. *The Development of Personality*, trans. R.F.C. Hull, Coll. Works, Vol. 17, Bollingen Series XX, New York Pantheon, 1954.

_____. "On Psychic Energy," *The Structure and Dynamics of the Psyche*, trans. R.F.C. Hull, Coll. Works, Vol. 8, Bollingen Series XX, New York, Pantheon, 1960.

_____. "On Psychological Understanding," *The Psychogenesis of Mental Disease*, trans. R.F.C. Hull, Coll. Works, Vol. 3, Bollingen Series XX, New York, Pantheon, 1959.

_____. *Psychology and Religion*, Terry Lectures, New Haven, Yale University Press, 1938.

_____. *The Secret of the Golden Flower*, London, Kegan Paul, Trench, & Trubner, 1935.

_____. *Symbols of Transformation*, trans. R.F.C. Hull, Coll. Works, Vol. 5, Bollingen Series XX, New York, Pantheon, 1956.

_____. *Two Essays on Analytical Psychology*, trans. R.F.C. Hull, Coll. Works, Vol. 7, Bollingen Series XX, New York, Pantheon, 1956.

Klausner, J. *The Messianic Idea in Israel*, trans. W.F. Stinespring, New York Macmillan, 1955.

Komroff, M. *The Apocrypha*, New York, Tudor, 1936.

LaBarre, W. "Materials for a History of Studies of Crisis Cults, A Biblographical Essay," *Current Anthropology*, XII, No. 1, 1971.

_____. "John Wilson, The Revealer of Peyote," Appendix 7 of *The Peyote Cult*, New York, Schocken Books, 1971.

La Cassagniere, C. *La Mystique du Prometheus Unbound de Shelley*, Paris, Lettres, Modernes, Minard, 1970.

Lame Deer, J. *Lame Deer, Seeker of Visions*, ed. R. Erdoes, New York, Washington Square Press, 1976.

Lanternari, V. *The Religions of the Oppressed*, Mentor Books, New York, New American Library, 1965.

Latourette, K.S. *The Chinese, Their History & Culture*, New York, Macmillan, 1946.

Legge, J. *The Four Books*, Shanghai, The Commercial Press, undated.

Levinson, D. *The Seasons of Man's Life*, New York, Ballantine, 1979.

Levy-Bruhl, L. *Primitive Mentality*, London, Allen & Unwin, 1923.

Lin Yu-tang *The Wisdom of the East*, New York, Random House, 1942.

Loomis, R.S. *Celtic Myth and Arthurian Romance*, New York, Columbia University Press, 1927.

————. *The Grail from Celtic Myth to Christian Symbol*, New York, Columbia University Press, 1963.

L'Orange, H.P. "Studies in the Iconography of Cosmic Kingship in the Ancient World," Cambridge, *Institutett for Sammenlignende Kulturforskning*, Harvard University Press, 1953.

Lovelock, J.E. *Gaia*, Oxford, Oxford University Press, 1979.

MacCana, P. *Celtic Mythology*, London, Hamlyn, 1970.

Markale, J. *King Arthur: King of Kings*, London, Gordon and Cremonesi, 1977.

————. *Women of the Celts*, London, Gordon and Cremonesi, 1975.

Maslow, A.H. *Religion, Values, & Peak Experiences*, New York, Viking, 1970.

Masson-Oursel, P. *Ancient India and Indian Civilization*, trans. Dobie, London, Kegan Paul, Trench & Trubner, 1934.

Mercer, S.A.B. *An Egyptian Grammar for Beginners*, Oriental Research Series, No. 1, London, Luzac, 1929.

Merchant, C. *The Death of Nature*, San Francisco, Harper and Row, 1983.

Mooney, J. "The Ghost Dance." *Report of the Bureau of American Ethnology*, XIV, 1872.

Mowinckel, S. *He That Cometh*, trans. G.W. Anderson, New York, Abingdon, 1954.

Muller, F.M. *Sacred Books of the East*, ed. F.M. Muller, Vol. 41, Oxford, Clarendon, 1900.

Needham, J. "Evolution and Thermodynamics," *Time, The Refreshing River*, London, Allen and unwin, 1943.

_____. "Human Laws and Laws of Nature in China and the West," *Journal of the History of Ideas*, XII, 1951.

_____. *Time, The Refreshing River*, London, Allen and Unwin, 1953.

Newstaed, H. *Bran the Blessed in Arthurian Romance*, New York, Columbia University Press, 1939.

Neumann, E. *The Origins and History of Consciousness*, Bollingen Series XLII, New York, Pantheon, 1954.

Nikam & McKeon *The Edicts of Asoka*, Chicago, University of Chicago Press, Phoenix, 1959.

Nygren, A. *Agape and Eros: A Study in the Christian Idea of Love*, trans. A.G. Herbert, London, Society for Promoting Christian Knowledge, 1952.

Ornstein, R.E. *The Psychology of Consciousness*, San Francisco, Freeman, 1972.

Pagels, E. *The Gnostic Gospels*, New York, Vintage Books, Random House, 1981.

Perry, J.W. "Emotions and Object Relations," *Journal of Analytical Psychology*, II, No. 2, 1937.

_____. *The Far Side of Madness*, Englewood Cliffs, Prentice-Hall, 1974.

_____. *Lord of the Four Quarters*, New York, Braziller, 1966.

_____. "The Messianic Hero," *Journal of Analytical Psychology*, Vol. 17, 1972.

_____. "Psychosis and the Visionary Mind," *Journal of Altered States of Consciousness*, Vol. 3, (1), 1977–1978.

_____. "Reconstitutive Process in the Psychopathology of the Self," *Annals of the New York Academy of Sciences*, XCVI, art. 3, Jan. 27, 1962.

_____. *Roots of Renewal in Myth and Madness*, San Francisco, Jossey-Bass, 1976.

_____. *The Self in Psychotic Process*, Berkeley, University of California Press, 1953.

Perry, W.J. *The Children of the Sun: A Study in the Early History of Civilization*, London, Methuen, 1923.

Prigonine, I. *From Being to Becoming*, San Francisco, Freeman, 1980.

Pritchard, J.B. *Ancient Near Eastern Texts Relating to the Old Testament*, ed. J.B. Pritchard, Princeton, University of Princeton Press, 1955.

Raghavan, V. "Hinduism," *Sources of Indian Tradition*, ed. W.T. deBary, New York, Columbia Univesity Press, 1958.

Raglan, F.R.S. *Jocasta's Crime*, London, Thinker's Library, 1940.

Rahula, W.S. *What the Buddha Taught*, New York, Grove Press, 1959.

Reinach, S. *Orpheus*, New York, Liveright, 1935.

Rhys Davids, T.W. "Dialogues of the Buddha," in *Sacred Books of the Buddhists*, London, Oxford University Press, 1899.

Robinson, J.M. *The Nag Hammadi Library*, New York, Harper and Row, 1977.

Saso, M.R., *Taoism and the Rite of Cosmic Renewal*, Washington State University Press, 1972.

Sayers, D.L. *The Song of Roland*, Baltimore, Penguin, 1957.

Schaerf, R. "Die Gestalt des Satans im Alten Testament," in C.G. Jung, *Gestalt des Geistes*, Zurich, Rascher, 1953.

Shelley, P.B. *The Poetical Works of Percy Bysshe Shelley*, ed. Mary Shelley, London, Edward Moxon, 1857.

Smith, M. *The Secret Gospel*, New York, Harper and Row, 1973.

Soothill, W.E. *The Hall of Light: A Study of Early Chinese Kingship*, New York, Philosophical Library, 1952.

Sullivan, H.S. *Schizophrenia as a Human Process*, New York, Norton, 1962.

Sundkler, B.G.M. *Bantu Prophets in South Africa*, London, Lutterworth, 1948.

Teilhard de Chardin, P. *The Phenomenon of Man*, New York, Harper and Row, Torchbooks, 1961.

Terry, P. *Lays of Courtly Love*, Garden City, Anchor Books, Doubleday, 1963.

Thomas, E.J. *The Life of the Buddha as Legend and History*, New York, Barnes and Noble, 1960.

Toynbee, A.J. *A Study of History*, Oxford, Oxford University Press, 1947.

Vaillant, G.C. *The Aztecs of Mexico*, Garden City, Doubleday, Doran, 1941; republished, Penguin, 1953.

Von Hagen, V.W. *Realm of the Incas*, Mentor Books, Ancient Civilizations, New American Library, 1957.

Von Vacano, O.W. *The Etruscans in the Ancient World*, trans. S.A. Ogilvie, London, Edward Arnold, 1960.

Wagner, R. *Parsifal*, trans. J.L. & F. Corder, New York, Rullman.

Wallace, A.F.C. "Stress and Rapid Personality Change," *International Record of Medicine and General Practice Clinics*, 169, No. 12, 1956.

————. *Culture and Personality*, New York, Random House, 1961.

Waley, A. *The Analects of Confucius*, New York, Vingate Books, Random House, undated.

————. *The Way and its Power*, New York, Grove Press, 1958.

Webb, T. *Shelley, A Voice Not Understood*, Manchester, Manchester University Press, 1977.

Weston, J. *Sir Gawain at the Grail Castle*, London, Nutt, 1903.

Whitehead, A.N. *Process and Reality*, New York, Macmillan, 1936.

Widengren, G. "The King and the Tree of Life in Ancient Near Eastern Religion," *Uppsala Universitets Arsskrift*, Vol. 4, Uppsala, Sweden, Lundequisttika Bokhandeln, 1951.

Wilber, K. *The Holographic Paradigm*, ed. K. Wilber, Boulder, Shambala, 1982.

Wilhelm, R. *The I Ching or Book of Changes*, Bollingen Series XIX, New York, Pantheon, 1950.

Williams, C. *The Figure of Beatrice*, New York, Noonday Press, 1961.

Wilson, J.A. *The Culture of Ancient Egypt*, Chicago, Phoenix Books, University of Chicago Press, 1960.

————. "Egyptian Observations," *Ancient Near Eastern Texts Relating to the Old Testament*, ed. J.B. Pritchard, Princeton, Princeton University Press, 1955.

————. "Egyptian Oracles and Prophecies," *Ancient Near Eastern Texts.*

————. "Proverbs and Precepts," *Ancient Near Eastern Tests.*

————. "Egyptian Secular Songs and Poems," *Ancient Near Eastern Texts.*

Wilson, M. *Shelley's Later Poetry*, New York, Columbia University Press, 1959.

Woodman, R.G. *The Apocalyptic Vision in the Poetry of Shelley*, Toronto, Toronto University Press, 1964.

Worsley, P. *The Trumpet Shall Sound: A Study of Cargo Cults in Melanesia*, London, 1957.

Young, A. *Shelley and Nonviolence*, The Hague, Paris, Mouton, 1975.

Zimmer, H. *The King and the Corpse*, ed. J. Campbell, Bollingen Series XI, Princeton, Princeton University Press, 1971.

Author Index

Subject Index